Windows on Early Christianity

Windows on Early Christianity

Uncommon Stories, Striking Images, Critical Perspectives

James W. Aageson

CASCADE Books · Eugene, Oregon

WINDOWS ON EARLY CHRISTIANITY
Uncommon Stories, Striking Images, Critical Perspectives

Copyright © 2016 James W. Aageson. All rights reserved. Except for brief Quotations in critical publications or reviews, no part of this book may be reproduced in any manner without prior written permission from the publisher. Write: Permissions, Wipf and Stock Publishers, 199 W. 8th Ave., Suite 3, Eugene, OR 97401.

Cascade Books
An Imprint of Wipf and Stock Publishers
199 W. 8th Ave., Suite 3
Eugene, OR 97401
www.wipfandstock.com

PAPERBACK ISBN 13: 978-1-4982-3391-0
HARDCOVER ISBN 13: 978-1-4982-3393-4

Cataloguing-in-Publication data:

Aageson, James W., 1947–

Windows on early Christianity : uncommon stories, striking images, critical perspectives / James W. Aageson.

xiv + 266 p. ; 23 cm. Includes bibliographical references and indexes.

ISBN: 978-1-4982-3391-0 (paperback) | ISBN: 978-1-4982-3393-4 (hardback)

1. New Testament—Introductions. 2. Church history—Primitive and early church (ca. 30–600). I. Title.

BR162.3 A25 2016

Manufactured in the U.S.A. 04/04/2016

The Scripture quotations contained herein are from the New Revised Standard Version Bible, copyright © 1989 by the Division of Christian Education of the National Council of the Churches of Christ in the U.S.A., and are used by permission. All rights reserved.

The reproduction of Mark 16:2–8 is from the Greek text of Nestle-Aland, 28th edition: Nestle-Aland, *Novum Testamentum Graece*, 28th Ed., edited by Barbara and Kurt Aland, Johannes Karavidopoulos, Carlo M. Martini, and Bruce M. Metzger in cooperation with the Institute for New Testament Textual Research, Münster/Westphalia, © 2012 Deutsche Bibelgesellschaft, Stuttgart. Used by permission.

Photographs of Ecclesia and Synagoga from Strasbourg Cathedral are from the Jewish Christian Relations website. Used by permission.

Photograph of the cave of Paul and Thecla is from Carl Rasmussen's Holy Land Photos blog. Used by permission.

The reproductions of works of art are determined to be in the public domain. All other photographs, charts, and diagrams are the work of the author.

This book is dedicated to all the students with whom I have had the privilege of working and learning over many years in many different settings.

Contents

Figures | viii
Acknowledgments | xi
Abbreviations | xii

Part 1: Foundational Issues
1 What You Should Know before Reading this Book | 3
2 Three Middle Eastern Religions: Dynamics in Belief and Practice | 12
3 Abraham and Sarah: Story and Counterstory | 26
4 The Births of Two Great Religions:
    Rabbinic Judaism and Early Christianity | 39

Part 2: Foundational Texts and Traditions
5 The Apostle Paul and the Early Church | 55
6 The New Testament Gospels: History, Story, and Claims about Christ | 73
7 The Church in Motion: The Acts of the Apostles | 95
8 Paul and the Next Generations of the Church | 111
9 Jesus and Other Gospels: Widening the Circle | 131
10 Jewish Apocalyptic Tradition and the Revelation to John | 148

Part 3: Foundational Topics
11 Render unto God and unto Caesar: The Problem of Empire | 167
12 People of the Book: From Text to Canon | 183
13 Location and Legacy, Church and Opposition, Function and Formation | 200
14 Worship and Religious Practice in Early Christianity | 215
15 Abraham's Children: Competition and Contention | 231

Epilogue | 247

Bibliography | 251
Index of Modern Authors | 257
Index of Topics | 259
Index of Ancient Sources | 261

Figures

Figure 1: Diagram of the Three Religions | 24

Figure 2: *Moses and the Tables of the Law*, Reni (1624). Wikimedia Commons | 25

Figure 3: Church of the Holy Sepulcher, Jerusalem. Photo by author | 25

Figure 4: Diagram of the Genealogical Backbone of Genesis 12–50 | 31

Figure 5: *Sacrifice of Isaac*, Caravaggio, 1602. Wikimedia Commons | 38

Figure 6: Cave of Machpelah, Tomb of the Patriarchs, Hebron. Photo by author | 38

Figure 7: Replacement Model of Christian Origins | 44

Figure 8: Offshoot Model of Christian origins | 46

Figure 9: Sibling Model of Christian Origins | 50

Figure 10: Paul's Actual Conversion | 58

Figure 11: Later Christian Interpretations of Paul's Conversion | 59

Figure 12: *Conversion of Saint Paul*, Caravaggio (1600–1601). Wikimedia Commons | 72

Figure 13: *Paul in Prison*, Rembrandt (1627). Wikimedia Commons | 72

Figure 14: Mosaic in the Archiepiscopal Palace of San Pietro Crisologoa Chapel in Ravenna, Italy (sixth century). Wikimedia Commons | 93

Figure 15: *The Savior*, El Greco (seventeenth century). Wikimedia Commons | 94

Figure 16: View of Antioch in Pisidia, where the remains of a church may be over an ancient synagogue. Photo by author | 110

Figure 17: Cave of Saint Paul at Ephesus: Paul and Theocleia, mother of Thecla. Photo by Carl Rasmussen, https://holylandphotos.files.wordpress.com/2013/08/twcseppt03.jpg/ | 130

Figures

Figure 18: Church of Saint Mary in Ephesus (fifth century). Photo by author | 150

Figure 19: Basilica of Saint John in Ephesus. Photo by author | 150

Figure 20: Apocalyptic Ages Old and New | 154

Figure 21: Christian Apocalyptic Ages Old and New | 155

Figure 22: Hot and Cold at Laodicea. Photo by author | 158

Figure 23: Reconstructed Altar from Pergamum. Photo by author | 159

Figure 24: Temple to Trajan. Photo by author | 172

Figure 25: Greek text of Mark 16:2–8 with textual apparatus. Nestle-Aland, 28th edition | 191

Figure 26: Tertullian. Wikimedia Commons | 213

Figure 27: Origen. Wikimedia Commons | 213

Figure 28: Ignatius of Antioch. Wikimedia Commons | 214

Figure 29: Synagoga (Synagogue) and Ecclesia (Church), column figures, South Transept Portal, Strasbourg Cathedral. Jewish-Christian Relations website photo. Used by permission | 245

Figure 30: Ecclesia, Strasbourg Cathedral. Jewish-Christian Relations website photo. Used by permission | 245

Figure 31: The Jewish Ghetto in Venice, described as the first Jewish ghetto in Europe. Photo by author | 246

Acknowledgments

This book is the fruit of my long collaboration with friends and colleagues, too many to name, but no less important to me and this project. My colleagues at Concordia College, Moorhead, Minnesota, have had a profound influence on my thinking and teaching and deserve a special word of appreciation. But colleagues near and far also have contributed much to my thinking in their writings and presentations, and by their friendship. Scholarship and teaching are collaborative activities practiced in communities of learning, and depend on the contributions of the participants for them to flourish. So I thank not only the people involved in my learning and teaching but also the learning communities themselves, which are greater than the sum of the individuals involved. May this book be a contribution worthy of their importance to me!

Abbreviations

BIBLICAL BOOKS

Old Testament

Gen	Genesis	Prov	Proverbs
Exod	Exodus	Eccl	Ecclesiastes
Lev	Leviticus	Song	Song of Solomon
Num	Numbers	Cant	Canticles
Deut	Deuteronomy	Wis	Wisdom
Josh	Joshua	Sir	Sirach
Judg	Judges	Isa	Isaiah
Ruth	Ruth	Jer	Jeremiah
1 Sam	1 Samuel	Lam	Lamentations
2 Sam	2 Samuel	Bar	Baruch
1 Kgs	1 Kings	Ezek	Ezekiel
2 Kgs	2 Kings	Dan	Daniel
1 Chr	1 Chronicles	Hos	Hosea
2 Chr	2 Chronicles	Joel	Joel
Ezra	Ezra	Am	Amos
Neh	Nehemiah	Jonah	Jonah
Tob	Tobit	Mic	Micah
Jdt	Judith	Nah	Nahum
Esth	Esther	Hab	Habakkuk
1 Macc	Maccabees	Zeph	Zephaniah
2 Macc	2 Maccabees	Hag	Haggai
Job	Job	Zech	Zechariah
Pss	Psalms	Mal	Malachi

New Testament

Matt	Matthew	1 Tim	1 Timothy
Mark	Mark	2 Tim	2 Timothy
Luke	Luke	Titus	Titus
John	John	Phlm	Philemon
Acts	Acts	Heb	Hebrews
Rom	Romans	Jas	James
1 Cor	1 Corinthians	1 Pet	1 Peter
2 Cor	2 Corinthians	2 Pet	2 Peter
Gal	Galatians	1 John	1 John
Eph	Ephesians	2 John	2 John
Phil	Philippians	3 John	3 John
Col	Colossians	Jude	Jude
1 Thess	1 Thessalonians	Rev	Revelation
2 Thess	2 Thessalonians		

IGNATIUS OF ANTIOCH

Ign. *Eph.*	*To the Ephesians*
Ign. *Magn.*	*To the Magnesians*
Ign. *Smyrn.*	*To the Smyrnaeans*
Ign. *Phld.*	*To the Philadelphians*
Ign. *Rom.*	*To the Romans*
Ign. *Pol.*	*To Polycarp*

SECONDARY REFERENCES

AB	Anchor Bible
ABD	*Anchor Bible Dictionary.* 6 vols. Edited by David Noel Freedman. New York: Doubleday, 1992
ABRL	Anchor Bible Reference Library
ANF	*The Ante-Nicene Fathers.* Edited by Alexander Roberts and James Donaldson. 1885–1887. 10 vols. Repr. Peabody, MA: Hendrickson, 1994
CBQ	*Catholic Biblical Quarterly*
CC	Continental Commentary
ECC	Eerdmans Critical Commentary
JETS	*Journal of the Evangelical Theological Society*
JSNT	*Journal for the Study of New Testament*

LCL	Loeb Classical Library
LNTS	Library of New Testament Studies
NTL	New Testament Library
NTS	*New Testament Studies*
SBLSymS	Society of Biblical Literature Symposum Series
WGRWSup	Writings from the Greco-Roman World Supplement Series

PART 1

Foundational Issues

1

What You Should Know before Reading This Book

INTRODUCTION

This book is introductory, but it is not an introduction to biblical content or to the history of early Christianity in the strict sense of the term. The marketplace is filled with books billed as introductions to the Bible, or to Judaism, Christianity, Islam, and various other world religions. But this book is different. Each of the chapters addresses a different aspect of early Christianity and provides its own perspective on the phenomenon we call Christianity. At the outset of each chapter, I pose a question or two appropriate to the topic at hand, which in turn becomes the focus of the chapter. As an introductory text, this book is suggestive rather than exhaustive, a prelude to further study for those interested in probing the materials and questions more deeply, and an interlude for those who pause briefly to study this material in the midst of otherwise busy lives. Insofar as possible, it is written with a nontechnical vocabulary and in a style that is accessible to those not particularly familiar with the material or the state of the scholarly and theological questions. It also recognizes that students and other people will come to this text with different religious backgrounds, agendas, and attitudes towards religion more generally. Nevertheless, it is hoped that readers will enter into these questions and discussions with constructive openness, most especially where fundamental differences of perspective exist and perhaps continue to persist after the reading of this book. As the discussion continues, it will become clearer where my sympathies lie and what questions are important for me.

METHOD AND APPROACH

The discussion that follows is a critical look at early Christianity through the lens of certain foundational questions, and in most cases the discussions begin not with theological questions but religious or historical questions, or both, that may in turn lead to wider theological and spiritual considerations. As a corrective to what often seem to me unreflective, perhaps even troublesome, theological and spiritual assertions about Christianity, I bring critical scholarly questions to the fore, even though I am well aware that it is precisely the personal, theological questions that often bring people to the study of this material in the first place. The expectation is that whatever one's own theological or spiritual sympathies and perspectives, the result of entering into these discussions will be a more sophisticated understanding of what historic Christianity is, how it came to function, and why it became such a powerful force for people in much of the world for almost two millennia.

But why begin the chapters with questions addressed to the material rather than introducing the content? What may be obvious to many, but forgotten by most when thinking about religion—or perhaps when thinking about many other areas of human investigation as well for that matter—is that the questions we first pose to the object of study, whether explicitly or implicitly, virtually always correspond to what we ultimately see in the material. To put it another way, the answers we draw about the material are relative to the questions that interest us. If that is true, we ought to be very attentive to the questions we ask, for if we pose superficial or, dare I say, largely irrelevant questions, the conclusions we draw will be less than significant. To illustrate, when people read the Bible and come to very different conclusions about the meaning, character, and significance of the material, the differences usually result from different questions being brought to the texts. Often these questions themselves are prompted and shaped by assumptions or preconceived notions about what the texts mean. If different people bring different assumptions and questions to the texts, it is likely, if not certain, that they will also draw different conclusions about them. This clearly suggests that any study of Christianity ought to be extremely mindful of and reflective about the questions being asked of the material. Therefore, it seems appropriate to be as explicit as I can about the questions that intrigue me. There is no suggestion here that these are the only significant questions that could be asked, but I would claim that these are important questions and that they help us break open the material in new and interesting ways.

What does it mean to say that I begin in the first instance with religious rather than theological questions? Perhaps I can best describe my academic approach to the study of early Christianity in a general sense as phenomenological. In the first instance, Christianity is a historical, literary, social, and intellectual phenomenon and is to be studied as any other historical reality. Any truth claims to be made about the tradition will follow from rather than precede those phenomenological considerations. Here the sequence is important. I am certainly not suggesting that theological claims are unimportant and have no place in reflections on early Christianity. But I am saying that to reverse the sequence and begin with theological questions can often have the tendency to privilege certain faith claims and in some cases make it difficult to look soberly at the tradition. It can sometimes even make it difficult for religious people to engage those with differing perspectives in serious, open-minded, and ecumenically respectful ways. I would also say that any truth claims that we might want to make about Christianity need to be juxtaposed alongside the counterclaims of those who hold contrary views, without resorting to absolutist claims about the singular, nonnegotiable truth of our own convictions. I am convinced we are better off learning from each other than we are asserting our own theological superiority and purity of faith. In short, I wish to be ecumenical rather than sectarian, without falling into thoroughgoing relativism. In that effort, I am sure each of us will benefit from finding fellow travelers from across religious boundaries and theological divides, people who wish to engage in serious conversation and respectful learning about things that often are very close to the heart and incredibly subtle. These conversations are extremely important because religion has enormous capacity to bring about the noble work of God in the world. But conversely, when it jumps the rails, religion and religious people can bring about unspeakable suffering. Hence, I wish to defer speculative truth claims about Christianity for the sake of analyzing the phenomenon we call Christianity.

During the forty years I have studied religion professionally, I have moved increasingly away from essentialist notions of religion toward more functionalist understandings of what religion is and how it operates. Religions are always changing, and in my view there is little about them than can reasonably be called an immutable essence. For example, the one thing we would identify as most central to Christianity, namely Christology, is always being understood in new ways. This is historically the case and seems to be the case still today.[1] Perhaps it would be fair to say that in recent decades social and dynamic understandings of religion have come to the fore among many scholars, whereas more normative and propositional understandings have tended to recede into the background, becoming less persuasive for many people who look into these questions. In other words, less and less seems to be hardwired into religious systems, and more and more appears to be in the process of reinventing itself in light of new circumstances and new ideas. This is not to say that over time there are no patterns of thought and practice that persist within a religious system. There clearly are. But again, over time even these things are continually being rethought and reimagined. In that sense, they too should not be identified as religious essences, in the sense of something immutable, singularly true, and immune from the winds of social and historical change. For some, the claim I am making clearly undermines the essential truth of religion, in this case Christianity. But for me just the opposite is the case. Instead of seeing Christianity, and other religions for that matter, as fixed entities, hovering above us and perhaps also removed from our questions and struggles, this opens the religion to dynamic engagement with people in the realities of their daily lives, both intellectually and personally. I do not think this approach necessarily wipes away the solid support and anchor that religion provides for many people, but I concede it probably changes how that support will be understood and manifested.

If it is the case that religion is not best explained by essentialist categories, it is also the case that much of what falls under the heading of our term *religion* is made up of various human constructs. In other words, it is socially constructed by human beings functioning in community. These constructs will in turn be made and remade over time. As we will see in the next chapter, religion in this sense is penultimate: it points to that which is ultimate but is not itself ultimate. There is something beyond it, and to which it struggles to point. Faithful and practicing Jews, Christians, and Muslims believe and trust, I would suggest, ultimately in Yahweh, God, and Allah, not in religion as such. Religion is the mechanism through which people seek to actualize and manifest that faith and trust. The study of religion is the study of these mechanisms. Strictly speaking, I would say it is theology's function to probe the claims about the ultimate reality that religions bring to the fore. It too is penultimate but explores more explicitly the faith claims and truths that religious people make about God and the world. In that sense, this book deals with religion, not theology.

---

1. See, e.g., Pelikan, *Jesus through the Centuries*.

What You Should Know before Reading This Book

But the study of religion may provide perspectives relevant to the work of theologians seeking to articulate faith claims about God and the world, and to give normative guidance about how to live in the world. I draw a sharp distinction between the study of religion and theology because, as I stated above, my preference is that the study of religion be preliminary to the more narrowly focused reflections of theologians. It is also much more historically, literarily, and socially based. In that sense, it is phenomenological.

It may also be clear that much of what passes in common parlance to be theological is in fact, according to my definition, talk about religion. It is also clear that many people today would not agree with my sharp distinction between the two. More important, however, my understanding of religion is thoroughly modern, and ancients would not have thought in these terms. Moreover, our concept of religion itself would have been foreign to them. They would have thought in terms of ethnic groups and peoples who inhabit certain regions, along with their beliefs and practices. They would not have conceived of religion as centered on faith communities and abstract belief systems, which stand alongside other communities and belief systems in diverse societies. And in the Greco-Roman world within which Christianity first emerged, the idea of religious exclusivity as we might know it would have been foreign to most people. So, when we today study Christianity and other ancient religions, we inevitably bring modern notions and experiences of religion to bear on the discussion. This is unavoidable and reminds us that we come initially to these investigations as outsiders and must not assume that the insiders thought much as we think.

While I would clearly assert that religions exist—indeed there is something to which our word *religion* points, and that stands behind our intellectual and linguistic representations—I would also assert that they do certain things. Religions function in certain ways to accomplish or transact various things for and among their adherents. In Christianity, for example, people ritualize participation in Christ, forgive sins, consecrate, include and exclude, console, worship God, and shape a sense of time, to name only a few. Writ large, Christianity is a spiritual mechanism to encounter the divine and represent the divine on earth in the lives of people, but it also operates politically in the world as it seeks to manifest, indeed in some cases enforce, its claims and social position. It is an earthly phenomenon exhibiting virtually all of the noble and frail markers of most human communities. As a religion, Christianity shapes a worldview and gives meaning and purpose to those who live under its sacred canopy and enact its rituals.[2] It also reinforces a way of being and acting in the world by lending ecclesiastical,

---

2. See the pioneering book of the same name by Peter Berger, *Sacred Canopy*.

if not divine, sanction to a moral framework for the lives of people. Along the way, Christianity also has generated an enormous amount of human energy and creativity. We only need to think of the volume of Christian art and music produced to represent the biblical stories, shape people's praise of God, display the wonders of the human spirit, and reinforce the narrative of salvation. These in turn function to nourish the faithful.

In this investigation, my approach is to identify, where possible, the structural relationships of the religion. In this case, the various aspects of the Christian religious and theological system operate in a set of structural relationships to one another, even where they appear less than coherent or thoroughly systematic. This, however, is not to deny that religions (in our case, Christianity) are constantly reinventing themselves and restructuring their religious systems and the relationships that enable them to operate. But how should we try to understand these structural relationships? One of the best ways is to look for comparisons and analogies. Comparison is a way of understanding through similarity and perhaps especially difference. By seeing how things are similar and in many cases different, we can begin to cast new light on how they function, what they mean, and why they may be important. For example, one of the best ways to understand one's native language is to learn another language. Or to understand more fully what it means to be an American or a European or an African, it is helpful to travel and live in another part of the world. Likewise, to appreciate the diversity and differences within Christianity, it is important to understand more clearly how various Christian groups respond differently to similar theological questions and how similar historical circumstances often affect people differently.[3]

A CRITICAL POSTURE IN THE FACE OF DIVERSITY

It is tempting to think that the way history turned out from our perspective was inevitable or the only possible option. Clearly this is not the case. Things could have been different, and among different groups often were. Call it the accidents of history, or simply different perspectives on Christianity's past, the result is similar. Diversity marks the religion and its narratives of the past, just as it will mark the future of the religion. It is in casting our eyes on this wider landscape that we learn about the character and complexity of Christianity and at the same time begin to understand more fully the

---

3. See Shedinger, *Was Jesus a Muslim?*, 49–71, for a critique of the comparative study of religion.

structural relationships at work in the religion, with its different expressions and histories. Simply sit for a couple of hours in the church of the Holy Sepulcher in the Old City of Jerusalem on a Sunday morning and experience the different practices, customs, and liturgies of the various religious groups to get a visceral sense of this diversity. A person quickly learns an appreciation for the many options available to Christians and how they practice their religion.

In response to this diversity, some people try to pull back and hunker down, retreating into their own worlds and comfort zones. For a great many people, this is self-defeating because life circumstances often have a way of piercing our attempts to protect ourselves from difference and otherness. In the modern world, we are simply bombarded by difference through social interactions and the media, which makes it all but impossible for most of us to retreat from it. For the person who wants to be a serious learner in these matters, it makes much more sense to be open to this difference, embracing it as an opportunity to learn, live, and grow in understanding. Denying difference and otherness certainly does not make them go away, and too often causes us to respond to them in unhelpful and what many would consider negative ways. Studying difference and similarity does more than cultivate a personal posture. More important, such study is a way of critically investigating religion as a phenomenon. Comparative approaches are fundamentally important to the study of religion and to thinking critically about things that are existentially close to the heart. To put it succinctly, comparison is one of those dimensions of critical thinking that allows us to probe religious phenomena with intellectual sympathy and at the same time with sober analytical skill that not only contributes to learning but also opens us to new ideas, to theological possibilities, and to people with different commitments and traditions. For someone within my system of values and sensibilities, these are generally thought to be good things both personally and intellectually.

The predictable criticism of my position, of course, will be that I have relativized the ultimate truth of Christianity, or any other religion for that matter, in the service of secular values and perspectives. The only honest answer is that, yes, there is a relativizing process that occurs when one embarks on this approach. In a culture that seems to place a premium on having clearly stated and strongly held convictions, even to the point of portraying them in stark black-and-white terms, it can be difficult to keep people's attention long enough to consider the subtleties of a religion or give much value to traditions that differ from one's own. If the strength of a person's unwavering conviction and vehemence becomes evidence of its truthfulness no matter how complicated the evidence in fact may be, it can be difficult to concede value to other perspectives and commitments, which is exactly what my approach does. In that sense and to that extent, my argument certainly does result in a process of relativizing. But does this mean that everything is relative and no better than anything else? Does it mean that truth must be abandoned where all we have left are opinions, none of which is any better than any others? Is it the case that to embark on this approach puts us on the slippery slope to a thoroughgoing relativism that removes all moral judgment and intellectual conviction in matters pertaining to religion? If that were to be the case, we would simply allow authoritarianism to slip in through the back door, because we would have no compelling moral or intellectual basis left from which to challenge those with the power to impose their will on us and our society. When ideas, no matter how suspect, are just as good as any others, we sacrifice the ability to discriminate and to stand for the noble, the true, and the virtuous.

When our only options become either resorting to absolutist certainties or abandoning all notions of truth, we face a dilemma both personally and intellectually as we approach the study of religion. It is clear that my approach pushes us to give up absolutist tendencies in the service of critical investigation. But does my critical approach to the study of religion invariably lead to extreme forms of relativism? I think not. Quite the opposite, it requires us to struggle in the middle ground between absolutism and relativism without slipping into either extreme—all the while critically investigating the evidence and mounting cogent arguments to explain the traditions in compelling and persuasive ways. To inhabit the middle ground can often be personally uncomfortable. But I suggest it is the most intellectually responsible position to take both in the critical study of religion and in theological reflection because it requires openness on the one hand and the search for truth on the other. This is no easy task, but a worthwhile effort nonetheless.

The use of the term *critical* may be a stumbling block for some who read this book. To begin, let me say the term has nothing to do with criticizing religion or religious or theological convictions. While I believe people are publicly accountable for their religious commitments and the consequences they may have, I am not in the business of criticizing religious convictions. I do hope, however, that people will examine their own ideas and attitudes and subject them to serious scrutiny. The term as I use it here has to do with critical thinking. That is, using one's rational skills to ask questions of religious traditions, to investigate and analyze the available evidence soberly, and to be precise about what the material might plausibly mean. It has to do with description and analysis in the service of understanding.

What You Should Know before Reading This Book

AUDIENCE

This book is written for nonspecialists who may have some familiarity with the traditions of Christianity, Judaism, and Islam. Other readers may have little or no knowledge of these traditions, their histories, or their religious dynamics. Many of the readers of this text will be students. Others will be people who are simply interested in learning more about Christianity. All are welcome to enter into the conversation. To the extent this book is used as a teaching book, each of the chapters might be used as independent, freestanding discussions. In that sense, they can be mixed and matched and used to investigate the respective topics independently. On the other hand, the chapters follow a logical narrative line and build from one to the next. The goal is to build in flexibility in the way this book may be used and in the way readers engage the material. In addition to the written text, graphic illustrations and diagrams also will be used to assist in making critical points along the way.[4]

I encourage readers to follow my example and generate their own questions to put before the material. To repeat, the questions and discussions here are intended to be suggestive and generative rather than comprehensive. They are intended to prompt alternative questions and responses in the hope that readers can master the art of asking ever more meaningful questions. In that way, the entire argument is intended to be open ended, inviting further conversation, not closing it down. The most effective way to use this book may be in group settings where discussion and debate, whether face-to-face or virtual, is possible. In that way, learning is not merely top-down but interactive, as readers engage the text and one another. Regardless of how this book is used, its goal is the critical analysis of the material and serious analysis of the religious phenomenon we call Christianity. The insights gained and the learning achieved may in turn contribute to theological reflection, even though the purpose of this book is not primarily *theological* in my narrower definition of the term. Likewise, in a world where our individual and social behavior can have far-reaching consequences, it is hoped that readers might think seriously about the ethical dimensions of Christianity. In this highly charged and globalized world, the human race's ability to survive and prosper may depend on it.

---

4. As an aid to readers, I have quoted where possible the relevant biblical and other primary texts in the body of the various discussions rather than simply citing the references. Reading the primary textual material is important in the study of early Christianity.

2

Three Middle Eastern Religions
Dynamics in Belief and Practice

*How does Christianity function as a religious system
as compared to Judaism and Islam,
both of which also operate as religious systems?*

In this chapter I am posing an explicitly comparative religious question designed to probe the structure and function of Christianity. While Christianity is the main focus of our investigation in this chapter, it so happens that Judaism and Islam exhibit certain similarities with Christianity on a foundational level in terms of their religious functions. Let there be no mistake: these three religions have significant structural differences and many quite different traditions and histories. There can and should be no attempt here to synthesize them, or to find the lowest common denominator, or to assume that they are always dealing with the same kinds of questions. To assume, however, that because these three great religious traditions are steeped in their own particularity they therefore have nothing at all in common religiously seems to me to be a mistake. I think it is also historically inaccurate. Again, I understand and appreciate the concerns of those who resist any attempts at comparison because they fear that comparisons will run roughshod over the differences in an attempt to find similarities and will end up drawing the conclusion that the three religions are basically alike. These comparative efforts can devolve very quickly into a kind of intellectual hegemony that has the result of eliminating difference in the service of commonality.[1] All of these concerns are legitimate. However, are there traits of the religious dynamics of these three great faiths that lend themselves to comparison? I think there are. And anyone who looks at religious phenomena, comparatively or otherwise, will do so through a particular methodological lens.

CHRIST AND CHRISTIANITY: BRIEF OVERVIEW OF A RELIGIOUS SYSTEM

If we examine the Christian storyline, it is fair to say that the center point governs its representation of the past and the future. That center point is, of course, the conviction that Jesus is the anticipated Jewish messiah. His followers early on began to read the Jewish Scriptures from the perspective of Christ as Messiah and Son of God. From Genesis to Revelation, the Christian canon of sacred Scripture, now called the Old and New Testaments, was shaped to tell the story of humankind's creation; its fall from grace; the prophetic expectation and promise that God was moving to redeem those lost in sin; the birth, ministry, death, and resurrection of Jesus as God's son; the kingdom of God, and finally the urgent expectation that God would intervene to bring salvation fully into the world at the end-times. In simple terms, this is the arc of the early Christian narrative. Virtually everything else was a matter of fleshing out the story and interpreting its meaning. During the early decades and centuries of the church, various aspects of the narrative would be elaborated to address new insights and issues confronting the Christ communities in the Mediterranean basin, as well as those farther to the East. Within three centuries, the church would rise from obscurity in the eastern Mediterranean to the pinnacle of political and religious power when Emperor Constantine would first legalize and then privilege Christianity.

This is an amazing story, but the question before us in this chapter is, how did the church emerge as a functioning religious system? Michael Goldberg, writing almost thirty years ago, argued that Matthew represents best the emergent Christian master story as he gives his account of Jesus,[2] probably based on Mark's earlier version of the Jesus story.[3] He begins his account of Jesus, unlike Mark, with a genealogy and the birth of Jesus:

---

1. See again the critique by Shedinger, *Was Jesus a Muslim?*, 49–71.
2. Goldberg, *Jews and Christians*, 135–212.
3. Aageson, *In the Beginning*, 35–42.

> [18] Now the birth of Jesus the Messiah took place in this way. When his mother Mary had been engaged to Joseph, but before they lived together, she was found to be with child from the Holy Spirit. [19] Her husband Joseph, being a righteous man and unwilling to expose her to public disgrace, planned to dismiss her quietly. [20] But just when he had resolved to do this, an angel of the Lord appeared to him in a dream and said, "Joseph, son of David, do not be afraid to take Mary as your wife, for the child conceived in her is from the Holy Spirit. [21] She will bear a son, and you are to name him Jesus, for he will save his people from their sins." [22] All this took place to fulfill what had been spoken by the Lord through the prophet:
>
> [23] "Look, the virgin shall conceive and bear a son, and they shall name him Emmanuel," which means, "God is with us." [24] When Joseph awoke from sleep, he did as the angel of the Lord commanded him; he took her as his wife, [25] but had no marital relations with her until she had borne a son; and he named him Jesus.

Without any doubt Matthew makes certain claims about Jesus's identity. He is Jesus, the one who saves his people from their sins (1:1, 21); the Messiah, the anointed one (1:1, 17); the son of David (1:1, 5), a son of Abraham (1:1–2), Emmanuel, God with us (1:23). The gospel writer clearly wants to make a statement about Jesus, who he is, and how he fits into the scheme of divine activity. Jesus is Son of God not only at his baptism, as Mark seems to suggest, but at his birth. He has both a human and a divine lineage, and the names and titles given to him provide readers a sense of what Jesus is to do as well as who he is. He is the fulcrum of redemptive history for Matthew, and as such he is the center of the gospel writer's master story of the church.

But what else is going on behind this story? Let me suggest that from the point of view of Matthew's religious system an entire view of the world informs this account. Although the ancients would not have made the same sharp distinctions we make between heaven and earth, nature and supernature, natural and supernatural, mundane and transcendent, God(s) and humans, it is clear Matthew positions Jesus as the touchstone between them. He is the descendent of Abraham and David, the son of Mary, but also the result of the Holy Spirit's activity. He is of God. He has both human maternity and divine paternity. Since the Enlightenment of the seventeenth and eighteenth centuries and the rise of modern science, we in the West have tended to make rather sharp distinctions between the natural world and the supernatural. Some would even deny that there is anything beyond the natural world. Everything that is and that might ever be can be explained in terms of natural forces and natural phenomena. The ancients in the eastern end of the Mediterranean, however, would have seen the boundary between the spirit world and earth as porous, constantly being crossed, where the forces of the two realms confront and interact with each other. The stories of demon possession and miraculous healing in the gospels clearly portray the reality of this world. If Jesus is of God and of woman, he bridges the two realms and brings the work of God to bear in and for the earthly world. What that in fact means the church will need to develop, both theologically and ritually. Theologically speaking, it will call this christological reality the incarnation, God taking on human form and flesh. The figure of Christ is the indispensable feature of the Christian religious system and the central agent in the life and practice of the church. Without him, the system would make little sense, and it certainly would not function as a religious system.

One of the great ironies of Christianity is that the central figure of the religion did not belong to the same religion as those who call themselves Christians. Jesus and his earliest followers were Jews. Jesus did not become the subject of worship and theological reflection among his followers until after his crucifixion, and the religion we call Christianity was not born until sometime later still. In short, Jesus practiced his life and worshiped as a Jew. We could perhaps debate what kind of Jew he was, but he certainly was not a Christian. In other words, Jesus and his earliest followers lived and were nurtured in a Jewish world, but when the church began reconfiguring its religious worldview and centering it in worship of Christ, tensions with other Jews were bound to appear. Ultimately Jesus came to be seen as more than just another Jewish teacher. His followers worshiped him as savior of the world. Not only did this change the intellectual imagery of Jesus's followers, but it altered their practice. To be sure, they continued to use the Jewish Scriptures, but now saw them as pointing forward to Christ and his followers. They saw oneness with Christ and participation in his death as ritually enacted in baptism and Eucharist, and they fully expected him to return in the last days. In those early years, the Christ followers were in the business of recentering their religious worldview and practice. In the end, the church refused to jettison the Jewish Scriptures from their sacred canon, but in many ways they Christianized their interpretations of those Old Testament texts and saw in them the fulfillment of Christ's life and work. Read, for example, Matt 1:22–23, 2:5–6, and 2:17–18 with the gospel writer's emphasis on the fulfillment of Old Testament prophecy in Christ:

> 1^{22}All this took place to fulfill what had been spoken by the Lord through the prophet^{23} "Look, the virgin shall conceive and bear a son, and they shall name him Emmanuel, . . ."

2:5 They told him, "In Bethlehem of Judea; for so it has been written by the prophet:

> 6 'And you, Bethlehem, in the land of Judah,
>   are by no means least among the rulers of Judah;
>   for from you shall come a ruler
>   who is to shepherd my people Israel.'"

2:17 Then was fulfilled what had been spoken through the prophet Jeremiah:

> 18 "A voice was heard in Ramah,
>   wailing and loud lamentation,
> Rachel weeping for her children;
>   she refused to be consoled, because they are no more."

Or read Isa 52:13—53:6 through the lens of Christ's life and death:

> 52:13 See, my servant shall prosper;
>   he shall be exalted and lifted up,
>   and shall be very high.
> 14 Just as there were many who were astonished at him
>   —so marred was his appearance, beyond human semblance,
>   and his form beyond that of mortals—
> 15 so he shall startle many nations;
>   kings shall shut their mouths because of him;
> for that which had not been told them they shall see,
>   and that which they had not heard they shall contemplate.
> 53:1 Who has believed what we have heard?
>   And to whom has the arm of the LORD been revealed?
> 2 For he grew up before him like a young plant,
>   and like a root out of dry ground;
> he had no form or majesty that we should look at him,
>   nothing in his appearance that we should desire him.
> 3 He was despised and rejected by others;
>   a man of suffering and acquainted with infirmity;
> and as one from whom others hide their faces
>   he was despised, and we held him of no account. 4 Surely he has borne our infirmities
> and carried our diseases;
> yet we accounted him stricken,
>   struck down by God, and afflicted.
> 5 But he was wounded for our transgressions,
>   crushed for our iniquities;

upon him was the punishment that made us whole,
  and by his bruises we are healed.
⁶ All we like sheep have gone astray;
  we have all turned to our own way,
and the LORD has laid on him
  the iniquity of us all.

It is not hard to see how this could be read by the early Christians as pertaining to Christ and to his treatment at the hands of the Roman soldiers, even though that does not appear to be what the text means in its Jewish scriptural context. One of the early debates in the church was how belief in Christ as Messiah related to the tradition of Moses and the practice of Torah by first-century Jews. We see this reflected in Matthew's account of Jesus's Sermon on the Mount in 5:17–20, and perhaps also in the so-called antitheses found in 5:21–48:

> ¹⁷ "Do not think that I have come to abolish the law or the prophets; I have come not to abolish but to fulfill. ¹⁸ For truly I tell you, until heaven and earth pass away, not one letter, not one stroke of a letter, will pass from the law until all is accomplished. ¹⁹ Therefore, whoever breaks one of the least of these commandments, and teaches others to do the same, will be called least in the kingdom of heaven; but whoever does them and teaches them will be called great in the kingdom of heaven. ²⁰ For I tell you, unless your righteousness exceeds that of the scribes and Pharisees, you will never enter the kingdom of heaven.

We might assume that Jesus and his earliest followers practiced the rituals and torah expectations of their respective Jewish communities,[4] but as the early church grew and spread to new peoples and lands, the question invariably arose regarding the place of Judaism's ritual and legal prescriptions for the lives of Christians. How should torah factor into the lives and practices of Christians, if they have a christocentric worldview with all of the beliefs and practices that go with that? We will learn more about this in chapters 3–5, but for now it is important to understand how the Christian religious system came to be structured, and how that system, at first Jewish, became generally less and less so over time. In the beginning, the Christ followers were thought to be simply another sect within Judaism, but later they would become something different, largely a freestanding and separate religion.

---

4. Vermes, *Christian Beginnings*, 51–60.

TORAH AND EARLY JUDAISM: BRIEF OVERVIEW OF A RELIGIOUS SYSTEM

Exodus is one of the primary master narratives of Judaism.[5] It covers some of the most important events in Israelite and Jewish memory, and it shapes Jewish identity. It also helps organize Judaism as a religious system. The narrative begins with stories about the Hebrews' bondage in Egypt (the people were called Hebrews at this point) and the appearance of Moses to lead the people miraculously across the Red Sea to freedom under the watchful hand of God. This all follows the plagues God had inflicted on Pharaoh to convince him to let the people go. As formative as this story has been for Judaism and Jews, it has also become an archetypical image for many other groups who have sought liberation from oppression: for example, American slaves who longed for their freedom. But Exodus is more than a story about liberation, for when the Hebrew people went into the wilderness of Sinai, they rebelled against Moses and struggled against the hardships of the desert that seemed worse than the bondage they had suffered in Egypt. More than a simple story about freedom from slavery, it is a story that couples liberation from oppression under Pharaoh with the freedom to serve God. It is not merely a story about being set free from constraint. Equally important, it is a story about freedom in the service of responsibility and obedience to God. And so the story continues with Moses's going up Mount Sinai and receiving the Ten Commandments from God, written on tablets of stone. It is a story of Moses's encounter with the awesomeness of God high on a mountaintop, symbolizing nearness to the divine, but it is also a story filled with various kinds of intrigue, faithlessness, frustration, and anger. Yet perhaps above all, Moses's encounter yields the commandments, a declaration of God's expectations for the people and their well-being. This becomes the centerpiece of the relationship or covenant between God and the people, sometimes called the Mosaic covenant. In imagery and symbol, it is foundational for the notion of Torah in Judaism. *Torah* is often translated into English as "law," but this only partially captures the full sense of the term. Torah includes stories of the people as the descendants of Abraham now inhabiting the promised land of Israel, as well as the expectations God has for how the people ought to live and observe the commandments, in both general terms such as the Ten Commandments, and in more specific terms such as the ritual and civic expectations set before the people of Israel. To be sure, different Jews understood and worked out the implications and expectations of Torah in

---

5. Goldberg, *Jews and Christians*, 25–118.

different ways, but it is hard to imagine Judaism as a functioning religion without some notion of torah.

In the exodus story, God ratchets up the seriousness of the plagues and sends the angel of death to take the firstborn of each house as the final demonstration intended to convince Pharaoh to let the Hebrews go from Egypt. Those with blood on the lintels of their doors, the Hebrews, are spared because the angel of death passes over those houses and does not take the firstborn. Hence, to this day, Jews celebrate the feast of Passover. In ritual and remembrance, observant Jews celebrate the memory of the exodus and the intervention of God to spare his people and lead them to freedom. It is a bold and powerful story, remembered and made real in ritual and meal, as the family and community sit before the table. In that sense, it is a story both ancient and contemporary, past and yet present.

However, religious systems are more than stories, more than expectations and guidance for life, more than ritual celebrations. They are made up of communities of people, and Judaism is certainly a case in point. Central to Judaism is the notion of the community, in some sense as the people of Israel, the people of the land, the people of some shared ethnic identity. And, of course, many Jews are not religiously observant, but they are still Jews. Most Jews are born into the ethnic Jewish community, whether they are religious or secular. Unlike Judaism, Christianity became a faith practiced by communities distinct from a particular ethnic or familial origin. To be sure, individuals can convert to Judaism and be adopted into the family, but Judaism by and large has not been a proselytizing religion as Christianity has historically been. It should also be noted at this point that contemporary Judaism, as well as Judaism down through ages, is a very diverse phenomenon. Jews' historic experiences and their religious traditions exhibit great variety. Even in Jesus's day, early Judaism was diverse, made up of different groups and sects: Pharisees, Sadducees, Essenes, Zealots, to name the more prominent ones. Therefore, when we think about Judaism, ancient and modern, we need to think about it in terms of a people, but a people that also displays great differences individually in terms of belief and practice.

Israel's emerging sense of monotheism and its covenantal relationship with God ultimately shaped its entire religious system and its notion of torah. It would be inaccurate to suggest that Israel's monotheistic belief (belief in one God) appeared full blown at the outset of its experience as a religious community. The Israelites did not necessarily deny the existence of other gods, but they clearly saw something special about Yahweh, and they believed that Yahweh saw something special about them. Over time their idea of God developed, and so did the idea that God is universal, creator and redeemer of the world. This conviction informed the Israelites' sense of their covenantal relationship with Yahweh, expressed most vividly in the stories of Moses (Exodus) and Abraham (Genesis). And as the years of wondering in the wilderness of Sinai came to an end and the Hebrew people settled in the promised land of Canaan, the land west of the Jordan River, their attachment to the land also came to be important to their imagination, identity, and sense of place in the world.[6] This sense of the land has had a long and tortured history for Jews, even to this day. But persisting throughout the experience of Judaism as a religion is the importance of torah, though it is understood and practiced quite differently in different corners of the community.

QUR'AN AND ISLAM: BRIEF OVERVIEW OF A RELIGIOUS SYSTEM

The Arabic words *Islam*, meaning "submission or surrender to God's will," and *Muslim*, meaning "one who submits or surrenders to God's will," are obviously linked to the religion we today call Islam, whose adherents comprise over a billion of the earth's inhabitants.[7] Historically, the prophet Muhammad appeared in the Arabian Peninsula in the seventh century of the Common Era. As Judaism and Christianity had before it, Islam became a diverse and complex religious phenomenon. Though born in the Arabian Peninsula, it has spread beyond the Arab world to much of South and Southeast Asia, Africa, and the West. Between 610 CE and 632 CE Mohammad received revelations from Allah (Arabic for God) through the angel Gabriel literally called the "recitation," Qur'an. Strictly speaking, only the Arabic can be called the Qur'an, even though the text has been translated into English and other world languages. Though the Qur'an was simply an oral recitation in the beginning, following Muhammad's death an authoritative written text of the Qur'an was produced. The Qur'an is considered to be the ultimate revelation of God.[8] More specifically, it is the revelatory centerpiece of Islam, and it displays and actualizes for Muslims the in-breaking of divine revelation into the world. To use the language of religious systems, Qur'an represents the foundation without which the religious system could not function, and it is that which gives the system its coherence.

---

6. More will be said about this in the next chapter.
7. For a good, accessible description of Islam, see Aslan, *No God but God*.
8. Hussain, *Oil and Water*, 69–78.

The five pillars of Islam define the practice of Muslims: 1) *the Shahadah* or statement of faith, "I bear witness that there is no God but God, and I bear witness that Muhammad is the messenger of God"; 2) *salat*, prayer, five times a day by observant Muslims; 3) *zakat*, charitable giving; 4) *sawm*, fasting during the month of Ramadan; and 5) *hajj*, pilgrimage to Mecca.[9] As one can see very quickly, Islam is a religion with a powerfully concise confession of faith, and at the same time it turns significantly on the practice of submission to Allah through clearly prescribed activities. Emphasis on monotheism is central to Islam, just as it is to Judaism, and both place great importance on religious practice, emanating from Moses and torah in the case of Judaism and Muhammad and *sharia* (law) in the case of Islam. But both presume that their obedience is to the will of God, Yahweh or Allah. Islam, however, is not merely a religion of individuals, because the concept of community is also fundamentally important. The term *ummah* expresses the basic unity of the Islamic community, a community made up of Muslims from different regions of the world and different ethnic groups. Here too Muslim community and tradition is historically diverse. The great historic division in Islam is between Sunni and Shia, a division that goes back to the early days of Islam following Muhammad's death. But even beyond that, historic Islam has a great many legal and philosophical traditions within its various religious communities, most of which are little known outside the traditional confines of Islam.

THREE RELIGIOUS SYSTEMS

Let me begin by being clear. This systemic comparison of religions is not intended to be comprehensive. Furthermore, it is intended primarily to help us understand the religious character and function of Christianity, without presuming that the questions important from a Christian point of view or an academic point of view are necessarily the same as those that animate Judaism and Islam, or even Christianity for that matter. In many cases they are not the same. To even bring these systems into conversation in the eyes of some runs the risk of bringing a kind of Western Christian, or perhaps even a secular, worldview to the conversation, which inevitably skews what we see. However, I repeat what I said earlier. We invariably bring our own questions to the study of religious material, and the only issues are which ones we bring and how we use them. Hence, I have tried to be explicit about my question and how I will try to use it; that is, comparatively. In short, I think that a question addressed to a religious phenomenon as part of a

9. Ibid., 87–100.

descriptive task has the best chance of dealing with the material responsibly. Moreover, I want to claim that from a religious and systemic point of view, these three religions have enough in common historically and religiously that comparison is a legitimate and productive effort.

If Christ is critical to the belief and practice of Christianity as a religious system, the same can be said about torah to Judaism and Qur'an to Islam, because in each case at some fundamental level the boundary between God and humans has been crossed, if not in fact bridged. Jesus is of God just as he is of woman. He is the living incarnation of God on earth, and that governs the Christian church's belief and practice. In him, heaven and earth touch. He is both a teacher of divine things and the redeemer of humankind. He is a man who walked the dusty paths of Galilee and was crucified on a rocky hill near Jerusalem at the hands of Roman soldiers. And for Christians, he is God's anointed, who was raised from the dead and now sits at the right hand of God. In him the kingdom of God has broken into the present. Following and trusting Jesus, Messiah and Son of God, is foundational to the Christian life. He is that without which Christianity would neither make sense nor function, and as such he is the lynchpin in the Christian religious conviction that God has entered into the world. In the decades and years following Jesus's life, the church would spend enormous amounts of intellectual energy working out the implications of this foundational conviction. How is it that he is God and man? What is the meaning of his crucifixion, a seemingly senseless execution? What is the significance of his teaching for the church? When will he return, and what does it mean to have faith? What is the nature of the Christian life and practice centered in Christ? Reflection on these kinds of questions would animate discussion and debate in the early church. It would result eventually in the church's great confessions of faith, namely, the Apostles' and Nicene Creeds, which were thought to summarize the orthodox Christian belief. And it is this christological conviction that would anchor Christian ritual practice in baptism and Eucharist. Through these ritual enactments, the faithful would participate in the body of Christ represented both mystically (symbolically and spiritually) and socially (in the visible church).

The church's Christology would prompt a particular debate that would ultimately shape orthodox Christianity and raise questions among Jews and Muslims about its monotheism. That is the notion of the Trinity, the belief that God is represented in three persons: Father, Son, and Holy Spirit. The belief in the Trinity would come ultimately to define most of Christianity and shape the three parts of the church's confession, with each focused on a different part of the Godhead. This theological confession would open the church to the charge of polytheism and set it apart from Jewish, and eventually Muslim, notions of God.[10] In this and other christological debates, the early church would establish the importance of theological reflection as it sought to work out the meaning of the faith. In the face of differing interpretations of the faith, early catholic Christianity came to prevail and establish orthodox Christian belief and practice. In short, orthodoxy (correct belief) came to be important to Christian life and tradition, unlike in Judaism and Islam, which seem to be compelled in daily life more by orthopraxy (correct practice).[11] This is certainly not to say, however, that practice is unimportant to Christians, or that belief is absent from Jewish and Muslim life. But it is a clear recognition that the three religions are driven by different foundational convictions that compel their life, thought, and practice.

To the extent that Judaism is driven by torah, this makes perfect sense. Again, torah is more than the English word *law* suggests, but among other things it is about expectations for living and the ritual patterns that go with them. So it is no surprise that Jews would be concerned about working out the implications of God's moral, civic, and ritual law. In short, obedience to divine rule and rules is tantamount to being holy as the Lord their God is holy.[12] In chapter 4, we will see how this eventually worked itself out in the emergence of rabbinic Judaism after the time of Jesus, but for now it is important to recognize that a religious system reflects and conforms to that which is thought to be centrally important to it. In this case, it is torah, not Christ, who is thought by Jews to be at most a wise teacher, prophet, or holy man, but not messiah. Structurally Jews operate within a similar religious framework as Christians do, but in terms of the details and particularities they are governed by different religious centers. This results in different religious practices, beliefs, and views of the world. While Christianity and first-century Judaism may have begun as sibling religions, over time they ended up being distant cousins, sometimes with tragic consequences, especially for Jews.

Though Islam historically came along later, its religious dynamic is much the same as the dynamics in Christianity and Judaism. Muslims view Jesus as a prophet but not Messiah or Son of God. And if Qur'an, not Christ or Torah, is the ultimate revelation of God for Muslims and a centerpiece of the faith, it follows that this is going to govern how Muslims will live and practice their religion. This is virtually self-evident, but too often forgotten. As we remember the five pillars of Islam, one of them focuses explicitly on

---

10. Compare the Muslim confession of faith about the oneness of God.
11. Hussain, *Oil and Water*, 90–91.
12. Neusner, *From Testament to Torah*, 6–7. See Lev 19:1–18.

belief, whereas the other four pertain to specific practices. This perhaps gives us a clue that Islam, like Judaism, is in many ways a religion of practice. However, a word of caution is in order here. Muslims have historically produced important philosophical and intellectual traditions that pertain to Islamic life, faith, and politics. Hence, it would be an error to think Muslims are only interested in sharia law. Whereas Christians and Jews living in the West have separated in more recent times their overt religious activities from the political life of their pluralistic democracies, in predominantly Islamic countries many Muslims have tended to see their religious, political, and social orders as much more of an undivided whole. To separate what we in the West would call religion from this unified whole would distort things from a traditional Muslim point of view.[13] In the beginning of the twenty-first century, this sense of unity among the religious, social, and political spheres is still an unfolding story in traditionally Muslim lands of the Middle East. Yet this sense of unity is a difference that separates many traditional Muslims from people in the West, and this needs to be acknowledged.

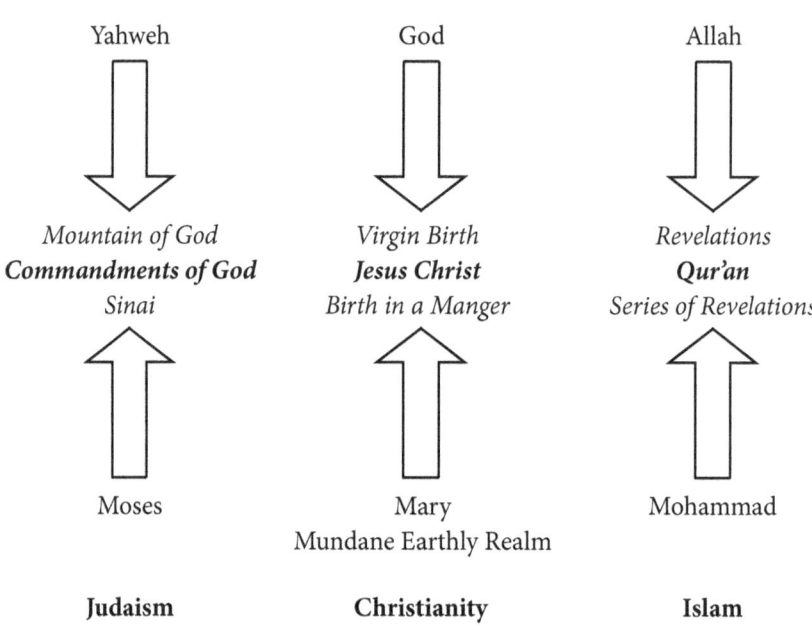

Diagram of the Three Religions

---

13. Shedinger, *Was Jesus a Muslim?*, 1–20.

Three Middle Eastern Religions

Moses and the Tables of the Law, Reni, 1624

Church of the Holy Sepulcher, Jerusalem

3

Abraham and Sarah
Story and Counterstory

What role does a progenitor, perhaps a founding figure, play in a religious system, and how does Abraham fulfill that function in Judaism and Christianity?

In this chapter, I will consider the ways religious communities tell the stories of how they came into being, together with the ways their ancient ancestors became mirrors reflecting the things that are important to them centuries later. If Moses and Jesus are critical to the master stories of Judaism and Christianity, it is Abraham who assumes the role of a founding figure for Judaism and in a quite different way perhaps also for Christianity. Referring to Mircea Eliade's expression "the prestige of origins,"[1] Jon Levenson writes about Abraham in the life of Judaism: "In that case, the goal is not so much to make a point about Abraham; it is to make a point about the importance and preciousness of the practices of Torah by associating them with the ancient and revered first father of the Jewish people."[2] That is an insightful comment and opens the question for us about how an ancient ancestor, in this case Abraham, functions in the two religions. If Christianity grows out of first-century Judaism, it is not surprising that the early church would be compelled to address the role of Abraham. But how it does so is clearly another matter. Once again, by juxtaposing the stories and counterstories,

---

1. Eliade, *Myth and Reality*, 21–38.
2. Levenson, *Inheriting Abraham*, 147.

we will learn about how they relate to each and what this says about early Christian thinking.

ABRAHAM IN BIBLICAL AND JEWISH TRADITION

The biblical account of Abraham (here called Abram) begins in Gen 12:1–3:

> [1]Now the LORD said to Abram, "Go from your country and your kindred and your father's house to the land that I will show you. [2]I will make of you a great nation, and I will bless you, and make your name great, so that you will be a blessing. [3]I will bless those who bless you, and the one who curses you I will curse; and in you all the families of the earth shall be blessed."

So begins the story of Abraham, and a little further on in 15:1–6, it is elaborated:

> [1]After these things the word of the Lord came to Abram in a vision, "Do not be afraid, Abram, I am your shield; your reward shall be very great." [2] But Abram said, "O Lord GOD, what will you give me, for I continue childless, and the heir of my house is Eliezer of Damascus?" [3] And Abram said, "You have given me no offspring, and so a slave born in my house is to be my heir." [4] But the word of the LORD came to him, "This man shall not be your heir; no one but your very own issue shall be your heir." [5] He brought him outside and said, "Look toward heaven and count the stars, if you are able to count them." Then he said to him, "So shall your descendants be." [6] And he believed the Lord; and the LORD reckoned it to him as righteousness.

In chapters 12–50, the focus of the entire Genesis narrative is the story of Abram (later renamed Abraham) and his descendants. The two texts just cited are perhaps the most poignant statements of what has come to be called the Abrahamic covenant in Judaism. Seemingly out of the blue, Abram is told to leave his family and his home and go to a land he will be shown. He is told that he will be made a great nation, that he will be blessed, and that in him all the families of the earth will be blessed. Abram does what he is requested to do, but as the story unfolds it is clear there is a problem. He is without an heir. Moreover, he and his wife are old, and she is beyond childbearing years. How can the promise be fulfilled? It seems impossible for him to be a great nation, let alone to be a blessing to the nations, without offspring. Much of the early part of the narrative is devoted to this dilemma. But God promises Abram that he will have an heir, and that his descendants will be as numerous as the stars in the night sky. Despite the surrogate mother arrangement proposed by Sarai, Abraham's wife, that results in the birth of Ishmael by Sarai's maidservant, Hagar (16:1–15), Abram is told that Ishmael will not be his heir. His wife, despite her age, will bear a child (17:1–22). The tension in the story is resolved only with the birth of Isaac (18:9–19; 21:1–7). But the tension escalates again with God's command to Abram to bind his promised son, Isaac, and offer him as a sacrifice (22:1–19). In the end, Abraham proves faithful to God by preparing to sacrifice his promised son, and he is told to unbind Isaac. Disaster and tragedy are averted, and the covenant will now play itself out in what might be called a genealogical narrative of the next generations (23–50).

Though Ishmael is sent away, God promises that he too will be a great nation (21:12–14; 25:12–18), even as Isaac is clearly Abraham's heir and the promised child. Isaac is the one through whom the line of Abraham passes, and through whom the story plots the genealogical progression. He and his wife, Rebekah, have twin sons, Esau and Jacob, and through deception by Rebekah and Jacob the birthright passes from Isaac to Jacob, instead of to Esau (27:1—28:5). As the story develops, Jacob ultimately has twelve sons; and at the Jabbok River, he wrestles with a man until daybreak. Though the man does not prevail against him, he strikes Jacob in the hip and puts it out of joint. At that point in the story, the man says to Jacob, "You shall no longer be called Jacob, but Israel, for you have striven with God and with humans and prevailed." (32:22–32). Jacob, now renamed Israel, calls the place Peniel, "For I have seen God face to face, and yet my life is preserved." Now the twelve sons of Israel become the progenitors of the twelve tribes of the people of Israel (49:1–33).

While this is a fascinating account, it is equally fascinating to think about the function of the story for the people of Israel down through the generations. Regardless of whether this is a legend, it certainly became legendary. It functioned to establish the identity of a people, much as any genealogy does. But in this case, it is largely the identity of the community, of which the individual Israelites are a part: who they are, where they came from, and perhaps equally who they are not. They are not the people descended from Ishmael and Esau. They are the people of God's promise now fulfilled. In the generations that follow, the people could think back to this story, first told orally and only eventually written down, and see in their very existence the fulfillment of God's promise to Abraham. They are numerous, and they are at times a great nation. Indeed the promise of God has been fulfilled. In terms of the covenant with Abraham, they are a blessed people. The story says something about the nature of God and God's faithfulness to the people of Israel. It is theological in that sense.[3] But it is also profoundly religious. There is in fact a community; we call them the people of Israel: and in myth, ritual, and imagination, they have a deep sense of who they are and whence they have come—something without which the community probably could not have endured. Over the generations and centuries, the people of Israel would suffer setbacks and various traumas, but I suggest that even when the people of Israel were stretched thin, perhaps on the verge of melting away and disappearing forever from view, the story of Abraham and God's promise to him continued to function at some deep psychological and sociological level to enable the people of Israel to survive. As we have seen in the previous chapter, there is much more to Judaism than the promise to the patriarch Abraham, but it certainly functioned as part of the religious whole we call Judaism. And over time the story continued to be revisited and reinterpreted, perhaps most especially the figure of Abraham himself.

The most thorough, recent study of Abraham in Judaism, Christianity, and Islam is the book by Jon Levenson, *Inheriting Abraham: The Legacy of the Patriarch in Judaism, Christianity, and Islam*. For a thorough investigation of Abraham in the history and tradition of the three religions, this book should be consulted. But for our purposes, we can focus on one aspect of the Abraham story that generated special interest among later interpreters and also seems to have influenced early Christianity. This is the account of God's command that Abraham bind his son Isaac and prepare to sacrifice him on a mountain in the land of Moriah. This is known as the Binding (*Aqedah*) of Isaac. On its face, it is a poignant and troubling story to say the least, and over time Jewish interpreters returned to it to make sense of what it might mean. Apart from any implications of child sacrifice or the cruelty of God in commanding a father to sacrifice his son, Jewish interpreters focused on Abraham's commitment to God's will. This was a story of obedience and surrender to God, now represented in the commandments of torah. We can see here how the torah tradition of Judaism and the Abraham tradition came together.[4] Though there is no direct reference to Abraham's faithfulness in Gen 22, it might be inferred from his actions that he has confidence God will fulfill what he had promised. And if that promise is to be fulfilled, how can Isaac in fact be sacrificed? There is an internal logic to the story that the killing of Isaac would seemingly violate. We should not try to psychologize Abraham's state of mind in the event, but it becomes clear that later interpreters will see in Abraham's willingness to bind his son and proceed with the sacrifice, as painful as it must have been, an act of extreme obedience.

---

3. Levenson, *Inheriting Abraham*, 6.
4. Ibid., 112.

Moreover, Abraham now reflects the Jewish concern for surrender to God expressed through obedience to God's will in the commandments of Torah. There will also be later speculation about Isaac's role in the episode, what he knew and when he knew it.[5] As Levenson says:

> If we remember that oath-taking and covenant-making overlap, and that "oath" itself can be a term for covenant, we will see that the Aqedah has now become the basis for the Abrahamic covenant, or, to state the reverse, the Abrahamic covenant has now become a consequence of the Aqedah. Abraham's great act of obedience stands to the benefit of the nation that derives from him for all time.[6]

What seems in the story to be an act of pure grace—or arbitrariness, depending on one's point of view—now becomes a matter of divine promise and human response. The Abrahamic covenantal relationship, in light of these interpretations, reflects a sense of reciprocal mutuality, perhaps more akin to the Mosaic covenant in that regard. In that way, Abraham lived on in Jewish life and imagination and became a reflection of later and wider Jewish sensibilities. To put it another way, not only are later interpreters trying to say something about Abraham, but perhaps more important, they are seeing something in Abraham that is important to them and their contemporary religious practice.

---

5. Ibid., 75–79.
6. Ibid., 84.

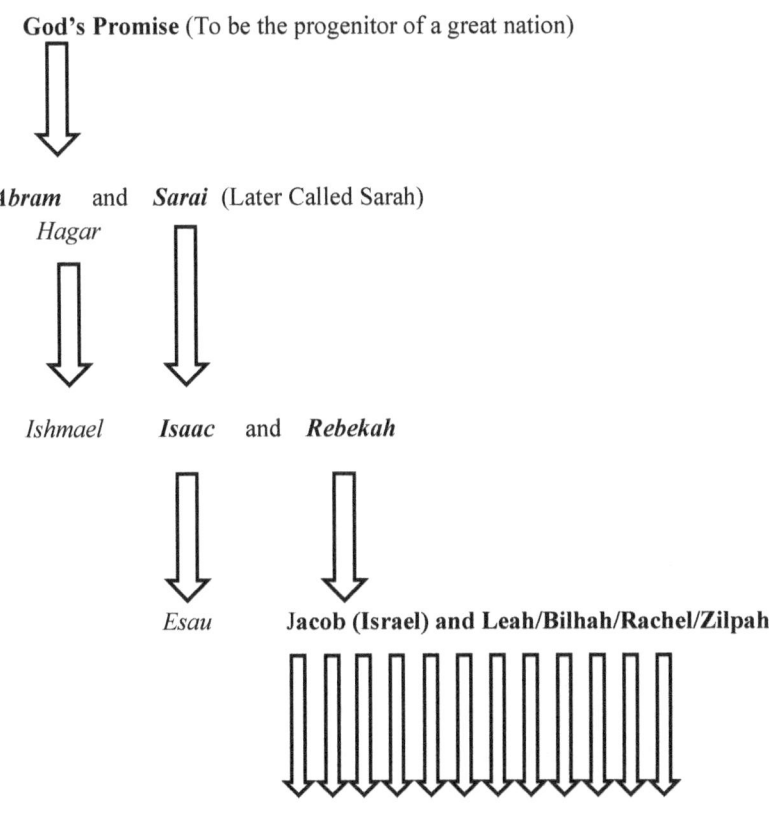

12 Sons, 12 Tribes of Israel, People of the Promise

Diagram of the Genealogical Backbone of Genesis 12–50

ABRAHAM IN NEW TESTAMENT TRADITION

In no sense could we meaningfully claim from a historical point of view that Abraham is the founder of Christianity. Jesus, or some might say the apostle Paul, are the candidates for this title. While Abraham has some claim to that title in Jewish biblical narrative, Christianity is a different case, because Christ is the center of the religious system, and Paul clearly set the early church on the trajectory that would eventually become Christianity. However, Abraham is still important to the early church as a theological ancestor, largely because the Jesus community emerged out of first-century Judaism and maintained the Jewish Scriptures as part of its sacred library. In this regard, Abraham assumes a role in Christian imagination and theology.

His role is not unimportant, and he is often brought to the fore to say something about the present circumstance of the church and its people. We can describe this process as having two different features. First, the early Christ followers turned to the scriptural texts dealing with Abraham, as they did with many other texts in the Jewish Scriptures, and sought to make sense of their faith and situation. In short, they interpreted and applied Scripture to their own context. Second, they also sought to give authority to their teaching and arguments by rooting them in Scripture and in the ancient traditions of Abraham. He gave authority to their teaching because its truth was there from the very beginning. In that sense, we may call him theologically foundational.

In some Jewish traditions, the Aqedah of Isaac came to be connected to the Passover sacrifice in Egypt.[7] The link between Jesus's death and Passover is clearly reflected in the Synoptic Gospel accounts of Jesus's crucifixion (Matthew, Mark, and Luke), and Paul writes in 1 Cor 5:7, "For our paschal lamb, Christ, has been sacrificed." The familiar John 3:16 passage also seems to reflect imagery from the Aqedah: "For God so loved the world that he gave his only Son, so that everyone who believes in him may not perish but may have eternal life." If one of the early impulses was to give meaning to the seemingly meaningless death of Jesus, the Aqedah of Isaac was at hand. Any parallels between Isaac and Jesus, however, are also matched by some obvious differences. Though God commanded Isaac to be bound and his father clearly complied, he is not finally sacrificed according to the Genesis account. But here is where the connection with the Passover story is probably important. In Exodus, God brings death to the firstborn of Egypt and through it brings freedom to the Hebrews. And in the annual Passover commemoration, Jews ritually celebrated this sacrifice on their behalf through story and symbol. In early Christian thinking, Christ, the Son of God, has been given and sacrificed by his Father in heaven for the redemption of the world.

In Gal 3:6–9, Paul cites Gen 15:6:

> [6] Just as Abraham "believed God, and it was reckoned to him as righteousness," [7] so, you see, those who believe are the descendants of Abraham. [8] And the Scripture, foreseeing that God would justify the Gentiles by faith, declared the gospel beforehand to Abraham, saying, "All the Gentiles shall be blessed in you." [9] For this reason, those who believe are blessed with Abraham who believed.[8]

---

7. Ibid., 91–99.
8. Cf. Rom 4.

Here Paul is deeply engaged in a debate about his mission to the Gentiles (non-Jews) and how they might become part of the Jesus community. Paul argues that they can come in on the basis of faith and not through torah observance, especially circumcision, Jewish dietary expectations, and the sacred calendar. This was one of the early church's important debates, and Paul clearly came down on the side of Gentile inclusion apart from the requirements of Torah.[9] In making his case to the Galatians, Paul turns to the story of Abraham in Gen 15:1–6. We recall that in that text, Abraham is lamenting the fact that despite God's promise he is without his own heir, and that Eliezer of Damascus will be his heir by default. But God takes him outside and reiterates the promise. Your descendants will be a many as the stars in the night sky. We are told Abraham believed God, and it was reckoned to him as righteousness. In other words, Abraham was reckoned to be righteous by his faith in God's promise, despite all the contrary evidence. Moreover, at the time Abraham was declared to be righteous, he was not yet circumcised (Gen 17): technically in Paul's view he was a Gentile. Paul makes this argument explicit in Rom 4:9–12:

> [9] Is this blessedness, then, pronounced only on the circumcised, or also on the uncircumcised? We say, "Faith was reckoned to Abraham as righteousness." [10] How then was it reckoned to him? Was it before or after he had been circumcised? It was not after, but before he was circumcised. [11] He received the sign of circumcision as a seal of the righteousness that he had by faith while he was still uncircumcised. The purpose was to make him the ancestor of all who believe without being circumcised and who thus have righteousness reckoned to them.

Unlike in Jewish tradition where Abraham became an example of obedience to the will of God (torah), he was seen to be an exemplar of faith (faith in Christ) in Paul's interpretation. And this reading of Abraham was put in the service of making the case for the church's mission to the Gentiles. Ultimately his efforts succeeded, and the church became overwhelmingly non-Jewish.[10]

In Gal 3:23–29, Paul takes the argument a step further:

> [23] Now before faith came, we were imprisoned and guarded under the law until faith would be revealed. [24] Therefore the law was our disciplinarian until Christ came, so that we might be justified by faith. [25] But now that faith has come, we are no longer subject to a disciplinarian, [26] for in Christ Jesus you are

---

9. This will be fleshed out much more fully in chapter 5.
10. More will be said about this in chapter 5.

all children of God through faith. ²⁷ As many of you as were baptized into Christ have clothed yourselves with Christ. ²⁸ There is no longer Jew or Greek, there is no longer slave or free, there is no longer male and female; for all of you are one in Christ Jesus. ²⁹ And if you belong to Christ, then you are Abraham's offspring, heirs according to the promise.

Here Paul brings together an explanation of the role of Torah in light of Christ (it is a temporary disciplinarian until the coming of Christ) and life through faith in Christ for the children of God (the people in the community of Christ's church). But Paul does not stop here. All those baptized have been baptized into Christ and have put on Christ, much as a person puts on clothes. In Christ, the old social distinctions have been removed. And those who belong to Christ are effectively Abraham's offspring and heirs according to the promise of God. We could say they are adopted as children of Abraham through Christ.[11] If the story of Abraham for Jews is about the familial line of descent, for Paul it is about incorporation into the line of descent and the promise of God through Christ. Here we can see that Paul interprets the Genesis text, but he also underscores the legitimacy of his argument by rooting it in the antiquity of Abraham, the forefather of the people of Israel, in order to make his point about the contemporary situation of the church. The success of Paul's argument would have a profound effect on the direction of the church and the formation of Christianity.

It is illustrative to contrast what Paul has said about Abraham with what he says about Moses in 2 Cor 3:7–18:

> ⁷ Now if the ministry of death, chiseled in letters on stone tablets, came in glory so that the people of Israel could not gaze at Moses' face because of the glory of his face, a glory now set aside, ⁸ how much more will the ministry of the Spirit come in glory? ⁹ For if there was glory in the ministry of condemnation, much more does the ministry of justification abound in glory! ¹⁰ Indeed, what once had glory has lost its glory because of the greater glory; ¹¹ for if what was set aside came through glory, much more has the permanent come in glory!
>
> ¹² Since, then, we have such a hope, we act with great boldness, ¹³ not like Moses, who put a veil over his face to keep the people of Israel from gazing at the end of the glory that was being set aside.¹⁴ But their minds were hardened. Indeed, to this very day, when they hear the reading of the old covenant, that same veil is still there, since only in Christ is it set aside. ¹⁵ Indeed, to this very day whenever Moses is read, a veil lies

---

11. Cf. also Gal 4:21–31.

over their minds; ¹⁶ but when one turns to the Lord, the veil is removed. ¹⁷ Now the Lord is the Spirit, and where the Spirit of the Lord is, there is freedom. ¹⁸ And all of us, with unveiled faces, seeing the glory of the Lord as though reflected in a mirror, are being transformed into the same image from one degree of glory to another; for this comes from the Lord, the Spirit.

In this text Paul does not juxtapose Abraham alongside Moses, but he clearly refers to the Sinai story in order to distinguish the ministry of the Spirit from the ministry of condemnation, as he describes it.¹² Even to the present day, says Paul to the Corinthians, a veil lies over the minds of the people of Israel when the old covenant is read. When one turns to the Lord, the veil is removed. What once had glory has lost its glory, because of the surpassing glory that has now come in Christ. Here Paul distinguishes the Christ community from the Israelite community, the ministry of the Spirit from the ministry of condemnation, the glory of the new age in Christ from the glory of God's covenant with Moses. The continuity Paul saw in the Abrahamic stories, rightly interpreted, with the Christ community is contrasted in this text with the discontinuity he apparently sees in the story of Moses, who met God on Mount Sinai and received the commandments. This illustrates how Paul and the early church struggled to figure out the role of the commandments and the Torah more broadly in the life of the church.

We can see in Jas 2:23-24 how this debate continued and how James sought to correct what he believed to be the error of Paul's interpretation of Genesis: "²² You see that faith was active along with his works, and faith was brought to completion by the works. ²³ Thus the scripture was fulfilled that says, 'Abraham believed God, and it was reckoned to him as righteousness,' and he was called the friend of God. ²⁴ You see that a person is justified by works and not by faith alone." James clearly refuses to abandon the importance of works of law for early Christians by asserting that works complete faith and that faith alone does not justify a person. For James, Abraham is not simply a man of faith but he is a friend of God. That implies he was also obedient to God. Once again, we glimpse how the early church debated the place of the law in the life of the community and how Abraham was used to make both the point and the counterpoint of the argument.¹³

Yet again, Abraham figures prominently in the ode to faith in Hebrews chapter 11. Apparently reflecting the Pauline emphasis on faith, the writer expands the story of faith to include the other patriarchs and worthy people

---

12. See the discussion above, pp. 18-19.
13. See the discussion below, pp. 58-61.

in Israelite history as well. But Abraham and his descendants are front and center, when the author writes in 11:8-12, 17-22:

> [8] By faith Abraham obeyed when he was called to set out for a place that he was to receive as an inheritance; and he set out, not knowing where he was going. [9] By faith he stayed for a time in the land he had been promised, as in a foreign land, living in tents, as did Isaac and Jacob, who were heirs with him of the same promise. [10] For he looked forward to the city that has foundations, whose architect and builder is God. [11] By faith he received power of procreation, even though he was too old—and Sarah herself was barren—because he considered him faithful who had promised. [12] Therefore from one person, and this one as good as dead, descendants were born, "as many as the stars of heaven and as the innumerable grains of sand by the seashore."
>
> [17] By faith Abraham, when put to the test, offered up Isaac. He who had received the promises was ready to offer up his only son, [18] of whom he had been told, "It is through Isaac that descendants shall be named for you." [19] He considered the fact that God is able even to raise someone from the dead—and figuratively speaking, he did receive him back. [20] By faith Isaac invoked blessings for the future on Jacob and Esau. [21] By faith Jacob, when dying, blessed each of the sons of Joseph, "bowing in worship over the top of his staff." [22] By faith Joseph, at the end of his life, made mention of the exodus of the Israelites and gave instructions about his burial.

The author of Hebrews retells the story of Abraham and his descendants from the point of their faith, not done in the peculiarly Pauline way of doing so, but certainly reflecting the emphasis on belief and trust in God. Whereas Paul uses the Abrahamic discussion to facilitate the inclusion of Gentiles into the Christ community apart from the observance of certain torah expectations, Hebrews generalizes about the patriarch's trust in God.

Returning to the Gospel of Matthew, we note again that Matthew explicitly identifies Jesus as son of Abraham and shows how his genealogy originates in Abraham (1:1, 2, 17).[14] This may mean nothing more than that Jesus was a Jew, but this is still a powerful claim about Jesus, and one that through the decades and centuries the church has continually needed to relearn. On the other hand, the Gospel of John portrays Jesus as locked in a debate with his Jewish opponents about who he is and who they are, and Abraham figures prominently in that contentious discussion as well (John 8:37-59). Perhaps we can summarize this as a debate about who the real

---

14. See above, pp. 13-14.

descendants of Abraham are. It is one thing to be a Jew, but it seems to be another to be a true Jew. These were debates that often went on in early Judaism, and here Jesus and his opponents appear to be engaging in their own version of this discussion. If this is reflective more broadly of discussions in the early church and early Judaism, it indicates another dynamic at work in the birth of early Christianity. At least in certain corners of the fledgling church, some followers of Christ wanted to lay claim to being the true children of Abraham, to being the true Israel.

In conclusion, it is interesting to see how the Qur'an, six centuries later, understands Abraham. We get a good sense of this in Surah 3:65-68 (Al-'Imran). The Qur'an states:

> 65. O people of the Scripture [Jews and Christians]! Why do you dispute about Ibrahim [Abraham], while the Taurat [Torah] and the Injeel [Gospel] were not revealed till after him? Have you then no sense?
>
> 66. Verily, you are those who have disputed about that of which you have knowledge. Why do you then dispute concerning that which you have no knowledge? It is Allah Who knows, and you know not.
>
> 67. Ibrahim [Abraham] was neither a Jew nor a Christian, but he was a true Muslim *Hanifa* [Islamic Monotheism—to worship none but Allah Alone] and he was not of *Al-Mushrikun* (See V.2:105).
>
> 68. Verily, among mankind who have the best claim to Ibrahim [Abraham] are those who followed him, and this Prophet [Muhammad] and those who have believed (Muslims). And Allah is the *Wali* [Protector and Helper] of the believers.[15]

According to this qur'anic text, Abraham was neither a Jew nor a Christian but a true Muslim, one who submits to Allah, and a devout monotheist. He worshiped Allah and Allah alone. Those who have the best claim to him are those who follow Abraham, namely, Prophet Muhammad and those who believed (Muslims). Again, we see how the ancient ancestor comes to reflect and endorse core religious convictions of a later system of belief, just as he did centuries earlier in Judaism and Christianity. One difference in the case of Islam, however, is that Genesis is not part of Islam's sacred text (Qur'an), even though Muslims acknowledge Jews and Christians as people of Scripture, people of the book.

---

15. Qur'an, Surah 3:65–68.

Sacrifice of Isaac, Caravaggio (1602)

Cave of Machpelah, Tomb of the Patriarchs, Hebron

4

The Births of Two Great Religions
Rabbinic Judaism and Early Christianity

*How did first-century Judaism in Palestine subdivide,
reinvent itself, and contribute to the origin of Christianity?*

Historically and religiously, the first century of the Common Era is critical for the development of Judaism and hence for understanding the origin of Christianity. To be sure, this is the time when Jesus and his early followers lived and when most of the New Testament documents were written, and the importance of these facts for understanding the origin of Christianity is beyond doubt. But for understanding the development of Judaism more broadly, it is probably the war against the Romans (66–70 CE) and the ultimate destruction of the temple in Jerusalem that left the most lasting imprint on the Jewish people in Palestine and beyond. The destruction of the temple, not to be rebuilt to this day, was to have a profound effect on Jews and Judaism and eventually gave rise to what we now call rabbinic Judaism. And if, as I have already argued, the church first emerged as a Jewish sect and neither saw itself nor was seen by others as an independent, freestanding religious phenomenon, it follows that the destruction of the temple also had serious implications for the formation of Christianity. It is my goal in this chapter to work out some of the implications of these events for the purpose of seeing more clearly how early Judaism and the early church were connected and how the church eventually became separate, even hostile to Judaism. This discussion will be organized around three different conceptual models for understanding the relationship between early Judaism and early Christianity. I note at the outset that these models are overarching ways of organizing the available historical and religious data, and they need to be evaluated on how well they account for that data. I also would argue that they need to be judged at times on the basis of the consequences they seemingly have generated and contributed to over time. Ideas have consequences, and when we shine the bright light of moral judgment on them, what do we see? Are we prepared to defend them, or are we not?

THE REPLACEMENT MODEL

The replacement model is a Christian theological way of understanding the relationship between Judaism and Christianity.[1] However, it is a Christian theological understanding with profound historical implications. In short, the replacement model asserts that the old Israel, Judaism, is now replaced by a new Israel, the church. Christ is the turning point of salvation-history, and in this new economy of divine activity Jews have no future apart from Christ, who is the Son of God and Savior of the world. As the diagram below indicates, there is theological and social disjunction between what was the case before and what is the case after the coming of Christ. Likewise, while the Jewish Scriptures were retained by the church, they were now called Old Testament and were juxtaposed alongside a New Testament, which testified to Christ and the theology of the early church. Even though the Jewish Scriptures were retained as part of the Christian Bible, they were now increasingly interpreted through the lens of Christ and New Testament texts. From this theological point of view, a new creation was in the making with the advent of Christ, and the old Israel represented in the Old Testament is preparation for this new reality.

By late in the first century and certainly into the second century and beyond, this way of describing the relationship between Judaism and Christianity began to take root in the church and increasingly governed how Christians would think about Judaism and interact with Jews.[2] In part it was a way for Christians to define who they were by making clear who they were not. They were not simply Jews; they were Christ followers, and the theological implications of this required explanation by the Christians. Increasingly over the decades and centuries, they turned to variations of the replacement model to make the case that they were the true people of God and heirs of salvation. It was not universally the case that Christians

1. Aageson. *Written Also for Our Sake*, 39–41.
2. Flannery, *Anguish of the Jews*, 28–46.

severed all ties with Judaism (e.g., the Ebionites and some people in the eastern reaches of Christianity), and we know that in the fourth century Chrysostom (which translates to "golden mouth") preached a series of sermons castigating church members in Antioch who continued to engage in Jewish ritual practices, thus suggesting that at least some Christians still had close relationships with Jews and Jewish life in that city. Be that as it may, it is still fair to say that the church was increasingly defining itself over and against Judaism in terms of the church having superseded the old Israel, now represented by the Jews.

When reading the New Testament through this lens, a number of New Testament texts seem to jump out and reconfirm the idea that the Jews, apart from Christ, stand under the judgment of God. Though we may see these interpretations as in fact circular, they seemed to have persuasive power in the early church. Even more, these ideas have persisted into the modern era of the church through contemporary forms of Christian anti-Judaism and anti-Semitism. Taking a look at some of the more poignant New Testament texts in this regard will illustrate how and why the replacement idea seemed to make sense to so many and have such power. We begin with a look at Matt 27:20–26:

> [20] Now the chief priests and the elders persuaded the crowds to ask for Barabbas and to have Jesus killed. [21] The governor again said to them, "Which of the two do you want me to release for you?" And they said, "Barabbas." [22] Pilate said to them, "Then what should I do with Jesus who is called the Messiah?" All of them said, "Let him be crucified!" [23] Then he asked, "Why, what evil has he done?" But they shouted all the more, "Let him be crucified!" [24] So when Pilate saw that he could do nothing, but rather that a riot was beginning, he took some water and washed his hands before the crowd, saying, "I am innocent of this man's blood; see to it yourselves." [25] Then the people as a whole answered, "His blood be on us and on our children!" [26] So he released Barabbas for them; and after flogging Jesus, he handed him over to be crucified.

According to this text, the Jews in Jerusalem, spurred on by their leaders, clamor for Jesus's crucifixion, whereas the symbol of Roman power, Pilate, says he finds no reason to execute him, but merely succumbs to Jewish wishes in order to placate the crowds and avoid a riot. Read through the lens of Christian replacement, the Jews appear to be guilty of killing God's only son. What could be more damning confirmation of the replacement of the Jews in salvation-history by Christ and his followers? Perhaps even more troublesome, the Jewish crowds in the story call down upon themselves and their children the blood of the crucified Christ. It is not hard to see how this could be used to reinforce virulent forms of anti-Judaism.

In a similar vein, the so-called Parable of the Wicked Tenants in Matt 21:36–44 seemingly supports the theology of replacement:

> [33] "Listen to another parable. There was a landowner who planted a vineyard, put a fence around it, dug a wine press in it, and built a watchtower. Then he leased it to tenants and went to another country. [34] When the harvest time had come, he sent his slaves to the tenants to collect his produce. [35] But the tenants seized his slaves and beat one, killed another, and stoned another. [36] Again he sent other slaves, more than the first; and they treated them in the same way. [37] Finally he sent his son to them, saying, 'They will respect my son.' [38] But when the tenants saw the son, they said to themselves, 'This is the heir; come, let us kill him and get his inheritance.' [39] So they seized him, threw him out of the vineyard, and killed him. [40] Now when the owner of the vineyard comes, what will he do to those tenants?" [41] They said to him, "He will put those wretches to a miserable death, and lease the vineyard to other tenants who will give him the produce at the harvest time."
>
> [42] Jesus said to them, "Have you never read in the scriptures:
>
>> 'The stone that the builders rejected
>>   has become the cornerstone;
>> this was the Lord's doing,
>>   and it is amazing in our eyes'?
>
> [43] Therefore I tell you, the kingdom of God will be taken away from you and given to a people that produces the fruits of the kingdom. [44] The one who falls on this stone will be broken to pieces; and it will crush anyone on whom it falls."

It appears that Matthew, writing toward the end of the first century, already reflects a type of replacement theology and does so in quite explicit ways.[3] By uncritically allowing Matthew's theology to take precedence and not placing the gospel in its wider historical and religious context, the interpreter easily slides into a replacement framework without much awareness of what is at stake for Matthew and his audience late in the first century. There is no sense of the debates going on in his community, or how the gospel writer, perhaps from a Jewish background himself, sought to articulate the Jesus

---

3. See below, pp. 232–34; 240–41.

story in his own context. This will become clearer in chapter 6 when we consider the literary character and genre of the New Testament gospels.

Matthew and the other gospel writers also relate the Jesus story to the destruction of the temple. In 24:1-2 Matthew writes: "As Jesus came out of the temple and was going away, his disciples came to point out to him the buildings of the temple.² Then he asked them, "You see all these, do you not? Truly I tell you, not one stone will be left here upon another; all will be thrown down." And in 26:59-61 he portrays the Jewish leaders seeking false testimony against Jesus: "Now the chief priests and the whole council were looking for false testimony against Jesus so that they might put him to death, but they found none, though many false witnesses came forward. At last two came forward and said, 'This fellow said, "I am able to destroy the temple of God and to build it in three days."'" Both of these texts relate Jesus to the destruction of the Jerusalem temple. By the time Matthew writes these words, the temple in all likelihood has already been destroyed for some time. The most common judgment is that Matthew was written well after 70 CE when the temple in fact was destroyed by the Roman army. By the way the text presents the words of Jesus, they appear to be an announcement of what will happen and obliquely relate the temple's destruction to Jesus's own resurrection, when they are in fact a retrospective theological explanation of the temple's demise. The temple and what it represents are under the judgment of Christ. Jews will come to terms with the temple's destruction in their own ways as we shall see below, but the early church too was compelled to provide some explanation because of its closeness to Judaism and its worldview. The temple's destruction was perhaps the most formative event in the life of first-century Judaism, and both Jews and the Jesus community had to come to terms with it. Once again, however, we can see quite easily how these texts could be used by the early church to support the notion that Judaism is being replaced as the true people of God.

I have spent time describing and illustrating in general terms the replacement model, not because I think it is the best or most accurate way of understanding the origin of Christianity, but because it is part of the historical record and has had some very pernicious historical consequences. I would assert that Christian anti-Judaism and anti-Semitism are the off-spring of this replacement theology,[4] and we all know the horrific consequences of this kind of thinking in recent times.[5] At the very least, this theology stands under the indictment of moral judgment. But it also illus-

---

4. For a broad look at the history of anti-Semitism, see Flannery, *Anguish of the Jews*.

5. The Holocaust, in the mid-part of the twentieth century, would be a most horrific example.

trates my point in the first chapter of this book, about giving methodological precedence in these matters to historical and religious investigation rather than to theological assertion. To state it another way, good theology will invariably follow from good scholarly investigation. Likewise, the example of these texts indicates that replacement theology has already crept into some of the New Testament material, which is part of sacred Scripture for Christians. This, of course, raises the stakes for many, but here too I would argue that Scripture itself must stand under critical investigation and judgment. If we do not investigate and make judgments about Scripture, then we cannot see the fuller picture of what was going on in the writers' worlds and can slip too easily into anti-Judaism, if not also anti-Semitism, which can be intellectually and socially toxic. Knowledge and historical understanding are not by themselves foolproof antidotes to anti-Judaism and anti-Semitism, but coupled with moral sensitivity and judgment they give us the best chance of resisting potentially destructive theologies or ideologies.

OFFSHOOT MODEL

The offshoot model is a historical way of understanding early Judaism and the origin of Christianity, and in some ways it may have most appeal from a Jewish perspective. It suggests that first-century Judaism continues in a fairly straight line of development from Israelite religion to various forms of Judaism that develop later, and that Christianity is simply a sectarian offshoot, if not a heretical aberration, of early Judaism. From my perspective, it is an improvement over the replacement idea because it begins with a historical concern, and it does not seem to lend itself to such potentially negative consequences. The main objection to this way of understanding early Judaism and Christianity is that it suggests, in my view, a much too direct line of development from Hebrew religion to Israelite and early Jewish religion—and perhaps most telling—to the rise of rabbinic Judaism after the destruction of the temple in the first century. The exodus, the Babylonian destruction and captivity in the sixth century BCE, the period of the Maccabees in the second century BCE, and the destruction caused by the Roman army in 66–70 CE and again in 132–135 CE had profound effects on this line of development, causing significant adjustments to the tradition.

While there is some continuity, Hebrew religion is not the same as Israelite religion, and Israelite religion is not identical with early Jewish religion, and early Jewish religion is not the same as rabbinic Judaism. And differences existed even during these chronological eras and within these religious categories. All this is to say that historically the rise of Christianity is a complex religious and social phenomenon and cannot be reduced to a single thing or a straight line.

From a Christian point of view, I would also suggest that the earliest Jesus community was likely a Jewish sectarian phenomenon, but it was a Jewish sectarian group alongside other Jewish groups and was deeply rooted in Jewish ideas, themes, and practices. Even where the early church was objecting to certain Jewish ideas or practices, Jewish issues were still setting the agenda. Once again turning to Matthew will help us illustrate the point (5:17–20):

> [17] "Do not think that I have come to abolish the law or the prophets; I have come not to abolish but to fulfill. [18] For truly I tell you, until heaven and earth pass away, not one letter, not one stroke of a letter, will pass from the law until all is accomplished. [19] Therefore, whoever breaks one of the least of these commandments, and teaches others to do the same, will be called least in the kingdom of heaven; but whoever does them and teaches them will be called great in the kingdom of heaven. [20] For I tell you, unless your righteousness exceeds that of the scribes and Pharisees, you will never enter the kingdom of heaven.

To be sure, Matthew is a deeply committed Christ follower, but he also feels compelled, as we see in this text, to address what the Jewish law and observance mean for followers of Christ. An important Jewish concern, namely torah observance, is something that Matthew and his community must think about. What does torah observance mean for those who believe in Christ? His answers in 5:17–20 and in the six antitheses in 5:21–48 define what he means by adherence to the law. The fourth antithesis will suffice to illustrate the point in 5:38–42:

> [38] "You have heard that it was said, 'An eye for an eye and a tooth for a tooth.' [39] But I say to you, Do not resist an evildoer. But if anyone strikes you on the right cheek, turn the other also; [40] and if anyone wants to sue you and take your coat, give your cloak as well; [41] and if anyone forces you to go one mile, go also the second mile. [42] Give to everyone who begs from you, and do not refuse anyone who wants to borrow from you.

Hence, it would be incorrect to suggest that Matthew and the other New Testament writers for that matter are simply abandoning Judaism and its questions. While Matthew and the others are certainly creating something new, they are not simply religious freelancers. The offshoot way of understanding early Christianity may be an advance on the replacement model, but it still leaves us with some concern, and causes us to seek a still better way of looking at first-century Judaism and the origin of Christianity.

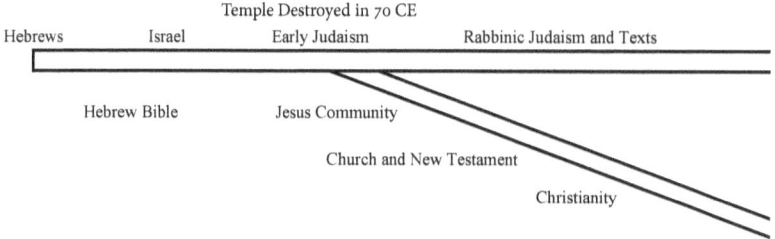

THE SIBLING MODEL

The sibling model begins with the premise that first-century Judaism gave birth to two great religions: rabbinic Judaism and Christianity.[6] Much as Rebecca's twin sons, Jacob and Esau, quarreled and went their own directions according to Genesis, so rabbinic Judaism and Christianity were born in the same religious environment but early on went different directions, often quarreling along the way. As with the offshoot model, the sibling model begins with the historical evidence of the first century and looks at the way the Jewish religious landscape changed following the destruction of the temple. Once again, the destruction of the temple was the precipitating factor in the origin of rabbinic Judaism and Christianity and allowed them to prevail over their closest religious competitors. They were the groups most successful in adjusting to the new religious circumstances following 70 CE.

We know that Judaism early in first-century Palestine was diverse, made up of different groups and sects. The best known were the Sadducees and Pharisees, but there were other groups as well. The Essenes, for example, may have been associated with Qumran, the site near where the Dead Sea Scrolls were found, and may have composed the community which hid the texts in the desert caves above the Dead Sea. Other Jews, often referred to as Zealots, were willing to take up arms against Roman occupation, often turning to religious zealotry to resist foreign domination. And messianic

---

6. See Segal, *Rebecca's Children*, 163–81.

figures appeared from time to time, who claimed to be the Messiah some Jews expected to arrive and to restore the fortunes of the nation according to biblical prophecy. The Jewish religious landscape was quite diverse early in the first century, and Jesus and his earliest followers were simply another group alongside all the others. Whether Jesus saw himself as the anticipated Jewish Messiah or not, very early on he came to be acclaimed and worshiped as the anointed one of God by his followers, most of whom in the early days were Jews. This was a complex time in Jewish life, marked by religious diversity and brutal foreign occupation, and it was in this environment that Jesus appeared.

As a result of Rome's suppression of the Jewish rebellion and the destruction of the temple, one by one most of these groups disappeared. The Zealots were subdued by Roman force, as was the Qumran community at the Dead Sea. The Sadducees, long associated with the temple and priesthood, were now effectively out of business, with the temple in ruins. The Pharisees, being a lay middle-class reform movement and not particularly beholden to the temple, were, however, well positioned to deal with this new reality. And they set about transforming themselves to deal with it. The Pharisees and the early rabbis (teachers)—hence the name rabbinic Judaism—retreated to Galilee and began an intellectual process of making sense of Judaism without a functioning temple in Jerusalem. They did so by turning to the study of torah, both written (Scripture) and oral (tradition), in order to work out its implications for daily life, and over time they produced a series of texts that would come to define rabbinic Judaism: the Mishnah (circa. 200 CE), the Palestinian Talmud (circa 400 CE), and the Babylonian Talmud (circa 600 CE). These came to represent the wisdom of the sages (rabbis) about torah and their debates over fine points of legal interpretation. At the very center of this emerging form of legal interpretation was Torah, represented in later rabbinic tradition as having been given to Moses on Mount Sinai in two forms: written and remembered oral tradition.[7]

The way rabbinic Judaism came to explain the destruction of the temple is fascinating and illustrates the rabbis' process of coming to terms with the temple's demise. By the time the Mishnah was written, the temple had been in ruins for 130 years, but the terms *temple*, *sacrifice*, and *priest* were still used by the rabbis in the Mishnah. Now, though, they no longer referred to a physical structure in Jerusalem or to the people and functions associated with it. The term *temple* now referred to the Jewish community, whereas *sacrifice* referred to acts of charity and study by members of the

---

7. See Neusner, *Rabbinic Judaism*, 31–43; and Neusner, *Judaism when Christianity Began*, 15–27.

community. And the *priests* are presently the wise men and teachers—in other words, the rabbis. The notion of a messiah does not figure prominently in the Mishnah,[8] and in its own way this underscores yet again the centrality of torah for rabbinic Judaism. In the early centuries of the Common Era, rabbinic Judaism would lay the foundations for most forms of Judaism that would follow.

On the other hand, Christianity too had to come to terms with the post-70 reality. Unlike rabbinic Judaism, it came to be defined by its belief in Jesus as Messiah and Son of God. He and his earliest followers were thoroughly Jewish, but the later religious community that came to worship him became increasingly non-Jewish and made sense of the temple's destruction in their own Christ-centered way. In addition to Matt 24:1–2 and 26:61 cited above, John 2:13–22 illustrates in especially poignant terms the community's attempt to relate Christ to the temple's destruction:

> [13] The Passover of the Jews was near, and Jesus went up to Jerusalem. [14] In the temple he found people selling cattle, sheep, and doves, and the money changers seated at their tables. [15] Making a whip of cords, he drove all of them out of the temple, both the sheep and the cattle. He also poured out the coins of the money changers and overturned their tables. [16] He told those who were selling the doves, "Take these things out of here! Stop making my Father's house a marketplace!" [17] His disciples remembered that it was written, "Zeal for your house will consume me." [18] The Jews then said to him, "What sign can you show us for doing this?" [19] Jesus answered them, "Destroy this temple, and in three days I will raise it up." [20] The Jews then said, "This temple has been under construction for forty-six years, and will you raise it up in three days?" [21] But he was speaking of the temple of his body. [22] After he was raised from the dead, his disciples remembered that he had said this; and they believed the scripture and the word that Jesus had spoken.

John portrays Jesus making explicit the identification of his own body with the temple. Certainly implicit, though not stated directly, Jesus's crucifixion is tantamount to a sacrifice, and the resurrection to the building of a new temple. If rabbinic Jews related the temple to the community, John relates it to Christ's body.

Later in the New Testament, the writer of Hebrews, in 2:17 and 7:27, develops this even more fully:

---

8. Neusner, *From Testament to Torah*, 62–63.

> [17] Therefore he had to become like his brothers and sisters in every respect, so that he might be a merciful and faithful high priest in the service of God, to make a sacrifice of atonement for the sins of the people.

> [23] Furthermore, the former priests were many in number, because they were prevented by death from continuing in office; [24] but he holds his priesthood permanently, because he continues forever. [25] Consequently he is able for all time to save those who approach God through him, since he always lives to make intercession for them. [26] For it was fitting that we should have such a high priest, holy, blameless, undefiled, separated from sinners, and exalted above the heavens. [27] Unlike the other high priests, he has no need to offer sacrifices day after day, first for his own sins, and then for those of the people; this he did once for all when he offered himself.

Here we see how the writer relates Christ to priests and sacrifices, and in this theology Christ appears to function as both priest and sacrifice on the high altar of the cross. Moreover, this sacrifice need not be repeated, unlike in the Jerusalem temple's sacrificial system; it has been done once for all. In this sense, Christ on the cross brings the sacrificial system to an end, and the believers now participate in that sacrifice through the body of Christ (Heb 10:8–10):

> [8] When he said above, "You have neither desired nor taken pleasure in sacrifices and offerings and burnt offerings and sin offerings" (these are offered according to the law), [9] then he added, "See, I have come to do your will." *He abolishes the first in order to establish the second.* [10] *And it is by God's will that we have been sanctified through the offering of the body of Jesus Christ once for all.* (italics added)

This has eucharistic overtones in Paul's theology when he records the words spoken over the bread and wine at communion (1 Cor 11:23–26):

> [23] For I received from the Lord what I also handed on to you, that the Lord Jesus on the night when he was betrayed took a loaf of bread, [24] and when he had given thanks, he broke it and said, "This is my body that is for you. Do this in remembrance of me." [25] In the same way he took the cup also, after supper, saying, "This cup is the new covenant in my blood. Do this, as often as you drink it, in remembrance of me." [26] For as often as

you eat this bread and drink the cup, you proclaim the Lord's death until he comes.

Following this line of thought through the various New Testament texts illustrates the way early church writers redefined temple, sacrifice, and priesthood and in the process made them thoroughly Christ centered. And in baptism and Eucharist, the church enacted its Christology in ritual practice. If rabbinic Judaism turned on the axis of torah and community, Christianity turned on the axis of Christ and church: each represented and developed different strands of first-century Judaism. After the first century, both developed significant bodies of literature and continued to work out the implications of their new religious circumstance.

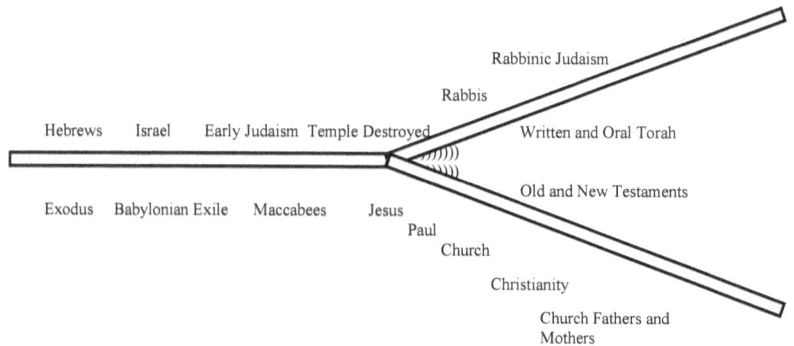

CONCLUSIONS

While I consider the sibling model to be the most accurate and productive way to view the origin of Christianity and it relationship with Judaism, there are objections to it. Some look at the broad sweep of Jewish and Christian history in the ancient world and their often acrimonious interactions and conclude that they are so different that they could not possibly be siblings. Likewise, there may be legitimate concerns on the part of some Jews that Jews and Christians might be seen erroneously as just one big, happy family, and that Christian issues and concerns might be viewed as pretty much the same as Jewish issues and concerns. To be sure, the relationship between Jews and Christians down through centuries has been tortuous, with Jews often being targets of Christian persecution. And there is no doubt that the particularities of rabbinic Judaism and Christianity display a great many differences. If rabbinic Judaism and Christianity began as siblings, over time they often became not so friendly distant cousins, each following quite different paths. To see them as coming from a common religious environment does not mean that we need to be blind to their individuality. I also believe it is incorrect to think that these paths followed straight historical lines. They most certainly did not, and there was considerable religious and social diversity within each of the religions themselves. It is worth mentioning in this context as well that as the early church began to pull away from Judaism, it was probably more akin to a rough edged tearing apart than a neat, clean parting of the ways.[9] It did not simply happen in one place at one time, but occurred in a rather uneven fashion over a period of time.

While the sibling model cannot be used as a rigid interpretive template for understanding early Christianity and rabbinic Judaism, I think it is a useful conceptual framework for positioning early Christianity in its proper historical and social context. And while it can be overdrawn, it can be a helpful interpretive lens for many people who wish to study the New Testament and early Christianity in greater detail. The sibling model also has a moral and ethical contribution to make. From a historical and religious point of view, early Judaism gave rise to two legitimate religious expressions, and each has sought to live out different aspects of first-century Palestinian Judaism. We need not determine which is right and by implication which is wrong. Both can be studied critically for what they are, and held to account when they fail to live up to their most noble aspirations. From a Christian point of view, it is critical to understand when reading the New Testament that the contentious things said by Jesus or the gospel writers about the Jews or Pharisees belong in some sense to intramural Jewish debates. These are in-house disagreements, perhaps born of religious conflict and competition. The Christ community is not yet a separate religion as it will become later. Hence, these quarrels are not Christian against Jew, Christianity against Judaism. Later the two sides will become more distinct, but they are not in this earliest period. This is especially important to keep in mind when reading such highly charged texts as the passion accounts of Jesus's arrest, trial, and crucifixion.

---

9. See for example, Dunn, *Jews and Christians*, 230–59.

PART 2

Foundational Texts and Traditions

5

The Apostle Paul and the Early Church

What was Paul's contribution to the early church, and was he the actual founder of Christianity?

Almost half the New Testament books are attributed to the apostle Paul, and in much of Acts, Luke's account of the early church, he is the principal figure of the narrative.[1] During both the New Testament period and beyond, Paul is a towering presence because of his missionary work and theological legacy.[2] Agree or disagree with Paul, he is close to the center of the early Christian story and can only be ignored at our peril if we want to understand the formation of the church and Christianity. I'll state it even more boldly: if it were not for Paul (or someone like him) and what he did, the early church would likely never have survived. We would be about as familiar today with the church as we are with the Sadducees, Samaritans, and Dead Sea community. The Jesus community and early church would be at most a historical novelty, its stories preserved in museums and history books. But that is not the way history turned out, and Paul is substantially responsible for that. He is an important link in the movement from the Jesus

---

1. The following New Testament epistles are attributed to Paul: Romans, 1 and 2 Corinthians, Galatians, Philippians, 1 and 2 Thessalonians, Ephesians, Colossians, Philemon, 1 and 2 Timothy, and Titus.

2. Aageson, *Paul, the Pastoral Epistles and the Early Church*, 1–17.

community (Jesus and his earliest followers) to Christianity (a full-blown and independent religion). It is that story we will investigate in this chapter.

But first we must orient ourselves to Paul. He was a Jew from Tarsus in Asia Minor (present-day Turkey), not Palestine, and he was not counted among Jesus's early disciples. As we shall see, he came late to Jesus's cause, and even then he did not enter without opposition from many in the church. Having been a persecutor of Jesus's followers, Paul, then called Saul, had developed a rather frightening reputation in the church. Following his dramatic experience on the road to Damascus, Saul changed from a persecutor into a follower, and to this day is a symbol of radical conversion. Unlike Jesus and his disciples, Paul was not from Palestine but from the Jewish diaspora: the Jews who lived outside the traditional Jewish homeland. If Jesus and his disciples were small-town folks from a backwater in the vast Roman Empire, Paul was an urbanite from a significant city in the Greco-Roman world. He was a literate, Greek-speaking Jew and was fairly well educated in the traditions of the Greeks. He was at home in the cities of the eastern Empire and knew his way around Roman urban culture. The contrast with Jesus is striking.

Three things help us situate the apostle Paul. First, he was a Jew by religion, and in my view he remained a Jew to his death. Second, Paul was thoroughly inculturated into Greek society—its language, thought, and views of the world. And finally, if we take Acts at face value we can say he was a Roman citizen. These are three aces for anyone who wished to spread the name and message of Jesus Christ through the eastern Mediterranean region of the empire. And again, the contrast between Paul and Jesus's earliest followers in Galilee could not be more striking. We now turn to Paul's Damascus Road experience and its meaning for him and the early church.

PAUL ON THE DAMASCUS ROAD

While on a mission of persecution to Damascus, Saul was struck down and blinded by flashes of light from heaven. He heard the voice of the Lord Jesus instructing him to enter the city where he would be told what he should do. Luke, in Acts 9:1–9, describes the scene this way:

> [1]Meanwhile Saul, still breathing threats and murder against the disciples of the Lord, went to the high priest [2] and asked him for letters to the synagogues at Damascus, so that if he found any who belonged to the Way, men or women, he might bring them bound to Jerusalem. [3] Now as he was going along and approaching Damascus, suddenly a light from heaven flashed

around him. ⁴ He fell to the ground and heard a voice saying to him, "Saul, Saul, why do you persecute me?" ⁵ He asked, "Who are you, Lord?" The reply came, "I am Jesus, whom you are persecuting. ⁶ But get up and enter the city, and you will be told what you are to do." ⁷ The men who were traveling with him stood speechless because they heard the voice but saw no one. ⁸ Saul got up from the ground, and though his eyes were open, he could see nothing; so they led him by the hand and brought him into Damascus. ⁹ For three days he was without sight, and neither ate nor drank.

For our purposes, the significance of this story is its religious meaning, not the psychological experience Saul may have had. Normally we have referred to this as the *conversion* of Saint Paul, but some have objected to this term, preferring instead the word *call*.³ Conversion clearly implies that Saul changed from one thing to something else, whereas a call suggests he was given a new mission but did not necessarily change religions. I am not categorically opposed to the use of the term *conversion* if we are precise about what we mean when we use the word. Very often Christians use the term as if Saul, the Jew, converted as a result of his encounter on the Damascus Road, thereby becoming a Christian and receiving his new Christian name, Paul. After the rise of Christianity, this seemed to make perfectly good sense, but if we look at Paul's own situation, this reading of events is problematic. When Paul became a follower of Christ, there was no such religious entity that we could accurately call Christianity. That was to come sometime later. So, if Paul did not change from Judaism to Christianity, we need to refine our understanding of his conversion. If he did not convert from Judaism to Christianity, what did he change from, and what did he change to?

By Paul's own admission, he was a Jewish Pharisee (Phil 3:5). As we have now already seen, the Pharisees were a reform faction in early first-century Judaism, and following the destruction of the temple they transformed themselves into the progenitors of rabbinic Judaism. In other words, Paul as a Pharisee was part of a specific group under the umbrella of first-century Judaism—still a Jew, but a particular kind of Jew. So, what did it mean that after his experience on the Damascus Road he became a follower of Christ? If as I have argued above, the Jesus community (early church) in this period was a Jewish sect alongside other Jewish groups, it follows that Paul did not convert to another religion but rather to another sect of Judaism. To put it another way, Paul's was a change or conversion

---

3. See the positions taken in Stendahl, "Paul among Jews and Gentiles," 1–77; and Segal, *Paul the Convert*, 3–33.

within Judaism itself. Before Damascus, he was a Jew, and after Damascus he is still a Jew, albeit a Jew of a different stripe. He is now a messianic Jew, believing that Jesus is the anointed one of God, the expected Messiah of the Jewish people. This distinction is subtle, but it makes all the difference in the world, because Paul did not necessarily become non-Jewish in order to become a follower of Jesus Christ, who, of course, was a Jew himself. From this foundational point of view, the idea of Pauline anti-Judaism sounds less and less plausible, even though Paul challenged Judaism and on occasion had some rather harsh things to say about his coreligionists. However, he is neither the first nor last to have said harsh things. In this line of thought, the pertinent question is, how did Paul's Judaism change after Damascus—not, why did he abandon Judaism? I close this section, with Paul's own personal description of his conversion in Gal 1:12–17:

> [13] You have heard, no doubt, of my earlier life in Judaism. I was violently persecuting the church of God and was trying to destroy it. [14] I advanced in Judaism beyond many among my people of the same age, for I was far more zealous for the traditions of my ancestors. [15] But when God, who had set me apart before I was born and called me through his grace, was pleased [16] to reveal his Son to me, *so that I might proclaim him among the Gentiles,* I did not confer with any human being, [17] nor did I go up to Jerusalem to those who were already apostles before me, but I went away at once into Arabia, and afterwards I returned to Damascus.

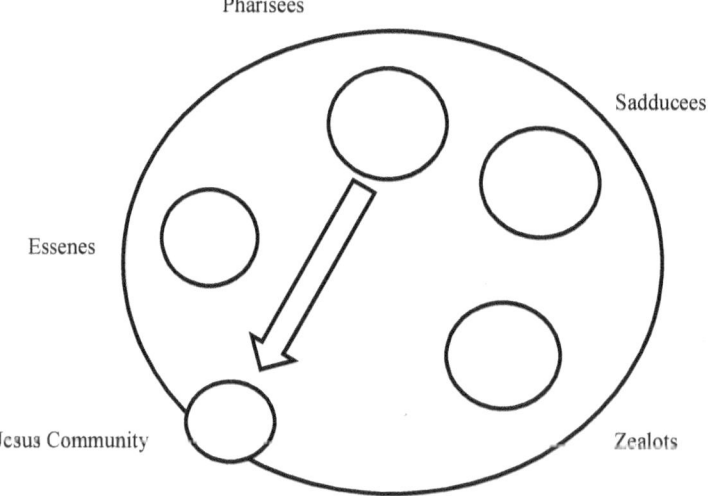

Paul's Actual Conversion
Judaism

Later Christian interpretations of Paul's conversion

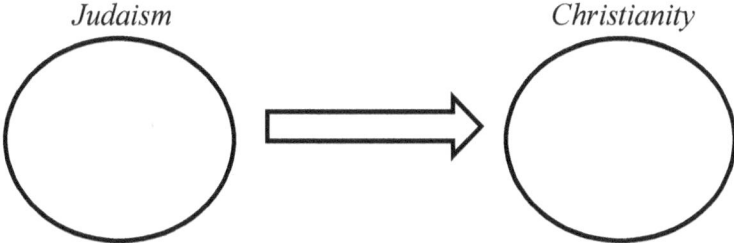

THE MISSION TO THE GENTILES

As Paul says in his own words, God revealed his Son to him in order that he might proclaim him among the Gentiles. He clearly understood himself to have been called and given a very specific mission. But how did he understand and enact this mission to the non-Jews? On what basis were the Gentiles to be included in the church? Did they need to become Jews before they could be included in the church, keeping the Jewish law and its ritual prescriptions? Paul answered categorically: no, they do not need to be converts to Judaism; they are included on the basis of faith. This was a bold step on Paul's part and aroused considerable opposition (see for example Acts 11:1–3; 15:1–29), but it enabled the church to move beyond its traditional religious and social confines within Judaism. I am convinced that Paul never intended to abandon Judaism (his life and missionary work in some sense may have been made much easier had he done so), but it is true that by including Gentiles in church on the basis of faith, he set in motion a process whereby the church in fact became more and more non-Jewish sociologically. That would have religious consequences and ultimately contributed to the church's move away from Judaism. In my view, that was a consequence, not a Pauline missionary strategy. We know that over time the church became less Jewish and more Gentile, and that the church thrived in the Gentile world. That is where it would make its mark on the Roman Empire.

But how did Paul make the case for this bold new theology and missionary strategy? He first turned to Scripture, in particular to Genesis and the stories of Abraham,[4] to argue that righteousness is on the basis of faith, not obedience to law. I quote again two texts respectively, one from his Epistle to the Galatians (3:6–9) and the other from Romans (4:1–3), both of which make reference to Gen 15:6:

---

4. See also above, pp. 32–34.

⁶ Just as Abraham "believed God, and it was reckoned to him as righteousness," ⁷ so, you see, those who believe are the descendants of Abraham. ⁸ And the scripture, foreseeing that God would justify the Gentiles by faith, declared the gospel beforehand to Abraham, saying, "All the Gentiles shall be blessed in you." ⁹ For this reason, those who believe are blessed with Abraham who believed.

¹ What then are we to say was gained by Abraham, our ancestor according to the flesh? ² For if Abraham was justified by works, he has something to boast about, but not before God. ³ For what does the scripture say? "Abraham believed God, and it was reckoned to him as righteousness."

Here we note that Paul saw Abraham as the exemplar of faith: a man who, even before he was circumcised and the law had been given to Moses, was declared by God to be righteous on the basis of his belief (probably also implying his trust) in God. In the context of Paul's Gentile mission, this provided scriptural support for his case about Gentile inclusion, because in effect Abraham too was a Gentile when he was made righteous on the basis of faith (Rom 4:9–12). As we saw in chapters 2 and 3, Jews read these Genesis texts very differently over time and certainly would not have drawn the same conclusions as Paul. Nevertheless, this provided the apostle's argument with scriptural grounding and rooted it in antiquity, in the very person who in myth and lore functioned as the progenitor of the Jewish people. How closely Paul's readers and hearers would have been able to follow this argument is unclear, but presumably many would have, especially those who were Jewish.

Paul in his own letters does not describe in any detail his missionary strategy in carrying the message of Jesus to the Gentiles, but Luke, writing in Acts, does. From the account of his conversion in Acts chapter 9 and on to the end of the book, the travels of Paul dominate the narrative. And each time as Paul enters a city, he goes first to the local synagogue where he preaches and at first receives a rather warm welcome. Later, the opposition mounts among the Jews, and they drive him out. From there he preaches to the Gentiles, where he has some success. According to Acts, as the story develops, some of his success appears to have been among a group of Gentiles referred to as "God-fearers," Gentiles who were attracted to Judaism and the life of the synagogue but who had never formally converted or become part of the Jewish community. Among males, the requirement of circumcision may have dissuaded them from going through the formal process of conversion. To those people, we can imagine how Paul's circumcision-free message of Christ may have had special appeal. The monotheistic belief and the Jewish Scriptures are all there in Christianity. Except for the onerous prospect of circumcision for adult males and dietary restrictions that may have had little appeal, the convert could receive most of the benefits of Jewish religion and social life. And in most cases, the fledgling church was not seen as really that much different from Judaism and the synagogue anyway.

It would be inaccurate to say that Paul's view was basically antilaw or that he cared little about people's behavior. Life in the Spirit and ethics are important to him, but torah obedience is not a requirement for inclusion in the church. In the main, it is the requirement of circumcision for males, the dietary stipulations affecting table life and fellowship, and the sacred calendar governing worship practices that are the parts of Jewish law and life that most trouble Paul.[5] Why? They are the parts of torah that most visibly and publically separate Jews from Gentiles, and Paul is most concerned that the community of Christ believers, the church, be united, whether Jew or Gentile. They are the body of Christ and as the body of Christ cannot be divided. We know that Paul's churches were often rent by social and theological differences, but he tries mightily to hold them together as the one body of Christ.

ON THE ROAD WITH PAUL

Sometime after his experience on the Damascus Road, Paul embarked on a series of journeys through Asia Minor and Greece, preaching and starting small Christ communities in many of the region's most significant cities. Whatever his missionary strategy may have been, Paul probably saw his travels in the Mediterranean region as fulfilling his call to preach Christ to Gentiles. To be sure, there were Jewish communities in most of the sizable towns and cities of the eastern Mediterranean, but it was a region—except for Palestine and perhaps also Alexandria—largely populated by non-Jews and people of different ethnic groups. It was a region where Greco-Roman religion was woven into the fabric of society. At the same time various religious cults and groups from North Africa, Syria, and Mesopotamia had made their way into the region. Far from being a religious vacuum, the region teemed with religious adherents, practices, and rituals that defined Greco-Roman life in the first century. Life in the empire was highly structured and hierarchical; as Ramsay MacMullen has said, people had the responsibility to preserve the social order and their place in it.[6] The emperor stood atop the hierarchical social pyramid, even at times appearing to have

---

5. Sanders, *Paul, the Law and the Jewish People*, 143–67.
6. MacMullen, *Roman Social Relation*, 105.

god-like qualities.[7] It was into this rich social environment that Paul came with the message of Christ. To even the most casual observer of the day, it must have appeared as though Paul's chances of success were slim to none. Nonetheless, driven by his passion for Christ and his call to preach him to the Gentiles, Paul set off: suffering hardship, struggle, opposition; and, yes, meeting some success as well. It is this story that Luke chronicles in the second book of his two-volume work—a set generally known as Luke-Acts. Paul himself, on the other hand, did not write narrative accounts of his travels or missionary work. What we have are a series of letters: thirteen in all are attributed to him, though some of these in fact may have been written by followers of Paul. Reading Acts, one would not know that Paul was a letter writer, but that is how he is best known to us today. Following his departure from the fledgling congregations he started, he continued to communicate with them via letters, perhaps delivered by his associates, in which he addressed theological issues and problems confronting the communities, and exhorted them to remain steadfast in the Spirit until the day of Jesus Christ.

Many of these letters were addressed to churches in the various cities, whereas others were addressed to individuals. In all, seven of the letters are generally thought to have been authored by Paul himself: Romans, 1 and 2 Corinthians, Galatians, Philippians, 1 Thessalonians, and Philemon. Among the others, there is some debate about whether Paul wrote them or someone in the Pauline circle of early Christians wrote them in his name: Ephesians, Colossians, 2 Thessalonians, 1 and 2 Timothy, and Titus.[8] In any case, in all thirteen, Paul is named as the author, and in the tradition they came to be seen as the corpus of Paul's writings. It was not until more recent times that scholars began to raise critical questions about their Pauline authorship—questions generated largely by the theology, vocabulary, and manuscript traditions of these letters. As they now appear in the New Testament, the community letters appear first, longest to shortest, followed by the letters to individuals, longest to shortest. Together they make up a significant portion of the New Testament and present us with some of the most important theological work of the early church.

Paul was a letter writer, and his letters display many of the formal characteristics of letters of his day, suggesting he had training in Greek rhetoric and persuasive argumentation. Given that much of his education was in Tarsus, this stands to reason. But the forms by themselves do not tell the whole story of Paul and his interaction with these early church communities. More

---

7. Aageson, "'Control' in Pauline Language and Culture," 86–89.

8. For further information, consult introductions to Paul's letters and commentaries to 1 and 2 Timothy, Titus, Ephesians, and Colossians.

important, it is the way these forms shape and communicate his theological and pastoral probing, and the way he uses them to exhort his audiences to live the life to which they have been called in Christ. For example, if we look at Romans and Galatians, following the greetings and introductions, Paul launches into his theological arguments, which in turn lead into his pastoral advice and exhortations. The Corinthian letters, not entirely unlike the other two in form and structure, exhibit some of their own characteristics, devoting much attention to pastoral advice based on questions that have come to him from the community in Corinth. Something similar could also be said of the Thessalonian correspondence. The Epistle to Philemon is the only letter undoubtedly written by Paul to an individual, Philemon, about his runaway slave, Onesimus, whom Paul has met in prison, and whom Paul is now sending back to Philemon as a brother in Christ. The epistle focuses on a single issue: slavery and the way fellowship in Christ may affect the relationship between a master and a slave. In this case, the slave Paul has befriended in prison, and the master he also knows and refers to as a beloved coworker. Given the vastness of slavery as an institution in the first century, it is not surprising that this issue should arise. Paul also addresses slavery in 1 Cor 7:21–24, though in a very different kind of pastoral context.

Perhaps the most important lesson of this discussion is that Paul's letters are deeply contextual, rooted in his relationship with the communities and churches he has founded or (in the case of Romans) will soon visit. Even though some of the letters began to circulate to other communities very early on, they are closer to personal correspondence than they are to treatises fit for general audiences with different needs and circumstances. After Paul's death, when the letters came to have authority in their own right, they were set on a path toward attaining the status of sacred Scripture and applicability across different contexts. However, in their origin they were personal correspondence; and when we now read them with that in mind, it is as though we are peeking into someone else's mailbox. If our goal is to understand Paul's letters in their original contexts, we need to understand not only what Paul was saying but also the questions and issues that stand behind his letters and generate the substance of his responses to these ancient audiences.

THEOLOGICAL AND ETHICAL THEMES

Perhaps the most thorough recent volume devoted to a systematic look at Paul's theology is by James D. G. Dunn, titled, *The Theology of Paul the Apostle*. Dunn, a longtime student of Paul, should be consulted for a full interpretation of the apostle's theology and major themes. Our purpose here is not to investigate in detail his theology or ethics. Neither is it to identify the theologies of any of the respective epistles on their own terms. For those interested in this approach, it is worth consulting the four volumes produced by a Society of Biblical Literature working group that considered the theologies of each of the letters respectively on the assumption that each is a self-contained argument addressing a specific context.[9] Our purpose here is more general. It is to identify a number of the major themes in Paul's letters and to see how they fit into his thought and missionary work more broadly. The power of Paul's theological legacy is demonstrated most vividly by the fact that at strategic points in the life of the church it is his thought that leads the way to reform, bursting back on the scene with dynamism. Augustine consulted Paul in the fourth century, Martin Luther and John Calvin cited him in the sixteenth, John Wesley read him in the eighteenth, and Karl Barth at the end of the First World War wrote his moving commentary, *The Epistle to the Romans*. At these important junctures in the life of the church, the apostle Paul's theology led the way, prompting new ways of thinking and addressing the church.

Theology and Christology, Continuity and Discontinuity

For Paul, the God and Father of Jesus Christ is also the God of the Jews and Jewish Scripture. Three times (Rom 3:30; 1 Cor 8:4; Gal 3:20) he echoes the opening words of the Jewish *shema*, "Hear O Israel the Lord our God is one" And almost a hundred times he explicitly cites the Jewish scriptures to make a theological, pastoral, or ethical point. God is one, and this God is revealed in Scripture.[10] Unlike Marcion, a second-century Christian who wanted to sever the church from Judaism and the Christian God from the Jewish God,[11] Paul sees a theological line of continuity from the Jewish Scriptures to Christ and beyond. Marcion's effort failed largely because the emerging Christian tradition, Paul's thought included, was deeply rooted theologically in the Jewish Scriptures and would make little sense apart from them. Hence, a line of thought runs through Paul's writing and displays theological and temporal continuity with what has gone before and what he expects to unfold in the future. To put it bluntly, Paul does not start over with a new God or a new religion.

---

9. See Bassler et al., *Pauline Theology*, vols. 1–4.

10. For a discussion of Paul's use of Scripture see Aageson, *Written Also for Our Sake*; and also Hays, *Echoes of Scripture*.

11. See below pp. 194–95, 244–45.

Nevertheless, it is important to remember that Paul is also a messianist, and he believes Jesus is the anointed one of God. In Christ, God has done a new thing, and that new thing divides theologically what has come before from what comes after. In short, salvation-history is disrupted by the Christ event. As Paul writes in 2 Cor 5:17-18: "[17] So if anyone is in Christ, there is a new creation: everything old has passed away; see, everything has become new! [18] All this is from God, who reconciled us to himself through Christ, and has given us the ministry of reconciliation." And again as he says in Gal 6:15: "For neither circumcision nor uncircumcision is anything; but a new creation is everything!" The old has passed away and the new has come, only waiting to be finally consummated when Christ returns and salvation is fully realized. Hence, Paul sees himself living between times—times sometimes referred to as the "now" and the "not yet." In Christ, salvation is here, and it is still not yet fully here. That is yet to come. What this means is that for Paul, and much of the early church for that matter, there is conceptual tension between the theological continuity represented by Judaism and Jewish Scripture, and the christological disruption resulting in a new creation for those who are in Christ. This conceptual tension weaves its way through Paul's thought and cannot be resolved in either direction without either severing Paul from his deep Jewish roots or depreciating for him the significance of Christ.[12]

Sin and Redemption

Paul has a lot to say about sin and seemingly somewhat less to say about individual sins. We find Paul's most vivid description of sin in Rom 5:12-21 where he connects Adam and Christ in order to describe the human condition of being lost in sin and yet redeemed in righteousness through Christ:

> [12] Therefore, just as sin came into the world through one man, and death came through sin, and so death spread to all because all have sinned— [13] sin was indeed in the world before the law, but sin is not reckoned when there is no law. [14] Yet death exercised dominion from Adam to Moses, even over those whose sins were not like the transgression of Adam, who is a type of the one who was to come.
>
> [15] But the free gift is not like the trespass. For if the many died through the one man's trespass, much more surely have the grace of God and the free gift in the grace of the one man, Jesus Christ, abounded for the many. [16] And the free gift is not like the

---

12. For a fuller discussion of this, see Aageson, *Written Also for Our Sake*, 22–26.

effect of the one man's sin. For the judgment following one trespass brought condemnation, but the free gift following many trespasses brings justification. [17] If, because of the one man's trespass, death exercised dominion through that one, much more surely will those who receive the abundance of grace and the free gift of righteousness exercise dominion in life through the one man, Jesus Christ.

[18] Therefore just as one man's trespass led to condemnation for all, so one man's act of righteousness leads to justification and life for all. [19] For just as by the one man's disobedience the many were made sinners, so by the one man's obedience the many will be made righteous. [20] But law came in, with the result that the trespass multiplied; but where sin increased, grace abounded all the more, [21] so that, just as sin exercised dominion in death, so grace might also exercise dominion through justification leading to eternal life through Jesus Christ our Lord.

While this is a dialectical discussion about Adam and Christ, sin and righteousness, death and life, it illustrates in vivid terms Paul's notion of sin, the realm of human existence at the head of which stands Adam. Human beings participate in this realm of sin and death,[13] but they also continue to establish its rule by their own disobedience. Opposite the transgression of Adam stands the obedience of Christ, and just as Adam stands at the head of humanity lost in sin, so Christ stands at the head of humanity made righteous. While many have died through Adam's transgression, much more has the grace of God abounded for many through Christ. In large measure, this discussion enables Paul to make a christological point.[14] Christ undoes what Adam did. However, sin is clearly a necessary part of the discussion in order for Paul to make his point. When Saint Augustine some three centuries later came to this text, he found the basis for his full-blown notion of original sin. Humans are conceived and born in sin. Though Paul may not go as far as Augustine, it is clear he too defines the human condition apart from Christ in terms of sin and death. Looking more broadly in Paul's writings, it is interesting to note that by and large he does not describe the remedy for sin in terms of forgiveness. He will speak in terms of new creation, reconciliation, and sacrifice of atonement, but not forgiveness. That is language found elsewhere in the New Testament, but it is not common in Paul.

---

13. See also Rom 3:23.
14. See Aageson, *Written Also for Our Sake*, 107–12.

Paul and the Jewish Law

If the Jewish law is not the basis for inclusion in the church, what is the role and function of the law for Paul? This is an important question, for if God by definition is faithful and trustworthy in the giving of torah and yet its full observance is not necessary for participation in the church, surely it must have some other purpose. But what is that for Paul? To this question he gives basically two, perhaps three, different answers. Following my common practice, I will quote three texts, Gal 3:19, 23–26; Rom 7:5–13; and Gal 5:14. Written to two different audiences, these passages illustrate most vividly how Paul seeks to explain the role of the law:

> [19] Why then the law? It was added because of transgressions, until the offspring would come to whom the promise had been made; and it was ordained through angels by a mediator.
> [23] Now before faith came, we were imprisoned and guarded under the law until faith would be revealed. [24] Therefore the law was our disciplinarian until Christ came, so that we might be justified by faith. [25] But now that faith has come, we are no longer subject to a disciplinarian, [26] for in Christ Jesus you are all children of God through faith.

In short, Paul is saying to the Galatians that the law had a temporary function. The Greek term *paidagogos* is here translated "disciplinarian"; the law functioned this way only until Christ came. Just as a minor who is heir of an entire estate requires a minder until reaching adulthood, so we, who were heirs with Christ before he came, needed the law as a guardian before his arrival. Hence, the law was good, right, and proper, but temporary. Though hardly a satisfying notion to most Jews of his day, Paul's explanation preserves the faithfulness of God on the one hand and the preparatory function of the law for the coming of Christ on the other. Here again we see the tension between the theological continuity and the christological discontinuity in Paul's thought described above. It is important to remember that this entire discussion in Galatians is set in a context of disagreement and debate over the necessity of Gentile Christ believers to keep the law. In Romans, Paul comes at the problem from a different direction:

> [5] While we were living in the flesh, our sinful passions, aroused by the law, were at work in our members to bear fruit for death. [6] But now we are discharged from the law, dead to that which held us captive, so that we are slaves not under the old written code but in the new life of the Spirit. [7] What then should we say? That the law is sin? By no means! Yet, if it had not been for the

law, I would not have known sin. I would not have known what it is to covet if the law had not said, "You shall not covet." [8] But sin, seizing an opportunity in the commandment, produced in me all kinds of covetousness. Apart from the law sin lies dead. [9] I was once alive apart from the law, but when the commandment came, sin revived [10] and I died, and the very commandment that promised life proved to be death to me. [11] For sin, seizing an opportunity in the commandment, deceived me and through it killed me. [12] So the law is holy, and the commandment is holy and just and good. [13] Did what is good, then, bring death to me? By no means! It was sin, working death in me through what is good, in order that sin might be shown to be sin, and through the commandment might become sinful beyond measure.

If in Galatians law serves a temporary function, in Romans it serves a negative function. Law arouses sin and brings it to life. As Paul says, without the law he would not have known what sin is. The law is not sin but brings it to life where it can be disarmed through the work of Christ. This is a complicated text in many ways, but for our purposes it is sufficient to note how Paul tries yet again to deal with the issue of Jewish law. Whether the churches in Rome found his discussion persuasive or not, this text illustrates what a creative thinker he was. Religiously and conceptually he was on the cusp of something new, and he sought with all his intellectual resources to make sense of this new reality. Only later would the church systematize its understanding of the relationship between Judaism and Christianity, the Old Testament and the New Testament, the law and the gospel.

Paul, however, does not advocate freedom in Christ without personal restraint. In Gal 5:13–14, he calls upon the Galatians to become servants of one another and not to use their freedom as an opportunity for self-indulgence. In good Jewish fashion, he then sums up the entire law: "You shall love your neighbor as yourself" (v. 14). In the verses following (5:16–26), Paul continues by distinguishing life in the Spirit from life in the flesh, listing the behaviors representative of each.[15] The attributes of each are clearly at home in Greco-Roman thinking, and here Paul incorporates them into his theological ethic of Spirit and flesh and thus provides later thinkers with a foundation for Christian ethics.

---

15. Life in the flesh is "fornication, impurity, licentiousness, idolatry, sorcery, enmities, strife, jealousy, anger, quarrels, dissensions, factions, envy, drunkenness, carousing," and such things, whereas "life in the Spirit is love, joy, peace, patience, kindness, generosity, faithfulness, gentleness, and self-control" (Gal 5:19–20, 22–23).

God's Covenant with Israel

In Rom 9–11, Paul engages in his most direct and sustained discussion of the place of Israel in the economy of God's salvation now that Christ has come. This is a long, circuitous, and some might say tortuous discussion in which Paul quotes Scripture more heavily than anywhere else in his letters. It is a fascinating argument that begins with his sorrow over the fact that most of his fellow Jews have not come to believe in Christ (9:1–3) and ends with what might be called a doxology expressing the mystery of God (11:33–36). Along the way, Paul denies that God has abandoned the people of Israel, for to them belong the adoption, the glory, the covenants, the giving of the law, the worship, the promises, and to them belong the patriarchs and from them the Messiah according to the flesh has come (see also 11:1). But he also holds them to account for their unbelief (10:1–21), all the while recognizing that there is a remnant of Israel that has been faithful to Christ (9:27–29; 11:1–6). Following his analogy of the tame and wild olive trees— the natural and grafted branches (11:17–24)—Paul writes in 11:25–26: "So that you may not claim to be wiser than you are, brothers and sisters, I want you to understand this mystery: a hardening has come upon part of Israel, until the full number of the Gentiles has come in. And so all Israel will be saved." While it is not entirely clear what Paul means by "and so all Israel will be saved," it is clear he does not think Israel has been abandoned by God, and does think that in some mysterious fashion all Israel will be saved. At the very least, we can say this statement calls into question the notion that the church for Paul has simply replaced Israel as the people of God.[16] The church eventually will go in that theological direction, but not Paul; and this entire discussion in 9–11 indicates the intellectual energy he devotes to thinking through the issue. Given the way Paul's theology and missionary activity developed, this is an issue he could not avoid, even if his answer is not completely satisfactory. But it is also an issue the church has continued to wrestle with for almost two thousand years, sometimes clearly with more grace and compassion than at other times.

CONCLUSION

All of Paul's major epistles were most likely written in the decade of the 50s of the first century, and he apparently died in Rome not long after. While not among Jesus' earliest followers, he was the first great thinker and theologian

---

16. For fuller discussions of Rom 9–11, see Aageson, "Scripture and Structure"; and Aageson, "Typology."

of the early church. Following his death, Paul became an extremely influential figure in Christianity through his letters and the memory of his personal presence. We might say that Paul the person became Paul the personage, and in that transformation his legacy was set for the church. He, along with Peter and Mary, became the most commonly cited figures from the early church, and his writings continued to be read and interpreted down through the centuries by Christian thinkers of many different stripes. When the New Testament was finally canonized, Paul's writings assumed a prominent place, and to this day have continued to be a wellspring of Christian theological thinking.

But was Paul the founder of Christianity? Generally, I am inclined to see Christianity as originating from a complex network of people, practices, and ideas that came together over time to produce the phenomenon we know today. Hence, I tend to look first at the question of origins systemically rather than to look for the great man or woman who may have founded the religion. But that is a philosophical and methodological preference as much as it is a historical conclusion. Nevertheless, many important figures in the early church made significant contributions to its emergence and growth. In addition to Jesus and Paul, we might think of Peter, Mary, the authors of the four Gospels, as well as countless others who may only be known to us in passing. If we look to the second century, other names come to the fore as important in the development of Christianity: Ignatius of Antioch, Polycarp, Barnabas, Clement of Rome, Irenaeus, Tertullian, and Thecla—to name only some of the best known. But in the first century, Jesus and Paul stand head and shoulders above the rest. While I am not able to argue the point here, my view of Jesus the itinerant preacher, prophet, and holy man is that he started a movement within Judaism but in no sense intended to start a new religion beyond the boundaries of Judaism. It was only after his life on earth that he became the subject of worship and spiritual devotion. If this view of the historical Jesus is correct, then Jesus the man could hardly be considered the founder of Christianity. He could be considered at most only a focus for Christianity insofar as his teachings, life and, death lived on in the experience of the church. If my view of the historical Jesus is not correct, then his role in the founding of Christianity is still an open question. Paul's Gentile mission, his sense of the Jewish law, his thinking about Christology, and his views of Israel all combined to move the fledgling church into the larger Greco-Roman world where it would grow and by the fourth century flourish beyond any reasonable expectation. If forced to choose just one person, I would say Paul is my prime candidate as the founder of Christianity, but not in the sense we might normally think. Paul did not set out to establish a new religion separate from Judaism, but he did put in play forces that may have contributed ultimately to that reality. To make this claim, we need to distinguish between intent and consequences.

72 Part 2: Foundational Texts and Traditions

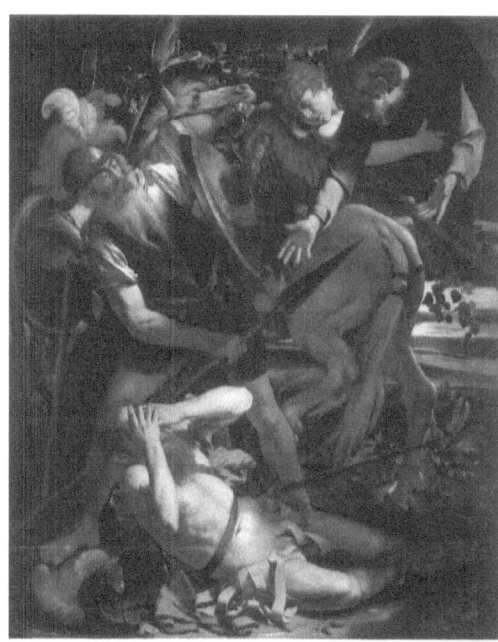

Conversion of Saint Paul, Caravaggio (1600–1601)

Paul in Prison, Rembrandt (1627)

6

The New Testament Gospels
History, Story, and Claims about Christ

*What are the New Testament gospels,
and what do they tell us about the early church?*

For general readers of the New Testament, the Gospels stand front and center. They not only appear first in the New Testament, but they tell the stories, parables, life, death, and resurrection of Christ. Unlike Paul's letters, they engage readers with compelling narratives that draw people into the drama of their stories. Taken seriously, they challenge readers on some deep and existential level. They have contributed to the doctrines of the church, and have been a wellspring for its art, music, and worship. So powerful was the gospel as a literary form that over time other gospels came to be written by various groups or individuals, although never included in the New Testament canon. The gospel as a form of literature is a hallmark of early Christianity, and in many ways it defines the way Christians imagine the origins of the church. Jesus, the Son of God and crucified messiah, called together his disciples, gathered the church, worked mighty wonders, died for the salvation of sinners, and rose from the dead to reign eternally with God. On one level, the Gospels seem to confirm this image of Christian origins, and for many people little more needs to be said. But our job in this chapter is to look more deeply at the questions posed above, and thereby to make the question of Christian origins more complicated but also presumably more representative of early Christian reality.

But before we turn to that task, the question may have occurred to some readers, why does this chapter on the gospels come after the chapter on Paul? Paul may be important, but the Gospels of Matthew, Mark, Luke, and John all come before Paul's letters in the New Testament. Moreover, they tell the stories of Jesus's life and ministry, whereas Paul deals with the theology and life of the church many years later. Would it not make sense logically to look at Paul and his letters after the gospels? Here we confront one of the ironies of early Christianity. Even though the gospels purport to tell the stories of Jesus's life and ministry during the first third of the first century, the general scholarly consensus is that they were probably not written until the final third of the first century. That places the texts of the gospels well after Paul wrote his letters and embarked on his Gentile ministry. This also means that in the case of the gospels we have a kind of double exposure, the narratives purport to tell the stories that took place early in the first century, but the audiences and readers of the gospels lived late in that century. The circumstances of the church had most certainly changed in those intervening years, and in the hands of the gospel writers the Jesus stories addressed new issues, problems, needs, and hopes. Just as preachers today try to bring the Jesus story to life among their contemporary hearers, so the gospel writers themselves were addressing the circumstances of a new day in the life of their audiences and the broader church. Likewise, the act of writing the gospel texts was not the same as canonizing them—that is, including them among the sacred writings of the New Testament. The canonization process took place much later, as we shall see in chapter 12. Hence, the order of the New Testament books bears no necessary relationship to the sequence in which they were written in history. These are two different things. In this case, the writing of Paul's letters in all likelihood predates the writing of the gospels; so, historically, the letters are the earliest documents in the New Testament. Therefore, our look at the New Testament authors and their texts began with Paul.

LITERARY GENRE AND CHARACTER OF THE GOSPELS

When we read the gospels, what kind of literary material are we reading? That is a critical question for every reader of literary texts, for it governs how we interpret and make sense of what we read. In that regard, the gospels are no different. While not unique in every respect, the New Testament gospels are an early, peculiarly Christian type of writing. They are narratives in which Jesus is the principal figure in the story line. They are certainly not historical writing in the way we think of history writing today. In fact, recent scholarship on the gospels has often argued that they are closer to narrative stories than they are historical texts or even redactions of earlier traditions and remembrances about Jesus.[1] Although some read the gospels as eyewitness reports, most serious scholars do not think they are in any way like journalistic accounts of what Jesus did and said. Far from it. The gospel writers are highly invested in the christological claims about which they write, and they are trying in story form to rethink the meaning and message of Jesus. He functions in the gospel accounts more like a character in a story and less like the subject of journalistic or historical reporting. Whatever historical material may stand behind the story lines produced by the gospel writers, students of the gospels need to attend to the literary features of the texts and to understand the texts as vehicles to communicate the message of Christ that the writer wishes to convey.

Does this mean there is little or nothing of historical value in the gospels? Not at all! But the Jesus material was shaped and passed on in the service of certain christological claims that the evangelists wished to make in the building up of the church. If the gospels were not written until at least fifty years after the death of Jesus, the most likely scenario is that between the time of Jesus and the writing of the gospels the stories and remembrances of what he did and said were passed down orally in early church communities and eventually were used by the gospel writers in composing their narratives. Many, if not most, of the early Christ followers could neither read nor write. Storytelling and memory were the mainstays of their world, and their ability to communicate across time was dependent upon their capacity to pass on orally the traditions about Jesus. At some point later in the first century, many of these oral traditions and stories were incorporated into the texts we call the gospels. While this may have been little more than an editing process, it seems more likely it was a process of molding these traditions into narratives with their own plot development, characters, perspectives, and points of view.

If the four New Testament gospels were not contemporaneous with the historical Jesus but later reflections on his life and ministry, it follows that they were not simply four independent, eyewitness accounts, each giving its own perspective on what was seen and heard. It is still possible that the gospels, each written later in the first century, could be independent from one another. That is a possibility, but certainly not the only way the process could have unfolded. Upon investigation, it seems especially unlikely that

---

1. See, for example, the works by Rhoads et al., *Mark as Story*; and Kingsbury, *Matthew as Story*.

the New Testament gospels were independent from one another. There is too much verbal and topical overlap among Matthew, Mark, and Luke (usually called the Synoptic Gospels because they can be lined up side by side and seen in synoptic fashion) to make this persuasive. While not completely unrelated, John is another matter.

In the eighteenth and nineteenth centuries, scholars proposed a hypothesis based on the literary dependence of the three Synoptic Gospels as a way of accounting for the evidence of the texts. We normally refer to it as the two-source hypothesis. While not subscribed to by all New Testament scholars, it is the most commonly accepted way of thinking about the relationships among the three Synoptics. It begins by noting that Mark was most likely written first because it is the shortest and written in the least developed style. Over time, written traditions tended to be elaborated and developed stylistically rather than simplified or condensed. Furthermore, almost all of Mark's material appears in either Matthew or Luke. How did it get there? The most likely explanation is that each of those gospel writers had access to Mark's Gospel but not to each other's work. Hence, Matthew drew material from Mark, as did Luke. In addition, Matthew as well as Luke each has material unique to their separate accounts of Jesus. This material is often referred to as M and L. Another result of synoptic comparison is to see that some material is common to Matthew and Luke but is not found in Mark. What is this material, and how did it get there? Backers of the two-source hypothesis call this material Q (for *Quelle* in German; the word is translated into English as "source"); they propose that Matthew and Luke both had access to this second source, Q. It was probably written, but is now known to us only in the material common to these two gospels.[2]

The two-source hypothesis helps us position the three Synoptic Gospels more precisely in the history of the first century. And if we can position Mark, the first gospel, more precisely, we will be in a better position to situate the others as well. Many scholars think Mark was written in or around 70 CE, and as we know from earlier discussions, this would place the gospel just before or just after the destruction of the temple. A number of factors converge in the church at this time, which may have prompted the oral gospel traditions to be written down. The trauma of the temple's destruction, the deaths of most or all of the eyewitnesses to Jesus's ministry, and the spread of the church to such an extent that the tradition about Jesus needed to be stabilized may have together prompted the writing of Mark's Gospel and subsequently the others as well. While we cannot be sure of all of the factors that prompted the writing of the gospel tradition, it is clear

---

2. Aageson, *In the Beginning*, 35–42.

that at some point later in the first century certain individuals in the church took the bold step of committing the tradition to writing. But they were far more than mere carriers of the tradition. They shaped the material in order to proclaim a Christology around which early Christians could live and worship.

A good example of this shaping in found in Mark 11:12–24:

> [12] *On the following day, when they came from Bethany, he was hungry.* [13] *Seeing in the distance a fig tree in leaf, he went to see whether perhaps he would find anything on it. When he came to it, he found nothing but leaves, for it was not the season for figs.* [14] *He said to it, "May no one ever eat fruit from you again." And his disciples heard it.*
>
> [15] Then they came to Jerusalem. And he entered the temple and began to drive out those who were selling and those who were buying in the temple, and he overturned the tables of the money changers and the seats of those who sold doves; [16] and he would not allow anyone to carry anything through the temple. [17] He was teaching and saying, "Is it not written,
> 'My house shall be called a house of prayer for all the nations'? But you have made it a den of robbers."
> [18] And when the chief priests and the scribes heard it, they kept looking for a way to kill him; for they were afraid of him, because the whole crowd was spellbound by his teaching. [19] And when evening came, Jesus and his disciples went out of the city.
>
> [20] *In the morning as they passed by, they saw the fig tree withered away to its roots.* [21] *Then Peter remembered and said to him, "Rabbi, look! The fig tree that you cursed has withered."* [22] *Jesus answered them, "Have faith in God.* [23] *Truly I tell you, if you say to this mountain, 'Be taken up and thrown into the sea,' and if you do not doubt in your heart, but believe that what you say will come to pass, it will be done for you.* [24] *So I tell you, whatever you ask for in prayer, believe that you have received it, and it will be yours.*

I have italicized the beginning and ending sections of the text to illustrate how Mark, unlike Matthew, sandwiched his account of Jesus in the temple between two parts of the fig tree story. Mark has literally split the fig tree story in two in order to bracket the temple scene. We normally refer to this text as the story of Jesus's cleansing of the temple. However, I would argue that this is anything but a cleansing story. It seems quite clearly to be Mark's announcement of the destruction of the temple. We have Jesus cursing the fig tree, followed by his casting out of the money changers, and finally his encounter with the withered fig tree. To make sense of Mark's editorial structuring of the text requires us to make a number of connections.

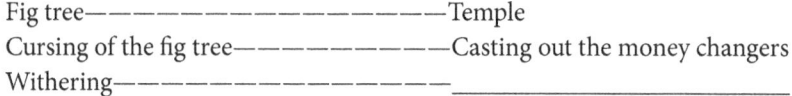

Not only does this illustrate that Mark is more than a carrier of the tradition, but it shows him making a claim about the temple's destruction. Far from being a cleansing-of-the-temple story, it is cast as a destruction story. To see this, interpreters must connect the analogous items and fill in the missing item. As the fig tree was cursed and withered, so the temple was cursed and now has withered. Its end has come. This recasting of the story of the money changers in the temple supports the argument that Mark's Gospel was written near the time of the temple's destruction, perhaps shortly after. As I indicated above,[3] the destruction of the temple was a trauma for Jews but also for the early followers of Christ.

According to the two-source hypothesis, Matthew and Luke would have written their gospels some time later still. Let's say sometime in the decade of the 80s. This would have given time for Mark's Gospel to circulate and become more widespread in the church. This time would have also provided opportunity for the church's Christology to mature and adjust to new realities late in the first century. It is not possible for us here to do more than illustrate some examples of how this christological development took place. One of the most conspicuous differences between Matthew and Luke and their predecessor Mark is that both Matthew and Luke have included birth accounts of Jesus. As we know, Mark begins his story of Jesus with the baptism of Jesus by John, but Matthew and Luke, each in quite different ways, record accounts of Jesus's lineage, birth, and early days. Whereas Jesus becomes Son of God at his baptism according to Mark, he does so at his birth in Matthew and Luke. The christological tradition is being expanded and elaborated. A fuller synoptic comparison would show many other instances of how this happens, but here I will illustrate the development with only two further examples.

The first is a subtle, technical modification that Matthew makes to Mark's text. The story is found in Mark 6:1–6 and Matt 13:54–58. The scene is Jesus's return to his home town of Nazareth where he preaches. At first, people are amazed at what he says but very quickly turn against him. The crowds know his family and so they think they know him. As the story ends, we are told that no mighty works were done that day in Nazareth,

---

3. See above pp.44, 47–48.

apparently on account of the people's unbelief. As Mark tells the story, "he could do no mighty works there" (6:5). The clear implication is that he could do no mighty works there, except for laying hands on some sick people and curing them, because of their unbelief. This makes Jesus's ability to perform mighty deeds dependent on the receptive response of the people. It portrays Jesus's power as limited, which, of course, has christological implications. Matthew reads this story in Mark and seems to sense the problem and ever so slightly modifies the text: "And he did not do many deeds of power there, because of their unbelief." Not only does Matthew make the implication of Mark's text explicit (the people's unbelief is the problem), but he makes clear that Jesus's power is not simply dependent on people's belief. Matthew senses the christological problem in Mark's wording of the story and wants to make sure his readers do not misunderstand Christ's power. Matthew ever so carefully tweaks the christological tradition and in so doing indicates the fluid nature of the tradition as it develops. Rather than something fixed at this early date in the church, it is still very much in the process of formation. We might even say that the process of christological formation and revision has continued in one form or another throughout the history of the church.[4]

The second example of christological development is much more dramatic. Each of the Synoptics ends with the tradition of the empty tomb, but only Matthew and Luke include appearances of the risen Christ. The original ending of Mark, most scholars think, is 16:1–8.[5] Here, Mary Magdalene, Mary the mother of James, and Salome come to the tomb, and finding it empty encounter a young man who tells them Jesus is risen. Overcome with fear, they flee and say nothing to anyone, contrary to the instruction they had been given. Here the original story apparently ended. Later, verses 9–20 were added to the text of Mark, perhaps to finish the story and make it conform more closely to Matthew's ending. As Matthew tells the story, the women find the stone in front of the tomb rolled away by a great earthquake and those posted as guards overcome with fear. The women are instructed by an angel to go tell the disciples that the risen Christ will go before them to Galilee and that there they will see him. On the way, the women encounter the risen Christ, and he too commands them to tell the disciples they will see him in Galilee. The Matthean resurrection story ends with what we normally call the Great Commission:

> [16] Now the eleven disciples went to Galilee, to the mountain to which Jesus had directed them. [17] When they saw him, they worshiped him; but some doubted. [18] And Jesus came and said

---

4. See Pelikan, *Jesus through the Centuries*.
5. Most English translations of this text discuss in their notes this textual issue.

to them, "All authority in heaven and on earth has been given to me. [19] Go therefore and make disciples of all nations, baptizing them in the name of the Father and of the Son and of the Holy Spirit, [20] and teaching them to obey everything that I have commanded you. And remember, I am with you always, to the end of the age."

Standing on a mountain in Galilee, the risen Jesus instructs his disciples. Not found in the other Synoptic Gospels, the Great Commission is a powerful christological and ecclesiological statement. All authority in heaven and on earth has been given to Jesus, and the disciples are charged to make disciples of all nations, baptizing them in the name of the Father, Son, and Holy Spirit, and teaching all that has been commanded by Christ. And then with words of reassurance, Christ tells the disciples he is with them to the close of the age. As the early Christians came to see themselves as heirs of Jesus's disciples and as followers of Christ, these words came to define their authority and the mission of the church. The Great Commission propelled them outward, reassured with the promise of Christ. It is hard to overestimate the influence of these words on the history of Christianity.

On the other hand, Luke tells the resurrection story quite differently from either Mark or Matthew, especially after the empty-tomb scene. While there are differences in the way Luke recounts the women's discovery of the empty tomb, it is his story of Jesus's encounter on the Road to Emmaus that marks his gospel. After Jesus's resurrection, two followers of Jesus are on the way to the village of Emmaus, some distance from Jerusalem, when they are joined by the risen Christ, though he is unrecognized by them. He inquires of them what they are discussing, and they tell him of the recent events in Jerusalem. The unknown Jesus then tells them of the necessity of these things and chastises them for their slowness of heart. As they approach Emmaus, the two men invite Jesus to stay with them, for it is evening. And we are told that in the eating of bread the two men recognize Jesus, and as they do so, he vanishes. Hastily, they return to Jerusalem and report what they had seen to the disciples, who are huddled in the city. As they are discussing these things, Jesus appears in their midst. Though they are understandably startled, he shows them his hands and feet and asks for something to eat. Jesus then teaches them and opens the Scriptures to them regarding the necessity of the Messiah's suffering and resurrection. In his name, repentance and forgiveness is to be proclaimed to all nations, beginning in Jerusalem. The eleven disciples, furthermore, are instructed to stay in Jerusalem until that which God had promised has come upon them, namely, the Holy Spirit. As we already know, Luke also wrote the book of Acts, and his account of the spread of the early church begins in Jerusalem, not in Galilee. Hence, the disciples' encounter with the risen Jesus, their stay in the city, and eventually their receiving the Holy Spirit all take place in Jerusalem. It is also hard to miss in the Emmaus story Luke's eucharistic imagery (the disciples' recognition of Jesus in the breaking of bread) and his emphasis on the proper interpretation of Scripture (it is written that the Messiah is to suffer and rise from the dead on the third day; and everything written in the Law, the Prophets and Psalms must be fulfilled). It seems Luke has shaped the tradition for his own theological and ecclesiological purposes. Once again, we see the Jesus tradition is both diverse and fluid.

John's Gospel is a very different kind of gospel. While following the same general arc as the Synoptics (Jesus's ministry, death, and resurrection), it uses very different kinds of imagery (e.g., light and darkness, the "I am" sayings, and a prologue rather than a birth account). The sequence of events is often quite different from the arrangement in the Synoptic Gospels (e.g., Jesus's demonstration in the temple takes place in chapter 2 rather than later in the gospel, and the Gospel of John portrays itself as a book of signs [e.g., 2:11, 20:30–31] rather than parables). John's Gospel is marked by long discourses, at least one of which runs for a number of chapters (the so-called Farewell Discourse, in which Jesus instructs his disciples prior to his departure (13:31—17:26), and the literary features of John's language are more sublime than is the language of the Synoptic Gospels. Instead of a Pentecost event as Luke describes the giving of the Holy Spirit, John speaks of a *paraclete* being given to the disciples following Jesus's departure. For all these reasons and many more, we can see that the Gospel of John stands in a class by itself in the New Testament gospel tradition and testifies yet again to the diversity of early Christianity's representation of Christ. Later than the Synoptics, John was probably written near the end of the first century or the beginning of the second. And apparently without much sense of contradiction, the early church lived with, perhaps even relished, the differences among the four gospels. Later, there was an effort by Tatian in about 170 CE to combine all four New Testament gospels into one supergospel called the *Diatessaron*. Though it was popular in some circles, the church at the end of the day preferred to maintain the diversity of the tradition represented by the fourfold witness of the New Testament gospels.

The Q material in Matthew and Luke is largely made up of teaching sayings attributed to Jesus. Little in this material suggests an interest in the crucified Messiah or his atoning death for the redemption of the world. The emphasis seems to be on Jesus the teacher of wisdom, and in that regard it bears some resemblance to the gnostic Gospel of Thomas, which presents

Jesus as a teacher of wisdom.⁶ There is no miraculous birth or crucifixion account in this gospel, which appears to reflect a strand of early Christianity called *Gnosticism*. Gnosticism focuses on Jesus as the teacher of divine wisdom and knowledge rather than on the suffering and crucified redeemer. It may be that Q and Thomas represent an early and alternate strand of Christianity that emphasized Jesus as a teacher of wisdom. Of course, each New Testament gospel presents Jesus as a teacher, but they clearly culminate in his death and resurrection. This is the christological tradition that came to prevail in early Christianity. To be sure, other, apocryphal gospels (not found in the New Testament) were produced in Christianity, each representing its own portrait of Jesus, but these did not prevail and were in the end marginalized by the emerging church.⁷

This illustrates that while there was diversity in the early church's Christology, there was also movement toward unity and consolidation as Christianity sought to define itself and its belief. Throughout the first four centuries, the church struggled to articulate Christian orthodoxy (correct belief) and to distinguish that from heterodoxy (incorrect belief). This process reached a crucial stage with development of the Nicene Creed (325, 381 CE). Having legalized Christianity, Emperor Constantine called the Council of Nicaea where it was expected the bishops of the church would establish orthodox Christian teaching, thereby reducing the forces of division that threatened both church and Roman Empire. While significant, the completion of the Nicene Creed did not end the church's search to define correct teaching. This search continues to this day as churches and individual Christians debate fine points of belief, practice, and ethics.

TWO WAYS OF READING THE GOSPELS

At the risk of oversimplification, I argue for two primary ways contemporary interpreters read and make sense of the New Testament gospels: literary approaches and historical approaches. Literary approaches focus on the gospel texts as literature, as narratives about Jesus in this case. The emphasis is on the internal features of the text. In narratives, emphasis falls on characters and character development, on the plot and plot development, on the perspective and point of view, on the literary settings and stylistic attributes of the text, on the narrator and implied author of the story, and on the meaning and message of the narrative. Speaking metaphorically, we

---

6. The English word "gnostic" comes from the Greek word *gnosis*, which translates as "knowledge."

7. To read these gospels, consult Hennecke, *New Testament Apocrypha*.

might say that reading the gospels literally is like standing before a pane of glass, and instead of looking through and beyond the glass we focus on the character of the glass itself.

Historical approaches ask different questions and look for different things. Who is the historical Jesus written about in the gospels, and how can we understand his world? Who is Mark or Matthew or Luke or John, and what are their worlds and communities like? Reading the gospels this way means bringing historical questions and critical evaluation of the evidence to the task of making sense of the material. However, for the person using modern historical methods the gospels present particular kinds of challenges. The primary purpose of the gospels is not to present raw historical evidence according to modern standards of historical evidence. On the contrary, the gospel writers are proclaiming a message about Jesus in narrative form, and the inclusion of historical material is rather incidental, I would argue, to that larger purpose. In other words, the historical reader's line of sight is refracted.

The modern historian using modern historical methods and assumptions must account in some fashion for the refraction of the evidence. This is not an uncommon problem for modern historians, and students of the historical Jesus have devised their own ways of dealing with this. For our purposes, the important point is that serious readers of the gospels cannot assume automatically that the narrative characterizations of Jesus in the gospel stories are identical with the historical Jesus who stands behind the gospel accounts. This distinction is fundamental and cannot be ignored by sophisticated modern interpreters, whichever approach they use. It is also the case that students of the historical Jesus do not limit their evidence to the New Testament gospels. They use all manner of Jewish and Greco-Roman material to help situate and understand who Jesus was.

THE LITERARY JESUS
ACCORDING TO MARK'S GOSPEL

Scholars have studied extensively each of the gospels from a literary perspective and have drawn interesting conclusions about their meaning and message. It is not possible for us to look literarily at each New Testament gospel, but it is important to illustrate by example some of the important literary features of at least one gospel, and at the way this type of literary reading might play itself out. Since Mark's account is presumably the earliest as well as the shortest of the four, it will serve as our example. As we have already noted, Mark's Gospel begins with the story of Jesus's baptism by

John the Baptist and ends with the women fleeing in terror from the empty tomb without saying anything to anyone. Between these two bookends, the story unfolds, with chapters 14 and 15 devoted to the events associated with Jesus's crucifixion and death. From 8:22 onward, the story moves inexorably toward Jerusalem and the death of Jesus. Because of this, the gospel has sometimes been described as a passion narrative with an extended introduction.[8] While this characterization is not accurate strictly speaking, it dramatizes the passion's importance in the Markan narrative. The story at strategic points is punctuated with claims about Jesus's divine sonship: at the baptism of Jesus (1:11) and at his transfiguration (9:7), a voice from heaven announces that he is the beloved son, and then at the end of the story (15:39) a similar confession is made by a Roman centurion as Jesus breathes his last, "Truly this man was God's son!" The irony of this confession, coming from the mouth of a Roman soldier, cannot be lost on readers. The three announcements of Jesus' divine sonship almost equally divide the narrative in half and leave readers in no doubt about Jesus' identity according to Mark. Shortly following the first of these announcements (1:15), Mark declares to the readers a theological claim that effectively serves as the theme of the gospel: "The time is fulfilled, and the kingdom of God has come near; repent and believe in the good news." The Son of God brings the kingdom of God near, and the dynamic of that Markan claim unfolds as the narrative develops.

In fact, the rhetorical device Mark uses to bring the story of Jesus and the kingdom of God to life is a journey that begins in 1:16–20 with the call of the first four disciples and ends in 16:1–8 with the empty tomb signifying the resurrection. The kingdom journey expands with the calling of Levi, the tax collector, in 2:13–17 and the appointing of the twelve in 3:13–19a. Along the way, as the entourage expands, Jesus casts out demons and heals those who are sick, possessed, or paralyzed. In the case of the unclean spirits they know who Jesus is. Those of the spirit world know one another, and Jesus prevails over those of Satan's world with clear and decisive action. And he runs afoul of the people's expectations about fasting, the Sabbath, and the people with whom he should or should not associate. At this early stage of the journey, Jesus appears largely as a healer and miracle worker who manifests the power of God's kingdom. This stage of the journey culminates in 3:31–35 with a redefinition of the family: "Whoever does the will of God is my brother and sister and mother."

The narrative and its kingdom journey become more complicated in chapter 4 with the parable of the Sower and its subsequent explanation. The

---

8. Martin Kahler's comment often repeated by others.

most perplexing verses in this chapter are 4:11-12, and they seem to suggest that Jesus tells the parables to confuse those on the outside, whereas to those on the inside the mysteries have been revealed.

> [11] And he said to them, "To you has been given the secret of the kingdom of God, but for those outside, everything comes in parables; [12] in order that (*for the purpose that*)
>
>> 'they may indeed look, but not perceive,
>>   and may indeed listen, but not understand;
>> so that they may not turn again and be forgiven.'"

Insiders are being distinguished from outsiders, and Jesus seems to see the parables much like riddles that perplex rather than merely teach. The disciples and those on the kingdom journey are given special instruction and privilege, making it all the more bewildering when the disciples themselves end up being without understanding and insight. We see this dramatically in chapter 5 when the disciples are terrified by the storm on the lake and exhibit fear rather than faith, and again in the section 8:22—10:33 where Jesus's passion is predicted three times and each time the disciples fail to grasp its meaning. Insight into the mysteries of the kingdom is in short supply among the disciples, and they often appear to be simpletons rather than stalwarts in the kingdom of God. More broadly, we might say that Mark's claims about the kingdom of God are, at the very least, provocative and edgy.

Looking more closely at 8:22—10:33, we see this even more powerfully. This section begins and ends with Jesus restoring eyesight. Apparently these men are not on the kingdom journey, but Jesus enables them to see. In my view, this sets the tenor and theme for this entire section. With Jesus's help and power, these two men see, but the disciples are blind to the mysteries of the kingdom, despite having been given special instruction. This is illustrated in spades in 8:27-38 where Jesus asks the disciples, "Who do people say that I am?"

> [27] Jesus went on with his disciples to the villages of Caesarea Philippi; and on the way he asked his disciples, "Who do people say that I am?" [28] And they answered him, "John the Baptist; and others, Elijah; and still others, one of the prophets." [29] He asked them, "But who do you say that I am?" *Peter answered him, "You are the Messiah."* [30] And he sternly ordered them not to tell anyone about him.
> [31] *Then he began to teach them that the Son of Man must undergo great suffering, and be rejected by the elders, the chief*

> *priests, and the scribes, and be killed, and after three days rise again.* ³² *He said all this quite openly. And Peter took him aside and began to rebuke him.* ³³ *But turning and looking at his disciples, he rebuked Peter and said, "Get behind me, Satan! For you are setting your mind not on divine things but on human things."*
>
> ³⁴ *He called the crowd with his disciples, and said to them, "If any want to become my followers, let them deny themselves and take up their cross and follow me.* ³⁵ *For those who want to save their life will lose it, and those who lose their life for my sake, and for the sake of the gospel, will save it.* ³⁶ *For what will it profit them to gain the whole world and forfeit their life?* ³⁷ *Indeed, what can they give in return for their life?* ³⁸ *Those who are ashamed of me and of my words in this adulterous and sinful generation, of them the Son of Man will also be ashamed when he comes in the glory of his Father with the holy angels."*

I have italicized the three important things in this text: 1) Peter confesses correctly that Jesus is Messiah, 2) he has little idea of the meaning of what he has just confessed, and 3) the kingdom of God, according to the kingdoms of this world, is upside down. The disciples show similar incomprehension during the second (9:30–37) and third (10:32–40) passion predictions. The disciples lack (in)sight, and the kingdom of God is a very different kind of kingdom relative to the kingdoms of this world. For those who follow Jesus on the journey, the first shall be last, those who lose their life for the sake of the gospel will save it, the ones who want to be first must be servants of all, and the positions of privilege are reserved for those who go the way of the cross. Mark's view of the kingdom of God is challenging, and on some deep existential level defies the disciples' ability to comprehend what they naively signed up for by following Jesus.

In chapter 11, Jesus enters Jerusalem and, as we discussed earlier, throws the money changers out of the temple. As the narrative plot now moves in unrelenting fashion toward its culmination on the cross, the die has been cast. Various events and teachings appear along the way—the parable of the Vineyard, the question about paying taxes, disputes with the Sadducees and scribes, the teaching about love of the neighbor, the dialogue with the disciples predicting the destruction of the temple, and the so-called little apocalypse of chapter 13—but the pace of the story now accelerates to its predicted end, with the events leading to Jesus's arrest, crucifixion, and death, where the centurion proclaims him Son of God. According to Mark, the kingdom journey passes through death on its way to the empty tomb, a confusing and daunting prospect for Jesus's disciples. Confusion and perplexity remain for later readers and hearers, especially given the way Mark ends the narrative. With the women fleeing in fear and keeping silent, the hearers of this story are left hanging. One of the great ironies of this is that throughout the story Jesus consistently enjoins the recipients of his power to maintain silence; but here they are commanded by the young man at the empty tomb to speak, and instead of speaking, they say nothing to anyone. The end—but is it? I suggest that even as the narrative ends in 16:8, the story continues on for the readers and hearers of the gospel as they seek to answer for themselves what this might mean and whether or not they will speak. In other words, how will they finish the story? Reading the Markan manuscript tradition indicates this is literally what happened. Scribes finished the story by adding longer endings, as we can see by reading the notes included at the end of Marks' Gospel in most modern editions of the Bible.

With the writing of Mark's Gospel, the early Christian gospel tradition was launched, and from then on this form of literature would mark the church and Christianity. It stands to reason that if Jesus Christ is the center of the Christian religious system, the stories and remembrances about him would be close to the center of Christian practice and imagination. To be sure, the early Christians would not be uninterested in historical questions, but they would continue to tell the stories of Jesus and to mine his words and deeds for theological insight and pastoral nurture, just as they would gather in worship to hear the gospel stories read and proclaimed.

THE HISTORICAL JESUS

The question of the historical Jesus has been around for a long time among scholars of the New Testament and early Christianity. In the nineteenth and twentieth centuries a number of the scholarly studies presented portraits of the historical Jesus that challenged traditional church teaching. By the mid-twentieth century that effort seemed to have run its course; the turn was to the Christ of faith, and a feeling prevailed that not much could be said about the historical Jesus. For example, the great German New Testament scholar Rudolf Bultmann devoted only about thirty pages of his two-volume *Theology of the New Testament* to the message of Jesus.[9] With new archeological discoveries and new interdisciplinary approaches, that changed yet again in the last half of the twentieth century, beginning with some of Bultmann's own students. This has continued into the twenty-first century, with a flurry of new interest and work. It is not my goal here to survey the scholarly chronology of the historical Jesus question[10] but rather

9. Bultmann, *Theology of the New Testament*, 1:3–32.
10. Powell, *Jesus as a Figure in History*; and Borg, *Jesus in Contemporary Scholarship*.

to illustrate the main features of two major and quite different strands of contemporary scholarship on this issue. There are many others, but it is not necessary for our purposes here to pursue these questions further. Again, my purpose is more suggestive and conceptual than it is historically exhaustive. Two points, however, need to be made at the outset. First, from the early days of Christianity, the implicit claim of the incarnation, God taking on human form and flesh, has been that in Christ God entered into human history. Thus, as a christological principle, the claim of Jesus's historicity is important, even if it is unclear precisely what that looks like. As the Nicene Creed puts it, he is true man and true God. This is not so much a historical statement as it is a confession of the claim that in him God entered into history. Second, as modern scholars using modern historical methods approach the question of the historical Jesus, what they end up producing are historical constructs, contemporary portraits created by historians based on the available evidence. In the process, these historians raise important philosophical questions about the nature of history.

John Dominic Crossan

Longtime New Testament scholar John Dominic Crossan burst on the historical Jesus scene in a new way in 1991 with his book *The Historical Jesus: The Life of a Mediterranean Jewish Peasant*. This was followed in 1993 by *Jesus: A Revolutionary Biography* (a condensed version of the earlier book), and in 2001 by *Excavating Jesus: Beneath the Stones, behind the Texts*, coauthored by Jonathan L. Reed. In these and many other written materials and presentations, Crossan has cut a wide swath through contemporary historical Jesus scholarship. Not only has his work shaped scholarly conversations in North America and abroad, but it has reached wider audiences of nonspecialists as well. Devoting careful attention to his method of evaluating the material, Crossan has sought to distinguish what can be attributed to Jesus himself from what was said about him and then placed back upon the tradition. He seeks to make sense of what the material means. Using archaeological techniques, Crossan works to identify the various layers of the Jesus tradition, from earliest to latest, much as archaeologists do when they expose different layers in a dig. He then makes judgments about which sources and materials fit into the different layers. Next he groups the various kinds of sayings attributed to Jesus, identifies the layer in which each cluster is first referenced, and notes how many times the cluster is independently attested. The earlier the material, and the more times it is attested, the closer the saying gets to something Jesus might have said. Having carefully worked through the material and made some judgments about what we might reasonably know about Jesus's teaching, Crossan sets about placing Jesus in a first-century Palestinian context, using interdisciplinary insights from social and cultural anthropology, anticolonial protest movements, and the character of preindustrial peasant societies. Subjecting the Jesus material to this analysis, Crossan concludes in his early work that Jesus was a peasant who spoke to other peasants; a Jewish Cynic, not unlike Hellenistic Cynics, who challenged convention; a healer who operated outside the traditional religious boundaries and expectations; and a man who practiced open table fellowship regardless of social status and convention, which in itself represented an alternate social vision in first-century Palestine. Crossan also concludes that Jesus was not an eschatological (end-times) figure—in order words, one who anticipated the kingdom of God's arrival in the near future.[11]

In their book *Excavating Jesus*, Crossan and Reed bring the discoveries and insights of archaeology to bear on the search for the historical Jesus. After looking at the layers of tradition, they examine the kingdoms represented by Herod the Great and Herod Antipas on the one hand and John the Baptist and Jesus on the other. The first they call a commercial kingdom and the second a covenantal kingdom. The imperial buildings of Caesarea, with their monumental facades and all they represented in terms of imperial power, contrast sharply with the peasant villages of Galilee, where Jesus lived, preached, and healed. In the covenantal kingdom, people lived close to the land, usually set apart from the commercial and social structures of imperial life. The structures and ways of life represented by these two competing kingdoms at certain points clashed, and it is in this highly charged world that Jesus's social vision and sense of justice took form. As an itinerant who took his healing power to the people, and as a person who invited all regardless of social rank to his table, Jesus represented a very different kind of kingdom from that represented by Herod and his imperial overlords. The Romans and their Jewish minions built for the purpose of imposing order and control on the land and its people, whereas Jesus welcomed all to his open table. This was a different kind of social dynamic, with a different mode of operation. On the spectrum of protesters and nonprotesters against Roman occupation, Jesus is situated on the interface between covenantal kingdom and martyrological protest, which puts him in a class of radical nonviolent resisters to imperial rule. If Galilee presented Jesus with its own imperial challenges, the clash of kingdoms was significantly more intense in Jerusalem, with its temple, priesthood, and Roman contingent. Not only

---

11. Borg, *Jesus in Contemporary Scholarship*, 32–36.

were imperial rulers honored in life, but in death as well, with monumental edifices and mausoleums. The contrast between Jesus's hasty burial and the elaborate ceremonies and monuments for dead emperors is striking, and indicative of Jesus's very different kind of kingdom. Only much later would the sites associated with Jesus's life and death be memorialized and celebrated with their own structures. Whereas the itinerant Jesus went out to the people, now the people came on pilgrimage to him, to the important sites associated with him and his ministry. The directional dynamic had now shifted. Crossan and Reed themselves wonder out loud how the fourth-century kingdom of Constantine (along with all the trappings of power it brought to the church) squared with the kingdom that Jesus represented in first-century Palestine.[12] This is an interesting question and one that indicates just how far the church had traveled in its first three hundred years.

The work of John Dominic Crossan is not without its critics, but he asks interesting questions and brings interdisciplinary insights to his work on the historical Jesus, which has changed the scholarly landscape. Even if Crossan's theory about the clash between the Roman Empire and the kingdom of God is correct (and there is much to commend this theory), one wonders how self-aware and programmatic the historical Jesus would have been about world forces and their implication for God's kingdom. Was Jesus simply caught up by forces that could only really be understood and appreciated from some distance—that is, by later observers of the tradition? Crossan walks this line very carefully. Yet these questions help us get to the heart of the distinction between history writing as reportage, which in the case of ancient historical figures seems unlikely, and history writing as construction based on available evidence and methodological theory. We now turn to a very different kind of interpretive construction of the historical Jesus, that of Geza Vermes.

Geza Vermes

Geza Vermes was one of the most important scholars of ancient Judaism in the last half of the twentieth century, having been a pioneer in Dead Sea Scrolls research, intertestamental Jewish literature, and early rabbinic tradition. Perhaps because of his own personal biography, he maintained a long-term scholarly interest in the historical Jesus. Beginning with *Jesus the Jew* in 1973, he published a series of books on Jesus over the next four decades: *The Gospel of Jesus the Jew* in 1981, *Jesus and the World of Judaism* in 1983, *The Religion of Jesus the Jew* in 1993, *The Changing Faces of Jesus* in

---

12. Crossan and Reed, *Excavating Jesus*, 97.

2000, *Jesus in His Jewish Context* in 2003, and *The Real Jesus: Then and Now* in 2010. Some of this material reappears in the early chapters of his book *Christian Beginnings: From Nazareth to Nicaea*, published in 2012, shortly before his death in 2013. As we see from the titles of these books, Vermes's interest is in the Jewishness of Jesus and his world. He has relatively little interest in the later christological and theological teaching of the church, except insofar as he needs to account for it in order to understand Jesus the Jew and his teaching and in order to explain the beginnings of Christianity.

Vermes's method can best be described as situational and comparative. It is situational in the sense he tries to position Jesus fully in his Jewish context, and he seeks to do this primarily through comparison with other figures and features of Jesus's Jewish world. At the end of chapter 1 in *Christian Beginnings*, he writes: "In short, without a proper grasp of charismatic Judaism it is impossible to understand the rise of Christianity."[13] After this conclusion, he titles the second chapter of this book "The Charismatic Religion of Jesus." Preceded by John the Baptist, who stood in the line of Elijah, Jesus emerges in the New Testament gospels as a spiritual healer, exorcist, preacher, and charismatic prophet.[14] For Vermes, this portrayal of Jesus is entirely consistent with the image of the "man of God" in charismatic Judaism. But Jesus was not simply a healer and doer of mighty deeds. He was also a charismatic teacher of the kingdom of God. As such, he was a Son of God in that he was close to God, but not in the sense of sharing God's divine nature. That would have been contrary to Jewish monotheistic belief. Vermes concludes that the religion of Jesus was the religion of Moses and the prophets, now adjusted to fit the needs of the eschatological age in which he found himself. In this, Jesus changed the normal priorities. The poor, prisoners, orphans, and widows now stand ahead of the pious. He gave special attention to the sick and the outcasts of society, those who had been marginalized.[15] His preaching focused on the imminent kingdom of God and the impending encounter with God the Father. As Vermes writes:

> The religion proclaimed by Jesus was a wholly theocentric one in which he played the role of the man of God par excellence, the prophet of prophets, the shepherd of the flock, the leader, revealer, and teacher without being himself in any sense the object of worship as he later became in the fully fledged Christianity created by Paul and John, and especially from the second century onwards . . . Christocentricity does not stem from the historical Jesus."[16]

13. Vermes, *Christian Beginnings*, 27.
14. Ibid., 33.
15. Ibid., 55.
16. Ibid., 60.

From this Jewish, charismatic Jesus, the church over the next centuries down to the council of Nicaea in the fourth century, according to Vermes, developed its christological dogma. Much as Crossan and Reed raise the question of what happened to the religion of Jesus over time, so too does Vermes. Their conclusions about who the historical Jesus in fact was differ greatly, but both seem to see the religion of Jesus and his teaching transformed, if not entirely replaced, by a different kind of religion. The covenantal kingdom of Jesus is replaced by the commercial and imperial kingdom of Constantine in the case of Crossan and Reed; and for Vermes, the charismatic Jesus is replaced by the christological dogma of the church. Apart from the methodological questions associated with the quest for the historical Jesus, perhaps the most important conceptual lesson to take away from this discussion is the seeming discontinuity between the Jesus of history and the Christ of the church's faith, at least in the two approaches to the issue discussed here. And even if at the end of the day we reject the portraits of Jesus painted by Crossan and Vermes, the persistent question for any investigation of Christian origins must address the relationship between the Jesus of history and the Christ of faith. For me, it is simply not sufficient to affirm the Christ of the church's teaching and faith and to summarily dismiss any concern for the historical Jesus. Without the historical Jesus, we are left with the speculative Christology of the church, or perhaps of the individual; and we are left without the possibility of a corrective for Christian theology—a corrective prompted, for example, by the study of the historical Jesus. Perhaps even more troubling is that any sense of the tension between the Jesus of history and the Christ of faith is then lost. The loss of conceptual tension is never a good thing, in my view. The loss of tension reduces the possibility of further creative thinking about the issues at stake. And if understanding is one of the goals of study, then the loss of constructive tension inhibits self-understanding, which in turn impedes learning and growth.

CONCLUSION

In this chapter, we have learned a number of important things about the New Testament gospels and their interpretation. From the question of their genre to their literary relationships with one another, we see how scholars argue hypotheses that affect how we read and understand them. But perhaps even more importantly, we see how these perspectives illuminate for us the origin of Christianity. We see how the gospels early on came to be identifying markers of Christianity, how the gospel writers tried to make sense of who Jesus is as the Messiah of God and to account for the destruction of the

Jerusalem temple. We see how the gospels can be read in different ways and for different purposes. This chapter has noted what the gospels say about the kingdom of God, the way the historical Jesus and the Christ of faith stand in relationship but also in tension, and the diversity and fluidity of the early Jesus tradition. Historically, the Gospels have anchored the New Testament, and much of Christian theology for that matter, even as they have occupied a privileged place in Christian worship. Just as Jesus stands at the center of Christianity as a religious system, so the Gospels take a central place in Christian practice because they testify most directly to him. No serious consideration of Christian origins can avoid study of the gospels.

Mosaic in the Archiepiscopal Palace of San Pietro Crisologoa Chapel in Ravenna, Italy (sixth century)

The Savior, **El Greco (seventeenth century)**

7

The Church in Motion
The Acts of the Apostles

*What was Luke's purpose in writing Acts,
and how did he tell the story of the early church's movement
into the first-century Greco-Roman world?*

As we now know, Luke wrote a two-volume work, the first dealing with Jesus and the second with the apostles and the growth of the early church. In the very beginning of Acts, Luke addresses someone named Theophilus and immediately rehearses in broad outline what took place at the end of the first book. As we saw in the previous chapter, the disciples in the Gospel of Luke saw the risen Christ in Jerusalem and were instructed to stay there until the Holy Spirit would come upon them. In this way Luke is unlike Mark and Matthew, where Jesus's appearances were to take place in Galilee. This gives us a clue that for Luke the geography of the Jesus story and perhaps more important the geography of the story of the early church is critical. Luke says as much in Acts 1:8 when he writes: "But you will receive power when the Holy Spirit has come upon you; and you will be my witnesses in Jerusalem, in all Judea and Samaria, and to the ends of the earth." This is about geography to be sure, but not only about geography. The statement gives us a thumbnail sketch of the entire book of Acts. It begins in Jerusalem; moves to Judea (the area around Jerusalem); then on to Samaria (the successor to the old northern kingdom of Israel); and finally to the ends of the earth, symbolized by Rome. And that is exactly the way the

Acts narrative unfolds, and at virtually any point along the way we can plot geographically where we are according to that sketch. However, Luke is not merely interested in geography, but writes a narrative that presumably interweaves some historical material with an interpretive theological agenda. For as we shall see, the movement of the church outward from Jerusalem is powered by the Holy Spirit, and along the way the Pauline Gentile mission is underwritten by Luke, if not the Holy Spirit as well. As this story develops, readers would never get a sense that there were Christ followers and churches in the lands east and north of Palestine or in North Africa. Luke has his eyes set on Rome, and that in itself presumably tells us something about what is important to him. To be sure, imperial Rome functioned as an economic and social magnet. Indeed, Luke portrays the church's growing and moving inexorably toward the capital city of the empire. Perhaps he thinks that for the church to survive and flourish it must make its way in the Roman world and come to terms with what that world represents for Christianity late in the first century. Hence, as important as Luke's account of the origins of early Christianity is, it is only part of a larger story, and it is as much, perhaps more, a theological rendering than it is a historical account of what happened.[1]

THE BEGINNING OF THE STORY OF THE APOSTLES

Before the story can go forward, there is according to Luke some unfinished business. After Judas's betrayal, the full complement of disciples must be restored, and Luke records the eleven casting lots to decide who should take Judas's place and thus round out the apostolate with the full number twelve. Having rehearsed briefly the ending of the gospel and taken care of unfinished apostolic business, Luke records the Pentecost scene in chapter 2, which in effect serves the narrative and the theology of Acts as the launching pad for everything that comes after. With the rush of a mighty wind and tongues of fire, the Holy Spirit descends upon the apostles, and they speak in languages not their own. Looking on are Jews from every nation who, though astonished and bewildered, hear the languages being spoken, and yet they understand in their own native tongue what is being said. The apostle Peter then stands up and preaches to the Jerusalem crowd that Jesus

---

1. For a recent major commentary on Acts see Pervo, *Acts*. For older works in the German and English scholarly traditions, see Haenchen, *Acts of the Apostles*; Dibelius, *Studies in the Acts of the Apostles*; Hengel, *Acts and the History of Earliest Christianity*; and Cadbury, *Making of Luke-Acts* .

is both Lord and Messiah and calls the people to repent and be baptized. Luke tells us that three thousand people were baptized that day. Whatever in fact happened on that occasion, Luke portrays an event of monumental proportions using vibrant imagery that, as far as he is concerned, can only portray divine power and action. It is vivid, hyperbolic language used for the purpose of describing something that astonishes and amazes, as only divine power can do. This is not the language of history writing, certainly not as modern historians practice their craft, but religious language, the only language adequate to an occasion of such magnitude. Thus, the language Luke uses to portray the Pentecost scene tells less about an accurate description of what took place on that day and more about the power and significance of the event for the apostles and the growth of the church. The apostles and the spread of the church go forth by divine intention and divine power. Whatever success the apostles achieve is not accidental, says Luke.

Shortly after the Pentecost event, Peter and John enter the temple in Jerusalem and there meet a lame beggar who asks for money. But instead Peter heals the man of his infirmity, which of course causes a stir. Peter in turn addresses the crowd and challenges them with the message of Christ. Not surprisingly, this annoys the priests, the captain of the temple, and the Sadducees. As a result, Peter and John are arrested and kept in prison until the next day. Again, we are told that in spite of this many who heard also believed—about five thousand in all. Peter and John are brought before the high priest and other priestly notables and questioned. Filled with the Holy Spirit, Peter proclaims Jesus and challenges his inquisitors who, for fear of the people, release them and charge them to stop preaching about these things. Already we can see a pattern beginning to develop. The apostles preach the message of Christ, many in the audience believe, opposition is aroused, and those preaching are arrested and imprisoned but emboldened by the Spirit live to preach another day. Luke clearly wants to convey the idea that despite opposition the proclamation of Christ was not and cannot be stopped. Many came to believe and were baptized. The message of Christ and the church are on the move. Perhaps one of the most astonishing things about early Christianity is that the church actually survived and grew. It may be that, among other things, Luke sought in Acts to give an account of this amazing and surprising thing, as he looked back from his vantage point late in the first century.

In 4:32–37, Luke gives us an interesting glimpse into what may have been part of early church life, when he writes:

> [32] Now the whole group of those who believed were of one heart and soul, and no one claimed private ownership of any

> possessions, but everything they owned was held in common. ³³ With great power the apostles gave their testimony to the resurrection of the Lord Jesus, and great grace was upon them all. ³⁴ There was not a needy person among them, for as many as owned lands or houses sold them and brought the proceeds of what was sold. ³⁵ They laid it at the apostles' feet, and it was distributed to each as any had need. ³⁶ There was a Levite, a native of Cyprus, Joseph, to whom the apostles gave the name Barnabas (which means "son of encouragement"). ³⁷ He sold a field that belonged to him, then brought the money, and laid it at the apostles' feet.

We cannot know for sure how accurate this description of common ownership is. Even if Luke is referring to something practiced in the early church, it is not clear how widespread it might have been. It is striking, however, that Luke seems to insert this comment out of the blue, as well as the story following—about the deceit of Ananias and his wife, Sapphira, withholding proceeds from the common treasury from the sale of a piece of property (5:1–11). The least we can say is, there seems to be no compelling literary or theological reason why Luke would include this unless there is some experience of common ownership rooted in the memory and tradition of the early church, which he wants to report for the sake of completeness.

In a similar vein, Luke in Acts 6:1–6 writes about the selection of seven upstanding individuals who are set aside to attend to the needs of the community's widows:

> ¹Now during those days, when the disciples were increasing in number, the Hellenists complained against the Hebrews because their widows were being neglected in the daily distribution of food. ² And the twelve called together the whole community of the disciples and said, "It is not right that we should neglect the word of God in order to wait on tables. ³ Therefore, friends, select from among yourselves seven men of good standing, full of the Spirit and of wisdom, whom we may appoint to this task, ⁴ while we, for our part, will devote ourselves to prayer and to serving the word." ⁵ What they said pleased the whole community, and they chose Stephen, a man full of faith and the Holy Spirit, together with Philip, Prochorus, Nicanor, Timon, Parmenas, and Nicolaus, a proselyte of Antioch. ⁶ They had these men stand before the apostles, who prayed and laid their hands on them.

In the case of the servers, we know from other sources that these functions came to be associated with the office of deacon, which gives some historical credibility to Luke's account. In any case, it is interesting to note that in these texts Luke gives us glimpses into his perception of two aspects of the early church's social life: common ownership of goods and service to others. We also know that over time the church came to be noted for the care of others, and that this became a marker of Christian communities, especially during times of distress and epidemic. As Rodney Stark has argued, during times of epidemic the mere act of keeping the sick hydrated (as Christians tended to do) as opposed to abandoning them (as many others did) could significantly increase the survival rate of the ill and thus the relative growth of the church.[2] Statistically over time, this one thing would be enough to make the church grow without ever making a convert.

Following these stories (6:8—8:1a), Luke embarks on a long discussion of the ministry and stoning of Stephen, the first Christian martyr. As Peter and John do before him, Stephen performs wonders and signs, only to be confronted by religious authorities who feel threatened by his wisdom and the Spirit that empowers him. Brought before the high priest, he is challenged to give account of himself. With a long speech that rehearses and reinterprets Old Testament history, Jewish unfaithfulness, and complicity in the death of God's righteous one, Stephen, refusing to back down, confronts his opponents. This enrages the authorities, who seize him and drag him out of the city to be stoned. Luke then reports that as Stephen is being stoned "the witnesses laid their coats at the feet of a young man named Saul" (7:58b). We might say that Saul was the coat checker at this distressing spectacle; and though he does not appear to be actively engaged in the stoning of Stephen, he presumably approved. In Acts, this is the first mention of the Saul who later became Paul. We are told a little later in 8:3 that Saul ravaged and persecuted the church. The stage is being set for what follows.

TO JUDEA, SAMARIA, AND BEYOND

As persecution of the Jerusalem church begins, many, except apparently the apostles, scatter to Judea and Samaria. According to Luke, the geographical reach of the church's missionary activity grows, even as persecution in Jerusalem seeks to contain it. In Luke's view of the church's mission, the Holy Spirit is not to be denied. We first encounter Philip in Samaria; he gathers a crowd by doing signs, exorcisms, and healings. He even amazes Simon the magician, who for a long time had attracted a following because of his wonder-working. Having paved the way for the church in Samaria, Peter and John go to them as well, proclaiming the word of the Lord. Samaria might be described as a land between, for it is not Judea proper, having

---

2. Stark, *Rise of Christianity*, 73–94.

descended from the old northern kingdom after the united monarchy had split into north and south; but neither is Samaria completely separate either. While the animosity between the north and south is well attested—see, e.g., the parable of the Good Samaritan—they share a common origin in the settling of the land by the twelve tribes and in the united monarchy under David and Solomon. The Samaritans are not Judeans, but neither are they truly Gentiles.

This is about to change in 8:26–40 as an angel of the Lord speaks to Philip and commands him to go toward the south to the road that goes from Jerusalem to Gaza, which he does. We pick up the story in 8:27–40:

> [27] So he got up and went. Now there was an Ethiopian eunuch, a court official of the Candace, queen of the Ethiopians, in charge of her entire treasury. He had come to Jerusalem to worship [28] and was returning home; seated in his chariot, he was reading the prophet Isaiah. [29] Then the Spirit said to Philip, "Go over to this chariot and join it." [30] So Philip ran up to it and heard him reading the prophet Isaiah. He asked, "Do you understand what you are reading?" [31] He replied, "How can I, unless someone guides me?" And he invited Philip to get in and sit beside him. [32] Now the passage of the scripture that he was reading was this:
>
> "Like a sheep he was led to the slaughter,
> and like a lamb silent before its shearer,
>   so he does not open his mouth.
> [33] In his humiliation justice was denied him.
> Who can describe his generation?
>   For his life is taken away from the earth."
>
> [34] The eunuch asked Philip, "About whom, may I ask you, does the prophet say this, about himself or about someone else?" [35] Then Philip began to speak, and starting with this scripture, he proclaimed to him the good news about Jesus. [36] As they were going along the road, they came to some water; and the eunuch said, "Look, here is water! What is to prevent me from being baptized?" [38] He commanded the chariot to stop, and both of them, Philip and the eunuch, went down into the water, and Philip baptized him. [39] When they came up out of the water, the Spirit of the Lord snatched Philip away; the eunuch saw him no more, and went on his way rejoicing. [40] But Philip found himself at Azotus, and as he was passing through the region, he proclaimed the good news to all the towns until he came to Caesarea.

Taken at face value, this is an interesting tale. Philip comes upon an Ethiopian eunuch, a court official of the Ethiopian queen, who had come to worship at the Jerusalem temple and is now returning home. While on this journey, he is reading from the prophet Isaiah. The court official invites Philip to ride along, and in so doing he inquires of the Ethiopian if he understands what he is reading. With a surprisingly open attitude, the eunuch invites Philip to explain the Isaiah text to him. Then Luke cites the Isaiah passage the man is reading, a version of 53:7–8, one of the so-called Servant Songs in Isaiah. In response to the eunuch's inquiry, Philip makes clear the Isaiah text refers to Jesus. Here, as we also saw at the end of his gospel, Luke makes the interpretive claim that understood rightly Israel's prophets testify to Jesus. (To most in the Christian community today, this may not be a very provocative claim, but in the first century this certainly would not have been self-evident, let alone accepted by anyone but a few of the early Christ followers.) Continuing along their way, the eunuch and Philip come upon some water, and the eunuch asks why he cannot be baptized—at which point they step down and Philip baptizes him. As the eunuch comes up out of the water, the Spirit descends upon the him and Philip disappears.

To be sure, this story has to do with the geographical spread of Christianity and with early Christian readings of Jewish Scripture, as we have seen; but in the literary and theological architecture of Acts, more is being said than first meets the eye. It is subtle and comes back to the Ethiopian eunuch's question, "What is to prevent me from being baptized?" Not only does the story take place outside of Jerusalem and Samaria, but the court councilor himself is non-Jewish—in other words a Gentile. Perhaps surprisingly, there is no discussion of the question by Philip and the eunuch. The eunuch simply commands the chariot to stop, the two of them get down, and Philip baptizes him. Apparently there is nothing to prevent this Gentile from being baptized. It happens immediately and without any serious consideration or delay. Furthermore, the first Gentile convert according to Acts takes place under the auspices of Philip, not Paul, the apostle to the Gentiles.

In Acts 10, this is reinforced in the story about the apostle Peter and Cornelius, another Gentile conversion-and-baptism story. Looking at the literary structure of Acts 8–10, we see that the so-called conversion story of Saul/Paul on the Damascus Road is sandwiched between two other stories of Gentiles in which Paul is nowhere to be found. Not only does Luke, as we saw in chapter 4, present his account of Saul being struck down in Acts 9, but he wants to make sure the Pauline record is clear. Paul's Gentile mission is divinely authorized. Once again, the language is hyperbolic religious language used to make a religious point, a point for which only this kind of language is adequate. On a more mundane level, Luke wants to make it clear that Paul, despite his call to take the message of Christ to the Gentiles, was not the first to cross the Jew-Gentile boundary. Philip and Peter, Jesus's disciple and the apostle to the Jews, were pioneers before him in this controversial endeavor.

To contemporary observers, the early church's crossing of the Jew-Gentile divide seems rather inconsequential and uneventful. What is the big deal? Let me say that in the first century it was a very big deal; and Luke, writing Acts late in the first century, is weighing in on this issue and trying to set the record straight. As we know, Paul and Luke won the day historically as the church became overwhelmingly non-Jewish. At stake in this issue was the very identity of the Christian church. Would it remain a small Jewish sect, or would it become something else? By the end of the first century the die on that question had probably already been cast, but Luke's contribution to the issue is unmistakable.[3] The Gentile mission was part of God's intention, and it has gone forth under the power of the Holy Spirit.

We now turn to the story of Peter and Cornelius in Acts 10 and to the problem of eating unclean food and Gentile baptism. For the sake of looking at the actual Lukan text, I quote Acts 10:1–35 in full:

> In Caesarea there was a man named *Cornelius, a centurion of the Italian Cohort*, as it was called. [2] He was a *devout man who feared God* with all his household; he gave alms generously to the people and prayed constantly to God. [3] One afternoon at about three o'clock he had a vision in which he clearly saw an angel of God coming in and saying to him, "Cornelius." [4] He stared at him in terror and said, "What is it, Lord?" He answered, "Your prayers and your alms have ascended as a memorial before God. [5] Now *send men to Joppa for a certain Simon who is called Peter*; [6] he is lodging with Simon, a tanner, whose house is by the seaside." [7] When the angel who spoke to him had left, he called two of his slaves and a devout soldier from the ranks of those who served him, [8] and after telling them everything, he sent them to Joppa.
>
> [9] About noon the next day, as they were on their journey and approaching the city, *Peter went up on the roof to pray*. [10] *He became hungry and wanted something to eat; and while it was being prepared, he fell into a trance.* [11] *He saw the heaven opened and something like a large sheet coming down, being lowered to the ground by its four corners.* [12] *In it were all kinds of four-footed creatures and reptiles and birds of the air.* [13] *Then he heard a voice saying, "Get up, Peter; kill and eat."* [14] *But Peter said, "By no means, Lord; for I have never eaten anything that is profane*

---

3. Aageson, *Paul, the Pastoral Epistles, and the Early Church*, 106–9.

or unclean." ¹⁵ *The voice said to him again, a second time, "What God has made clean, you must not call profane."* ¹⁶ This happened three times, and the thing was suddenly taken up to heaven.

¹⁷ Now while Peter was greatly puzzled about what to make of the vision that he had seen, suddenly the men sent by Cornelius appeared. They were asking for Simon's house and were standing by the gate. ¹⁸ They called out to ask whether Simon, who was called Peter, was staying there. ¹⁹ *While Peter was still thinking about the vision, the Spirit said to him, "Look, three men are searching for you.* ²⁰ *Now get up, go down, and go with them without hesitation; for I have sent them."* ²¹ So Peter went down to the men and said, "I am the one you are looking for; what is the reason for your coming?" ²² They answered, "Cornelius, a centurion, an upright and God-fearing man, who is well spoken of by the whole Jewish nation, was directed by a holy angel to send for you to come to his house and to hear what you have to say." ²³ So Peter invited them in and gave them lodging.

The next day he got up and went with them, and some of the believers from Joppa accompanied him. ²⁴ The following day they came to Caesarea. Cornelius was expecting them and had called together his relatives and close friends. ²⁵ On Peter's arrival Cornelius met him, and falling at his feet, worshiped him. ²⁶ But Peter made him get up, saying, "Stand up; I am only a mortal." ²⁷ And as he talked with him, he went in and found that many had assembled; ²⁸ and he said to them, *"You yourselves know that it is unlawful for a Jew to associate with or to visit a Gentile; but God has shown me that I should not call anyone profane or unclean.* ²⁹ *So when I was sent for, I came without objection.* Now may I ask why you sent for me?"

³⁰ Cornelius replied, "Four days ago at this very hour, at three o'clock, I was praying in my house when suddenly a man in dazzling clothes stood before me. ³¹ He said, 'Cornelius, your prayer has been heard and your alms have been remembered before God. ³² Send therefore to Joppa and ask for Simon, who is called Peter; he is staying in the home of Simon, a tanner, by the sea.' ³³ Therefore I sent for you immediately, and you have been kind enough to come. So now all of us are here in the presence of God to listen to all that the Lord has commanded you to say."

³⁴ Then Peter began to speak to them: *"I truly understand that God shows no partiality,* ³⁵ *but in every nation anyone who fears him and does what is right is acceptable to him.*

The italicized sections indicate the important parts of this story for our purposes. Cornelius is in Caesarea and Peter is in Joppa, many miles to the south. Cornelius sends messengers to Peter and in the meantime, Peter has a vision in which he is instructed to kill and eat things considered unclean by observant Jews. Only after Peter is instructed three times to eat does the observant apostle relent. What God has called clean should not be treated as profane, but it takes divine intervention to get through to Peter. The message about clean and unclean, Jew and Gentile is unmistakable. Despite his stated sense that Jews are not to associate with Gentiles, Peter goes to Caesarea with Cornelius's emissaries. While he is there, he states explicitly that God shows no partiality, and that any nation that fears God and does what is right is acceptable. Not only is the Holy Spirit poured out upon Cornelius and his Gentile household, but Peter orders them to be baptized. Peter is actively engaged, though as a result of divine prodding, in converting and baptizing God-fearing Gentiles.

If the story of Philip and Gentile baptism is oblique and subtle, the story of Peter and Cornelius is explicit. But as if to leave nothing to chance, Luke records the criticism Peter gets for his actions from the Jewish believers in Jerusalem in 11:1–18. There, Peter is forced to describe and defend his actions, which he does, and at the end of the scene the critics are silenced and praise God, implying their acceptance of the Gentile mission. Before Paul ever sets out on his travels and his work among the Gentiles, the message of Christ has already spread to the non-Jews. From Acts 13 to the end of the book, Paul and his travels to the Gentile lands are front and center in Luke's narrative.

At the beginning of chapter 13, we find Paul in the city of Antioch in the region of Syria, just north of Palestine but not far from his hometown of Tarsus. Antioch is an important city in the history of early Christianity, and according to Acts 11:26 is the place where the followers of Christ were first called Christians. It is also the city from which Paul embarked on his travels into Asia Minor and Greece. Looking at a map of Paul's journeys in any Study Bible, we can see that he first traveled to Cyprus and then on to Perga and Antioch in the region of Pisidia. Barnabas and Paul arrive in Antioch, enter the synagogue of the city on the Sabbath and sit down until the law and prophets have been read. The leaders of the synagogue then send a message to Paul and Barnabas asking them to give a word of exhortation to the people. Without hesitation, Paul stands up and launches into a lengthy sermon in which he rehearses, much as Peter had done in Jerusalem, the story of Israel's history, Christ's death and resurrection, and the blindness of the people of Jerusalem who prompted Pilate to execute Jesus. Paul notes that this took place to fulfill the words of Scripture. Initially, it appears the message is well received. Many of the Jews and converts to Judaism urge the two men to continue in God's grace and return the next Sabbath, which they do. With more than a little hyperbole, Luke tells us that on the next Sabbath the whole city gathered to hear what they had to say. Those Jews who had apparently received them well the previous week are now jealous and speak against what Paul had said. But Paul and Barnabas announce to the Jews that it was necessary that the word of Christ be spoken to them first. Since they have rejected it, showing themselves to be unworthy of eternal life, the two evangelists will now turn to the Gentiles. Unlike the people of the synagogue, the Gentiles who hear Paul and Barnabas gladly receive the word and praise the Lord. That day, Luke tells us, many believed, and the word of Christ spread throughout the region. Some of the local members of the synagogue incite opposition to Paul and Barnabas and drive the two men out of the city. Shaking the dust from their feet in protest and filled with the Holy Spirit, the men head to Iconium to continue their work.

In this passage, we see a pattern repeated in Acts. Paul preaches in the synagogue and receives a favorable hearing, only to be turned against and driven from the community, often also arrested and imprisoned first. In other words, Luke claims the message of Christ went first to the Jews, and only when they had rejected it do the evangelists go to the Gentiles. Again, Luke seems to cast the Jews of the synagogue in a negative light. But I suggest he does this in order to make a case about the Gentile mission, its authorization by the Holy Spirit, and its necessity driven by the Jews' rejection of the message of Christ. It may also be that Luke realizes by his time, late in the first century, that the future of the church is in the Roman rather than the Jewish world. We might even go so far as to suggest that the book of Acts is an apologetic for the church in the Roman world.[4] The fact that the lengthy speeches in Acts seem to be rather stylized and relatively similar from situation to situation suggests that they are not mere transcriptions or accounts of what supposedly happened, but are interpretations of what propelled the church's growth. (The Holy Spirit, the Gentile mission authorized by divine power, and the prospect that the church will—indeed must—find a home in the Roman imperial world.) By the time Luke writes Acts, it may already be clear to him that the church is not going to grow and thrive primarily within the confines of Judaism. If this is correct, Luke then intends to show interpretively how this happened and what it means for the lives of Christ's followers in the empire. It is unfair to say that Luke simply fabricated his account of the church's growth out of whole cloth. What is clear is that he produces a narrative blending memories and traditions of things that happened with theological interpretations of what these things

---

4. See below, pp. 169-75.

mean. It is less an objective record of events and more an attempt to discern and expound the meaning of things.

Following a similar experience in Iconium, the men go on to Lystra where it seems there was a great commotion. Much to their irritation, they are treated as gods after Paul heals a man crippled from birth. Certain Jews from Antioch as well as Iconium arouse the crowds against Paul and Barnabas. Paul is stoned, dragged out of the city, and left for dead. Attended to by the disciples, Paul is taken into the city, and the next day Paul and Barnabas depart for Derbe. Eventually retracing their steps, they return to Antioch, the city from which they began their journey. In Antioch, certain people from Judea are teaching that the Gentiles cannot be saved unless they are circumcised according to the stipulations of Moses. As one might expect, this stirs controversy and debate between these teachers and Paul and Barnabas. Paul and Barnabas, along with some of the others, are appointed to go to Jerusalem to discuss the situation with the apostles and elders in that city. They are well received by the elders and apostles, and there is much discussion, including with those who believe circumcision is necessary for salvation in Christ. Peter is the first to speak, and as recorded in Acts 15:7, says: "My brothers, you know that in the early days God made a choice among you that I should be the one through whom the Gentiles would hear the message of the good news and become believers." Clearly Luke portrays Peter supporting Paul and Barnabas, and they respond by recounting all the wondrous things God has done among the Gentiles. When they had finished, James, the brother of Jesus, who by then had become the leader of the church in Jerusalem, rose to speak (Acts 15:19–22):

> [19] Therefore I have reached the decision that we should not trouble those Gentiles who are turning to God, [20] but we should write to them to abstain only from things polluted by idols and from fornication and from whatever has been strangled and from blood. [21] For in every city, for generations past, Moses has had those who proclaim him, for he has been read aloud every sabbath in the synagogues.

This conference is often referred to as the Jerusalem Council. Four things are especially important about this passage for our purposes. First, we see in the Lukan account that the Gentile mission of Paul is ratified by the authorities in Jerusalem who have emerged in the narrative as a kind of centralized apostolic authority for the fledgling church. We know that by the late first century and into the second century the church had developed other kinds of authority structures. At this stage, however, Jerusalem and the apostolic authority centered there have considerable sway in the life of the church. Over time, that would of course change as the demographic center of the church shifted into the Gentile lands. Second, James, Jesus's brother, has assumed leadership of the church, and as we see, he is the one who renders the decision to accept the Gentiles with certain stipulations. Third, the list of four things from which the Gentiles should refrain—things polluted by idols, fornication, things strangled, and blood—appears to echo the so-called Noahide commandments of Jewish tradition, stipulations intended for Gentiles as well as Jews (cf. Gen 9:4-6; Lev 17-18).[5] From a Jewish point of view, this list of stipulations for Gentiles would make sense. The mission to the non-Jews could minimally expect them to observe the things that all Gentiles were expected to observe. Fourth, Paul gives us his own direct account of what the authorities in Jerusalem decided and expected of him and the Gentiles in Gal 2:7-10. As we can see, it is at variance with what Luke says:

> [7] On the contrary, when they saw that I had been entrusted with the gospel for the uncircumcised, just as Peter had been entrusted with the gospel for the circumcised [8] (for he who worked through Peter making him an apostle to the circumcised also worked through me in sending me to the Gentiles), [9] and when James and Cephas and John, who were acknowledged pillars, recognized the grace that had been given to me, they gave to Barnabas and me the right hand of fellowship, agreeing that we should go to the Gentiles and they to the circumcised. [10] They asked only one thing, that we remember the poor, which was actually what I was eager to do.

What we see in both accounts is that the decision is the same. The mission to the non-Jews is affirmed. What differs in the two accounts is the expectation placed upon the Gentiles. We need not try to reconcile here the two accounts, but to recognize that at this point there seems to be a discrepancy between Luke and Paul, not in terms of the legitimacy of the Gentile mission but the stipulations that go with it.

Paul ultimately embarks on two much more extensive journeys to Asia Minor and Greece. The successes as well as the trials and tribulations of Paul are made abundantly clear by Luke. This part of the Acts narrative (chapter 20) ends when Paul returns to Jerusalem and on the way stops in Miletus. There he summons the elders from Ephesus to meet him and has an emotional farewell with them. Paul does not know what kind of reception awaits him in Jerusalem but suspects it will not be good. He rehearses his ministry on behalf of Christ for the elders, and exhorts them to keep watch

---

5. See Segal, *Paul the Convert*, 187-223.

over the church. In doing so, he passes the mantel of leadership to the next generation. His example is his legacy for them. There is no suggestion that his legacy involves a body of letters or anything else written. His example and exhortation are what he now leaves them as he heads to Jerusalem and an uncertain future.

Soon after he arrives in Jerusalem, Paul's fears are confirmed. Much of this section of the narrative focuses on his arrest, plots against his life, his self-defense, and his appeal to the emperor as a Roman citizen to be tried in Rome. Chapters 27–28 are devoted to his treacherous journey under arrest to Rome and his time in the capital city meeting with the brethren. We are told he lived for two years in Rome, meeting people who came to him and preaching the kingdom of God with confidence and without interference. The common historical assumption and tradition is that Paul died in Rome. Later traditions known to us today as the Acts of Paul continue the Pauline story and fill in the record by adding all sorts of additional details. These stories were written much later and are clearly legendary. What they indicate, however, is that interest in Paul continued in the church and that the impulse to fill in details about his life and ministry persisted. As we shall see later, they also give us glimpses into things that concern the later church and in turn are overlaid onto Paul and his memory.

From the beginning of Acts to the end, Luke sees early Christianity changing from a Palestinian, Jewish, torah-observant phenomenon into a diaspora, non-Jewish, nonobservant religious expression. Though it is never severed from its Jewish theological foundation, the church throughout Acts is becoming more universal. As has been said, Paul expected the resurrection of the dead more urgently than the restoration of Israel.[6] This seems to be true, but Luke also sees Paul as a link between Jewish Christianity and the more universal Gentile Christianity spreading through the Empire on its way to Rome. Though we know Paul had hoped to travel to Spain (Rom 15:14–29), Acts gives no hint he ever made it. *The Acts of Paul* do indicate he fulfilled that hope. Luke presents Paul primarily as a missionary, model convert, and preacher engaged in bringing the message of Christ to the Gentile lands of the Mediterranean from Antioch all the way to Rome. Paul perseveres in the face of trial and tribulation, and fought the good fight to the end. Paul is not noted as a letter writer or as a theologian of righteousness by faith. That is the domain of his own letters, especially those to the Romans and the Galatians. Anthony Blasi writes that the Lukan portrayal of Paul is of a man who sees visions, makes converts, gives speeches, heals the

---

6. Aageson, *Paul, the Pastoral Epistles, and the Early Church*, 104; and Schwartz, "End of the Line," 21.

sick, fulfills prophecy, walks astride worldly affairs, addresses political leaders, debates with Greek philosophers, and advises sea captains. He honors Jewish religious requirements and conducts Christian worship, just as he exemplifies Judaism and functions as a Christian founder. He is heroic but also imprisoned and beaten.[7] To be sure, Luke portrays Paul as a complex and many-sided character.

LUKE'S PURPOSE IN WRITING ACTS

But beyond his defense of the Gentile mission and his theological understanding of the Holy Spirit's power in carrying the message of Christ outward into the larger Mediterranean world, what was Luke's political agenda in writing Acts? Steve Walton summarizes the various scholarly positions. First, Luke writes Acts as a defense of the church to Rome. Second, he writes Acts as an apology for Rome to the church. Third, Luke tries to assure Christians that their faith is not incompatible with allegiance to Rome. Fourth, he tries in Acts to prepare the church for life in the empire and to equip Christians for the trials that undoubtedly are ahead. Fifth, Luke in Acts has no political agenda at all.[8] Walton concludes that in Acts Luke is presenting Christians with various perspectives on how the empire might act toward them and how they in turn might respond. According to Acts, however, there is no doubt that Christ rules supreme, even over Caesar. This is an audacious claim for Luke to make, and one that would set the church at various times on a collision course with the empire. Even though Luke exhibits openness to the empire and his portrayal of Paul shows him embracing it, Luke also depicts Paul turning inward to the church and the faithful followers of Christ. Perhaps the message for us here is a word of caution against oversimplifying Luke's view or reducing his political perspective to just one thing. Walton's five options, however, give us lenses through which to read Acts, and they help us understand some of the early church's concerns, issues, and struggles.

---

7. Blasi, *Making Charisma*, 69, 75.

8. Walton, "State They Were In," 2–12. See also my discussion of this in Aageson, *Paul, the Pastoral Epistles, and the Early Church*, 104–5.

View of Antioch in Pisidia,
where the remains of a church may be over an ancient synagogue

8

Paul and the Next Generations of the Church

What happened to Paul after Paul, and how was his legacy shaped in the early post–New Testament period?

When we think about the origins of Christianity, it is important not to stop with the first century, in other words the apostolic and New Testament periods of the church. An important part of the story of early Christianity is also what happened to the church in the second and third centuries. How did the apostolic legacies develop in the next generations, and what were the problems and issues that confronted the church during this period? How did the church respond to the empire, and how did the empire respond to the church? Once the original disciples and associates of Jesus died, who became the leaders of the church, and how did the church structure itself as an institution when Christ did not return as soon as originally expected? The so-called delay of the parousia (the coming) required the church to prepare itself for being in the world much longer than originally expected. In light of that, how did the church transform itself from a charismatic movement into an institution with authority structures and official leadership positions? These questions too are part of the story of Christian origins and help us understand the phenomenon we call Christianity.

When I first began studying the apostle Paul seriously, it was often said that after the earliest period of the church Paul's legacy was kept alive primarily among the heretics. According to this view, in the more orthodox parts of Christianity there was a resounding Pauline silence, partly because the more suspect elements in the church had sidled up too closely to Paul and co-opted him. As I have studied the issue more closely, I have come to the conclusion that this view of things distorts the Pauline legacy in the second and third centuries. To be sure, some of the more marginal elements of the church certainly used Pauline material for their own religious purposes, but many influential mainline figures did too. We think of Irenaeus (in Gaul, present-day France), Tertullian (in North Africa), and Clement of Alexandria and Origen (in Alexandria, Egypt)—all important thinkers in the early church who used Paul's letters extensively. Likewise, Ingatius of Antioch and Polycarp of Smyrna, both bishops of the church in Asia Minor during the second century, thought very highly of Paul and made use of his letters. And then there is the fascinating story of Paul and Thecla in the Acts of Paul, which tells of Thecla's fascination with Paul and of women's authority in the second-century church. This is clearly legendary material, but it points to the struggle of women to find their place in the church and to challenge patriarchal authority. Early on, the church had apparently moved away from the equalitarian notion of Paul's statement in Galatians that in Christ there is no longer male and female, and had backslid into more patriarchal patterns of behavior and authority. All these people are important to the development of second-century Christianity and think highly of Paul. Not only does Paul's theology have authority for these people, but so does his personal example of perseverance in the face of opposition and tribulation. Ignatius of Antioch, for example, writes a number of letters to local churches in Asia Minor as he is being taken under arrest to Rome where he will be martyred. In these letters, which are still available to us, Ignatius refers to Paul's writings and clearly holds the apostle in highest esteem. Similarly, Polycarp is eventually martyred, and he too revered Paul and his example for the church. In the second and third centuries, there was hardly a Pauline silence in the church.

THE PASTORAL EPISTLES

Let me be clear at the outset: the Pauline legacy is much too extensive and complex to deal with fully in this chapter. That is not possible, and it is not my goal. I will simply chart one line of thought through this material. A second clarification is that I think it highly probable that the Pastoral Epistles, 1 and 2 Timothy and Titus, were not actually written by Paul, but by someone else in the early Pauline tradition. It might also be that these three letters were not in fact written by the same person either. These are issues discussed extensively in recent scholarship, and those interested can consult virtually any reputable commentary for a discussion of these matters.[1] Hence, I will treat the Pastoral Letters as part of Paul's legacy rather than as texts he himself actually wrote. As I noted earlier, the Pastorals are ostensibly written by Paul to his coworkers Timothy and Titus, giving them instructions, and exhorting them to remain steadfast. They are letters to individuals, though they may have circulated and been read by Christian communities as well.

I also see no compelling reason to date these letters to the second century, as many scholars do. They may well have been written in the first century. If this is correct, then the Pastorals give us an earlier rather than a later glimpse into the development of the early church. In any case, the Pastorals show us a church dealing with a new set of issues and confronting a new set of challenges. As I have written elsewhere:

> A comparative analysis of theological patterns illustrates that even as the Pastoral Epistles represent Paul and his theology in new contexts, they also reflect and foreshadow the significant issues confronting the church in the first two centuries. Among these issues are the nature of the true faith, the relationship of the church to Judaism, Christian asceticism, the prospect of church unity and the threat of disunity, the formation of the canon, the balance between scripture and tradition, the place of women, and the role of authorized leaders in preserving the true faith and practice of the church. These are pressure points of early Christian debate, and the Pastoral Epistles mark all of them in varying degrees. In this sense, the Pastorals serve as a kind of sourcebook for identifying, and in some cases detailing, the points of contention that characterize the church in the first three centuries. Perhaps no other set of documents in the New Testament point to such a broad range of conflicted issues in the early church as do the epistles of 1 & 2 Timothy and Titus.[2]

As a sourcebook for early church life, the Pastoral Epistles display concerns that bedevil the Pauline tradition in the next generations. We see, in Paul's own case, the course of his transformation from a persecutor of the church into a saint of the church, and in his letters from occasional writings into epistles that have authority and continue to inform the life, thought, and practice of Christians. These issues are not limited to the Pastoral Letters,

---

1. See for example Collins, *1 and 2 Timothy and Titus*; Johnson, *First and Second Letters to Timothy*; and Quinn and Wacker, *First and Second Letters to Timothy*.

2. Aageson, *Paul, the Pastoral Epistles, and the Early Church*, 15–16.

THE THEOLOGY OF THE PASTORAL EPISTLES

The Deposit of the True Faith

One of the most conspicuous features of the Pastorals is their concern with sound teaching and truth. This concern is largely a matter of principle, as the content of this sound teaching is not elaborated extensively. For example, we read in 2 Tim 1:12–14: "But I am not ashamed, for I know the one in whom I have put my trust, and I am sure that he is able to guard until that day what I have entrusted to him. [13] Hold to the standard of sound teaching that you have heard from me, in the faith and love that are in Christ Jesus. [14] Guard the good treasure entrusted to you, with the help of the Holy Spirit living in us." The sound teaching is portrayed as a good treasure that has been handed on and is now entrusted to Timothy. Reflected in this text and running through the Pastoral Letters is a concern for correct teaching and belief. Throughout Paul's ministry, he often battled with his opponents over the nature of the gospel, but now in the Pastorals we see reflected the idea of a deposit of correct belief. We might call it orthodoxy. This sound teaching is to be observed and handed on as the deposit of true faith. This is an issue precisely because the church in this period is struggling with diverse beliefs and teachings that some Christians consider to deviate from the true faith of Christianity. In other words, we see the church here struggling with the tension between correct and incorrect belief, orthodoxy and heterodoxy. The church is growing, and it should not surprise us that there are differences of belief and debates about the nature of the true faith. To put it differently, there is in this period and well beyond a struggle about what Christian faith and practice is, and how the differences will be negotiated. We see this most dramatically in the fourth century when Emperor Constantine assembled the bishops at Nicaea to hammer out a creed summarizing the Christian faith. As we see in the Pastorals, the tension between doctrinal unity and diversity was also going on in the church well before the council at Nicaea in 325.

The Church

In 1 Cor 12:12–31, Paul compares the church to a body, with its many parts. For him, the church is the body of Christ. But in 1 Timothy and Titus the metaphor for the church changes dramatically. Here the church is described as the household of God, presumably patterned after the Greco-Roman household.[3] This shift in images is interesting, for now it seems the image of the church as a household conforms to an actual feature of Greco-Roman life with its structures and expectations. Most dramatically, the church begins to assume the hierarchical pattern of the household. Just as the patriarch of the household is the head, God stands at the head of the church as a household of God. Under God, of course, stand those leaders who have special responsibilities for leadership in the church. As it turns out, this leadership structure appears to be highly patriarchal. As the church turned from a charismatic movement into an institution, it adopted patterns from the culture as models to inform how it would structure itself. Even as the church develops institutionally, we lament the loss of Paul's own egalitarian and inclusive vision of the church As the church became an institution, it lost the egalitarian and inclusive vision of Paul's own writings. We can lament this loss, but we also can recognize that the church was trying to organize itself for the longer term in an alien culture. What were its models, and what was required to survive over time? These are complex questions, and to many modern people it appears in retrospect the church accommodated too quickly to the prevailing culture. However it chose to do so, the church needed to make significant adjustments if it was to survive the delay of Christ's return.

Further, we see in 1 Timothy and Titus concern about the qualities leaders in the church should exhibit. In these two epistles, three offices are described: *episcopoi* (overseers or bishops), *deaconoi* (deacons or ministers), and *presbuteroi* (elders). The author of Timothy gives instructions to overseers and deacons (3:1–13) and Titus includes qualities for elders alongside those for overseers (1:5–9). Together 1 Timothy and Titus reflect what is called the threefold ministry of the church. The offices of bishop, deacon, and elder, in one way or another, are still represented in churches today. However, it would be a mistake to assume that in the early church these positions had the same connotations and authority structures they have now. For example, the bishop in the contemporary Roman Catholic Church has much different and more regal authority than did the overseer in the ancient church. This is underscored by the fact that 1 Timothy and Titus clearly do not give job descriptions for these positions. Rather, they give the personal qualities required for these leaders. Only later will the church define these institutional offices and the authority that goes with them. Here the emphasis is on personal attributes not institutional authority structures. But we

3. Ibid., 23–25.

can see clearly from the Pastorals the direction of the institutional church. Developing these leadership positions (bishops, deacons, and elders) is an important step for a church on the path to becoming the powerful institution so familiar later in history.

The Nature of Scripture

Nowhere in the seven undisputed Pauline letters or in the whole of the New Testament, for that matter, is there a more direct and poignant statement regarding the authority and function of Scripture than in 2 Tim 3:15–17: "And how from childhood you have known the *sacred writings* that are able to instruct you for salvation through faith in Christ Jesus. [16] *All scripture is inspired by God and is useful for teaching, for reproof, for correction, and for training in righteousness,* [17] so that everyone who belongs to God may be proficient, equipped for every good work." Much in this statement is unclear to us, but what does seem clear is that the author thinks these writings are sacred or holy and are God breathed. Furthermore, they have clear and useful functions: instruction for salvation, teaching, reproof, correction, and training in righteousness. It is less clear which works the author includes among these sacred writings—the Hebrew Scriptures, certain Christian writings, other texts? The Hebrew Scriptures must be included. But beyond that, it is not clear which texts the author may have had in mind. In any case, we can probably detect in 2 Tim 3:15–17 movement in the church toward the idea and development of a Christian canon. A word of caution is in order, however: the emerging Christian writings, including Paul's own letters, were coming to have authority even before they became part of an officially sanctioned Christian Bible. So, there may not always be in the early church a clear and sharp distinction between Scripture and tradition as there would be later in the church[4]—especially, for example, during the Protestant Reformation in the sixteenth century.

Women

Perhaps the most provocative and for many of us most distressing statement in the Pastoral Epistles and the early Pauline tradition is 1 Tim 2:8–15:

> [8] I desire, then, that in every place the men should pray, lifting up holy hands without anger or argument; [9] also that the

---

4. See Hoffman, "Authority of Scripture and Apostolic Doctrine in Ignatius of Antioch."

women should dress themselves modestly and decently in suitable clothing, not with their hair braided, or with gold, pearls, or expensive clothes, ¹⁰ but with good works, as is proper for women who profess reverence for God. ¹¹ Let a woman learn in silence with full submission. ¹² I permit no woman to teach or to have authority over a man; she is to keep silent. ¹³ For Adam was formed first, then Eve; ¹⁴ and Adam was not deceived, but the woman was deceived and became a transgressor. ¹⁵ Yet she will be saved through childbearing, provided they continue in faith and love and holiness, with modesty.[5]

In general terms, we can see that the text represents an accommodation to the more conservative and patriarchal elements of Greco-Roman culture. Women are to dress modestly and learn in silence with full submission. As if to drive the point home, women are not to have authority over a man but must keep silent. Whatever the immediate circumstances were that prompted this statement, it seems clear the author is defaulting to the more patriarchal elements of the society. It may be a turn by the author to more conventional norms, but it may also be a desire on his part not to provoke opposition to the church by allowing women to step out of their socially accepted roles. In other words, let's not bring attention to ourselves, which has the potential to create hostility to us. As noted above, the contrast with what Paul himself says in Gal 3 is striking. As we shall see below, this decidedly patriarchal turn by certain elements in the church would eventually create its own backlash from some women in the church.

The author's justification for not allowing women to have authority over a man in the church is that Adam was created before Eve and that she, not Adam, transgressed God's command. In short, the order of creation according to Genesis gives priority to the man because he stands first in the sequence. To modern ears, this is a very strange argument to support patriarchal authority. And the idea that only Eve was deceived and transgressed God's command is certainly a selective reading of the Genesis text. As if to add an exclamation point to the argument, the author announces that women will be saved through childbearing, but only if they continue in faith, love, and holiness with modesty. If the earliest stages of the Jesus movement represented a rather striking inclusion of women in the life and work of the various church communities,[6] as we see in the gospels and letters of Paul,

---

5. For a fuller discussion of this text see Aageson "Genesis in the Deutero-Pauline Epistles," 118–24.

6. See the formative work by Elisabeth Schüssler Fiorenza, *In Memory of Her*. This book prompted a whole generation and more of further work on the roles of women in the early church.

the next generations of the church undoubtedly represented powerful patriarchal tendencies. These would influence the church for centuries to come.

The writer of 1 Tim in 5:3–16 also instructs concerning widows. We see here that in Christian communities of the period there was concern about the place and role of older women, widows in particular. We can imagine that men for various reasons may have tended to die younger than their spouses, and that raised questions for Christian communities about how these widows should behave and what qualities they should exhibit; in the same way, questions surrounded the behavior and character of men appointed overseers, deacons, and elders. Singling out widows may strike modern readers as strange, but we can appreciate that this issue was of very practical concern for people in households—in this case for people in the household of God.

Asceticism

The author of 1 Timothy indicates in 4:1–5 that there are some followers of Christ who refrain from marriage and abstain from certain foods, perhaps reflecting a type of ascetic impulse:

> [1] Now the Spirit expressly says that in later times some will renounce the faith by paying attention to deceitful spirits and teachings of demons, [2] through the hypocrisy of liars whose consciences are seared with a hot iron. [3] They forbid marriage and demand abstinence from foods, which God created to be received with thanksgiving by those who believe and know the truth. [4] For everything created by God is good, and nothing is to be rejected, provided it is received with thanksgiving; [5] for it is sanctified by God's word and by prayer.

We know that early Christianity over time would be influenced by various kinds of ascetic movements. We think primarily of the desert monastic tradition in the Middle East. In this case, it is hard to argue that the text reflects a full-fledged ascetic movement, but it does suggest that certain people in the church were withdrawing from normal social and dietary expectations. The writer categorically rejects these behaviors, for everything created by God is good and should not be refused. To reject marriage and perhaps also certain foods made a larger cultural statement that the author rejects. For example, the refusal to marry in Greco-Roman society might well be considered tantamount to treason, especially when the birthrate and social stability needed to be maintained. For the writer of 1 Timothy, the theological justification for not refusing such things is clear and concise. They are created by God and therefore are good, provided they are received in thanksgiving.

Jewish Practices

Two texts in Titus suggest that some of the opposition encountered in Crete relates to Jews and Jewish issues. In 1:10–11 and 13–14, the writer states:

> [10] There are also many rebellious people, idle talkers and deceivers, especially those of the circumcision; [11] they must be silenced, since they are upsetting whole families by teaching for sordid gain what it is not right to teach . . . [13] That testimony is true. For this reason rebuke them sharply, so that they may become sound in the faith, [14] not paying attention to Jewish myths or to commandments of those who reject the truth.

Clearly some in the church in Crete are creating problems. They are "rebellious," "idle talkers," and "deceivers," and they are identified as people "of the circumcision," which is a euphemism for Jews. The author warns Titus and the Cretan Christians not to be led astray by Jewish myths. We know little beyond this, but the text indicates that as in Paul's own day there was conflict between the church and certain Jews.

Later on in the letter to Titus, the author writes in 3:4–5 about works and righteousness: "[4] But when the goodness and loving-kindness of God our Savior appeared, [5] he saved us, not because of any works of righteousness that we had done, but according to his mercy, through the water of rebirth and renewal by the Holy Spirit. [6] This Spirit he poured out on us richly through Jesus Christ our Savior." This is hardly reminiscent of Paul's concern with Gentile inclusion by faith into the church and not by works of law, but it does echo the apostle's argument that righteousness is not by works. Salvation is according to the mercy of God, says the writer. This is not a sustained argument about righteousness such as we find in Romans or Galatians, but the text touches in passing the Pauline concern with works, righteousness, and the mercy of God. While the issue of Gentile inclusion on the basis of faith seems to have receded into the background, this text may indicate that the issue of works was still of peripheral concern in the church.

All the issues here identified give us glimpses into the Pauline tradition and into parts of early Christian life. Even more broadly, many of these issues have continued to occupy the Christian church to this very day. Early in the post-Paul generations of the Pauline tradition, the church glimpses many of the contentious issues that will need to be addressed and negotiated as the church becomes increasingly an institution prepared for life in the world. One of the axes upon which the church turns in this period and beyond is the struggle between unity and diversity of thought and practice. This struggle will ebb and flow, but it will persist in one form or another for generations yet to come. The more the church gains a public place in Greco-Roman society, the more it must consider not only internal pastoral and communal matters but also external issues, structures, and forces. In other words, its attention will be both inward and outward.

IGNATIUS OF ANTIOCH AND POLYCARP OF SMYRNA

Ignatius, the bishop of Antioch, wrote a series of letters, most to churches along his route as under arrest he is taken to Rome where he will be martyred. The first set of letters, written from Smyrna, were sent to the churches in Ephesus, Magnesia, Tralles, and Rome; and the second set, written from Troas, were sent to Philadelphia, Smyrna, and the elderly Polycarp. All were in Asia Minor except, of course, Rome. Ignatius's journey to Rome probably took place later in the reign of Emperor Trajan (98–117 CE), and hence his letters date from that time period. A number of scholars note the connection between Ignatius and Paul, observing that Ignatius was greatly influenced by Paul and that the Pauline letters exercised considerable sway over the bishop.[7] William Schoedel observes that the churches to which Ignatius wrote have moved beyond the Pastoral Epistles, but only a step beyond them.[8]

In both Ign. *Eph* 12:2 and Ign. *Rom* 4:3, Ignatius makes direct reference to Paul. He writes to the Ephesians: "You are the passage for those who are being slain for God, fellow initiates of Paul, who was sanctified, approved, worthy of blessing, in whose footsteps may I be found when I reach God, who in every epistle makes mention of you in Christ Jesus." Here Ignatius overlays his suffering and impending martyrdom onto Paul's suffering and apparent martyrdom, and sees himself as walking in the footsteps of Paul. The Ephesians are his passageway to expected death in Rome. In fact, 2 Tim 1:12, 2:9, and 3:11 refer to Paul's suffering, and in 1:8, 2:3, and 4:5 the author exhorts Timothy to suffer as Paul has suffered. Here we can see that the apostle Paul endured suffering and martyrdom and that Timothy is exhorted to follow Paul's example of suffering. Now Ignatius too explicitly models his own experience of suffering and expected martyrdom

---

7. Aageson, *Paul, the Pastorals, and the Early Church*, 123–24.
8. Schoedel, *Ignatius of Antioch*, 22–23.

on Paul's. A clear line of suffering and martyrdom, in which Paul is the exemplar and standard, runs through the early Pauline tradition. And for the church, this whole tradition of suffering is predicated on the suffering and death of Christ. In his letter to the Romans, Ignatius writes in 4:3: "I do not command you as Peter and Paul; they are apostles, I am a convict; they were free, but I until now a slave. But if I suffer I shall be a freedman of Jesus Christ and shall be a free man in him. Now I am learning as one bound to desire nothing." In the context of a plea to the Romans not to hinder his martyrdom and thereby prevent the fulfillment of his sacrifice, Ignatius distinguishes himself from Peter and Paul on the basis of their apostleship. He goes to his death willingly and desires no one to intercede on his behalf but hesitates to command them as the apostles Peter and Paul might have done. He will never be an apostle as they were, but through his sacrificial death he will attain the status of a disciple. Here we see the church moving into the postapostolic era where identification as an apostle is no longer available. As I have stated elsewhere,

> From Paul to Ignatius, a post-apostolic generational shift takes place, and in the line of 2 Timothy, Ignatius sees suffering and martyrdom as something to be embraced according to the pattern of those apostles who have gone before him. Implicitly, Ignatius sees himself as following the example of Peter and Paul who have gone before him to their deaths in Rome. The references to suffering in Paul's letters to the Roman, Corinthian and Philippian churches are enhanced in the letter to 2 Timothy. The emphasis is not on following Christ's example but almost exclusively on following Paul's example of suffering. Ignatius extends this even further. He overlays his own imminent martyrdom symbolically with that of the apostle in his epistle to the Ephesians, but he also distinguishes his achievement of true discipleship in his letter to the Romans from the apostleship of Peter and Paul. The apostolic age is now at an end historically, but as we shall see it persists theologically in the structure and ministry of the church.[9]

In his letter to the Philippian Christians, Polycarp in 3:3 writes:

> For neither am I nor any other like me, able to follow the wisdom of the blessed and glorious Paul, who when he was among you formerly face-to-face taught accurately and steadfastly the word concerning truth (word of truth), who also when he was

---

9. Aageson, *Paul, the Pastorals, and the Early Church*, 125–26.

absent wrote epistles to you, from the study of which you will be able to build yourselves up into the faith which was given to you.

Polycarp holds Paul in the highest regard and knows he is the Philippian's apostle. Paul was a teacher of truth and wrote letters able to build up the faith of the Philippians, perhaps most especially his letter to them written decades earlier. In both Pol. *Phil* 3:2 and 11:2, Polycarp identifies Paul as a teacher, a designation also used of Paul in the Pastoral Epistles and in the post-Paul Pauline tradition. Ultimately, Polycarp, too, would be martyred, which indicates that by the second century certain church leaders had suffered the ire of some, if not many, people in the Roman Empire. Even if not massively widespread, martyrdom was a reality for Christians in this period, and a tradition of support developed to model and encourage Christian steadfastness in the face of possible suffering.

Looking further into the writings of Ignatius and Polycarp, we see a number of themes and concerns that echo those of the Pastoral Epistles: true and false teachings and teachers, the ministry of the church and qualities appropriate for its leaders, and the relation of Scripture and tradition. The movement toward notions of Christian orthodoxy continues in Ignatius and Polycarp, and the need to pass on the faith continues to be reinforced. It is to be guarded and handed on, not altered. The Pauline tradition lives on in the writings of these two church leaders and martyrs. They give us glimpses into the development of Christianity in second-century Asia Minor, and help us understand what became of Paul and his legacy after his death. In short, we see in them the church's continued movement from a charismatic Jewish sect to an independent, institutionalized religion seeking to make its way in an imperial world that is sometimes hostile to it.

IRENAEUS AND TERTULLIAN

Irenaeus became bishop of Lyon in southern Gaul not long after his arrival in the city, perhaps 177 or 178. Though born in western Asia Minor, presumably in Smyrna, Irenaeus attests to having seen Polycarp, who taught the things he had learned from the apostles—things the church had handed down and which alone are true. The line of Christian truth had been passed down from the apostles to Polycarp and on to the wider church. The bishop of Lyon now sees himself in that line through Polycarp, the bishop and martyr who held firm to the truth in the face of Valentinus, Marcion, and various other gnostic heretics, whom Irenaeus late in the second century seeks to refute. In a real sense, Irenaeus spans the divide between the church in the East, Asia Minor, and the church in the West, Gaul. With his roots in the East, he is linked to Paul's legacy both theologically and geographically. According to Rolf Noorman, Irenaeus exhibits a wide-ranging reception of Paul's letters, and his use of Pauline material stands squarely in the developing Pauline tradition.[10] Since Irenaeus attempted to combat the claims of various gnostic heretics and to do so in part using Paul's letters and theology, it is difficult to argue for the notion of a Pauline silence in the second-century church. And as a bishop, Irenaeus is part of what can perhaps be called emerging normative Christianity.[11] To defend his understanding of the Christian church, he appeals to the church's unity and to the trustworthiness of the tradition preserved and passed on by it in order to refute these gnostic claims.[12]

Irenaeus's major work is titled *Adversus haereses* (*Against the Heresies*), and it is here that he engages in a detailed defense of the church and a refutation of the gnostics. For him, theological unity and ecclesiastical unity are connected. Hence, the unity of the church cannot tolerate the kind of theological diversity now represented by the gnostics. Through the line of succession from the apostles now represented by the hierarchy of the church, Irenaeus sees the truth of Christ being preserved. Not only is this a truth claim about the church, but it represents an emerging Christian authority structure that has marked the Catholic Church to this day. The church and its structure of authority are the repository of Christian truth and as such unite all in this one truth. In *Against the Heresies*, Irenaeus uses the expressions "canon of truth" and "rule of truth" to designate the one truth of the one true church. He writes in 1:22:1 and 1:9:4 to refute the gnostics:

> The *rule of truth* (regulam veritatis) which we hold, is, that there is one God almighty, who made all things by his word, and fashioned and formed, out of that which had no existence, all things which exist (1:22:1).

> In like manner he also who retains unchangeable in his heart the *rule of truth* (regulam veritatis) which he received by means of baptism, will doubtless recognize the names, the expressions, and the parables taken from the scriptures, but will by no means acknowledge the blasphemous use which these men make of them . . . But when he has restored every one of the expressions quoted to its proper position, and has fitted it to the *body*

---

10. Noormann, *Irenäus als Paulusinterpret*, 517, 520.

11. This does not mean that there was still not great diversity in the church. There certainly was.

12. Aageson, *Paul, the Pastoral Epistles, and the Early Church*, 159.

of truth (veritatis corpusculo), he will lay bare, and prove to be without any foundation, the figment of these heretics (1:9:4).[13]

What began in the Pastoral Epistles as a church described as the household of God with overseers, deacons, and elders, who needed to exhibit the proper personal qualities of leadership, now becomes in the view of Irenaeus a church with definite authority structures, clear notions of Christian truth, and unity rooted in an integrated theology and ecclesiology. In Irenaeus, we see the struggle between unity and diversity in the church playing itself out; and in his refutation of the gnostics' claims, we see how far the church has come as an institution in little more than a hundred years.

Tertullian, a slightly later contemporary of Irenaeus, was born in the city of Carthage in 155 and in 207 became part of the Montanist movement.[14] As a North African, Tertullian was one of the most important thinkers in Western, Latin Christianity, and (except for Augustine, many decades later) may have been the most important early Latin Church thinker. As others were before him, Tertullian too was heavily dependent on the apostle Paul, both on his thought and on his personal image. Tertullian focused especially on Paul's Damascus Road experience, his confrontation with Peter in Antioch, his missionary journeys, and his personal suffering. Tertullian portrays Paul as a proclaimer of the Spirit and the fruits of the Spirit. For Tertullian discussing Paul, revelation comes through both natural and divine means, and the focus on the end-time is another Pauline theme Tertullian emphasized. As Irenaeus did, Tertullian also emphasized the rule of faith (regula fidei). This deposit of Christian teaching was left for his followers by Christ and has been passed down through the church's line of succession. For Tertullian, there are certain unalterable truths of the faith, and these can be condensed and summarized. The core of the church's faith is unchanging. It is the full revelation of God and runs back to the apostles themselves. The false teachings currently being propagated neither stem from nor conform to this apostolic deposit for Tertullian. Tertullian in *De praescriptione hereticorum* 20–21 rehearses the early history of the church as the repository of Christ's truth and the guardian of his revelation.[15] He writes:

> and after first bearing witness to the faith in Jesus Christ throughout Judea, and founding churches there, they next went forth into the world and preached the same doctrine of the same faith to the nations. They then in like manner founded churches in every city, from which all the other churches, one after another,

---

13. Ibid., 164.
14. See below, pp. 202–3, 214.
15. Quasten, *Patrology*, 2:331.

derived the tradition of the faith, and the seeds of doctrine, and are every day deriving them, that they may become churches... Therefore the churches, although they are so many and so great, comprise but the one primitive church, founded by the apostles from which they all spring. In this way all are primitive, and all are apostolic, whilst they are all proved to be one, in unbroken unity... Since the Lord Jesus Christ sent the apostles to preach, our rule is that no others ought to be received as preachers than those whom Christ appointed... If, then, these things are so, it is in the same degree manifest that all doctrine which agrees with the apostolic churches—those moulds and the original sources of the faith must be reckoned for truth.

As David Rankin states, Tertullian does not explicitly endorse the idea of the "one holy, catholic, and apostolic church," but he comes closer by implication than those Christian thinkers before him.[16] Echoing Paul's language of heavenly citizenship in Phil 3:20, Tertullian asserts that the citizenship of the Christian martyr is in heaven.[17] We might say still further that those who belong to the one true church themselves belong to a different realm. Once again, we see the continued institutional development of the church in the direction of what I called above emerging normative Christianity.

PAUL AND THECLA

The body of material known as the Acts of Paul describes a series of events in Paul's life associated with various places: Antioch, Iconium, Myra, Sidon, Tyre, Ephesus, Philippi, Corinth, and Rome. One of these episodes, beginning in Iconium and then moving on to Antioch (whether Syrian or Pisidian Antioch is not entirely clear) is the story of a young woman betrothed in marriage when she hears Paul preach. Being overcome with emotion and devotion to him, she breaks off her engagement and vows to follow Paul. The importance of this story is not its descriptive historical accuracy concerning Paul's life and ministry. On the contrary, it is a story that gives us important insights into the role of women and their leadership in the early church, perhaps late in the second century. We have already seen the church's turn to patriarchy in the Pastoral Epistles and elsewhere, and it should not surprise us that this caused a reaction. I think we can put the story of Paul and Thecla in that category, reflecting concerns for chastity, resurrection, and women's

16. Rankin, *Tertullian and the Church*, 92.
17. Ibid., 98.

authority and place in the church. In the Acts of Paul and Thecla, it is fair to say that the establishment of orthodoxy is not the primary concern of the story. Rather, this story presents a challenge to the patriarchal expectations of emerging normative Christianity, and perhaps to the wider Greco-Roman culture. In other words, we must read through the text to the subtext of the story if we are to get its full import for the origins of Christianity.

Having heard that Paul was coming to Iconium, a man named Onesiphorus goes out to meet him in order that he might receive him in his house. We are told that he saw Paul coming, "a man of small stature, with a bald head and crooked legs, in a good state of body, with eyebrows meeting and nose somewhat hooked, full of friendliness." When Paul enters the house of Onesiphorus, we hear there was great joy, bowing of knees, breaking of bread, and the word of God concerning continence and the resurrection. Paul then announces a number of blessings to the gathered assembly:

> Paul said, 'Blessed are the *pure in heart*, for they shall see God; blessed are those who have *kept the flesh chaste*, for they shall become a temple of God; blessed are the *continent*, for God shall speak with them; blessed are those who have kept *aloof from this world*, for they shall be pleasing to God; blessed are *those who have wives as not having them*, for they shall experience God.' (Acts of Paul and Thecla 5)

The beatitudes clearly signal what the Paul of this story thinks important: purity of heart, chastity, sexual continence, and living as though one has no wife. These behaviors are linked to the experience of God (resurrection?). The turn to sexual restraint here is unmistakable. While Paul is speaking, Thecla, a young woman engaged to a man named Thamyris, sits by an open window and listens day and night to Paul speaking the word of the virgin life. For three days and three nights she sits listening to Paul. Thecla's mother and Thamyris, of course, are troubled by this state of affairs, offended by Paul's preaching and by Thecla's infatuation with him. They try to talk sense into her but to no avail. She remains enthralled by Paul. We are told that Thamyris inquires who this deceiver is, and he is informed, "He deprives young men of wives and maidens of husbands, saying: 'Otherwise there is no resurrection for you, except you remain chaste and do not defile the flesh, but keep it pure'" (Acts of Paul and Thecla 12). Thamyris proceeds to take matters into his own hands by arousing opposition to Paul, after which Paul is bound and taken to prison. Undaunted, Thecla goes to Paul in prison. After Thecla is discovered in Paul's presence, both Paul and Thecla are commanded to come before the judgment seat of the governor, where Paul is scourged and banished from the city, and where Thecla is sentenced to be burned at the stake. Paul is condemned as a sorcerer, and Thecla, being under the spell of the deceiver, has defied convention. The protagonists are identified and the stage is set. Thecla willingly climbs the pyre and making the sign of the cross prepares to die. But instead of being burned and consumed by the fire, Thecla is spared by a rain and hailstorm that douses the flames. Thecla is saved, and she sets out to find Paul. He prays that she be spared, and when she appears before him we are told there is much love and rejoicing.

But Thecla's adventure is still not yet over. She accompanies Paul to Antioch, where upon entering the city she catches the eye of a Syrian named Alexander. He is one of the leading citizens of Antioch and immediately falls in love with Thecla. He tries to win Paul over with gifts and money, apparently assuming he is the male who has authority over Thecla. Paul disavows this and claims not even to know her. Is this a Pauline betrayal or an affirmation of Thecla's status as an independent female? Perhaps it is both, and as if to test fate yet again she rebuffs Alexander, making a laughingstock of him. His humiliation is not to be forgotten. Alexander reports her affront to the governor, who condemns her to the beasts. The other women in attendance are incensed and cry out, "A godless judgment." A rich woman, Tryphaena, whose daughter had died, takes Thecla under her protection and finds comfort in her. As the beasts are led in procession into the arena, Thecla is strapped to the back of a lioness as Tryphaena follows her. But instead of attacking her, the lioness licks her feet. The one charged with sacrilege is spared yet again, and the women in the arena cry out against the impious judgment that has been passed upon Thecla. The young female, Thecla, is spared by the female lion, and the women of Antioch raise their voices in support of her, and challenge the governor's unjust judgment. The patriarchal world is being defied.

But Thecla is not yet free, for the next day she is brought to the arena once again. Alexander's humiliation, not to be forgiven, frames the spectacle, and he comes to escort her to the waiting beasts. But a lioness dies to protect Thecla against a bear and a trained lion. The women in the crowd mourn the death of the lioness. After praying, Thecla sees a pool of water and declares, "Now is the time for me to wash . . . In the name of Jesus Christ I baptize myself on the last day." Because there are seals in the pool of water, the women in the crowd and even the governor laments that she will be killed by them. But the seals float as if dead on the surface of the water. Other animals are set loose upon Thecla, but again and again she is spared. She is brought before the governor, who inquires of her who she is. To which she replies:

> I am a handmaid of the living God. As to what I have about me, I have believed in him in whom God is well pleased, His son. For his sake not one of the beasts touched me. For he alone is the goal of salvation and the foundation of immortal life. To the storm-tossed he is the refuge, to the oppressed relief, to the despairing shelter; in a word, whoever does not believe in him shall not live, but die for ever. (Acts of Paul and Thecla 37)

The governor has clothes brought to her, and she is released, being identified as the pious handmaid of God. At which the women in the crowd again raise their voices: "One is God, who has delivered Thecla" (Acts of Paul and Thecla 38).

Thecla is spared from death by God and supported by women, even as she defies social expectations and refuses to conform to the wishes of men. To put it more sharply, it seems she is spared and defended precisely because she is devoted to the one God and does not conform to social convention. Thecla conforms to neither the expectations of the Greco-Roman household nor the Christian household of God. In terms of sexual and social expectations, the proper way for Thecla to respond to the Greco-Roman world is through separation and nonconformity. Thecla's behavior makes a striking contrast with the commands of the Pastoral Epistles that women should remain silent and never be in authority over a man, and that they will be saved through childbearing. In short, the heart of the Pauline gospel according to the Acts of Paul and Thecla is belief in one God, sexual purity, chastity, and the resurrection.[18] Did the Thecla story draw a reaction from emerging normative Christianity? Yes, indeed. Tertullian all the way from North Africa wrote:

> But if the writings which wrongly (falsely) go under Paul's name, claim Thecla's example as a license for women's teaching and baptizing, let them know that, in Asia, the presbyter who composed that writing, as if he were augmenting Paul's fame from his own store, after being convicted, and confessing that he had done it from love of Paul, was removed from office (*De baptismo* 17:5).[19]

The origin of Christianity is a complicated and in many ways conflicted story, and the roles for women in the church were in contention from the very early

---

18. For a fuller discussion of the Acts of Paul and Thecla, see my argument in Aageson, *Paul, the Pastoral Epistles, and the Early Church*, 192–206. See also the commentary by Pervo, *Acts of Paul*.

19. Tertullian, *ANF* vol. 3; see also http://www.earlychristianwritings.com/text/tertullian21.html/.

days, perhaps much as they have been throughout most of the church's history. The story of Thecla, however, reminds us that no matter how patriarchal the early church became, counterstories show us that at least some women pushed back against convention and male authority.

CONCLUSION

As we sketched a line through the early post-Paul tradition associated with the Pauline legacy, we have observed many of the features that marked the church as it transformed itself from a charismatic Jesus movement into an institutional community. Institutional leadership structures began to develop, and there was a clear turn toward patriarchy as those structures became hierarchical. Instead of imaging itself as the body of Christ, the church increasingly modeled itself on the Greco-Roman household—a household where God stood as the paterfamilias (head of the family). Not only are institutional structures developing, but there is concern for preserving the truth and handing on the sound teaching from generation to generation. By the time of Irenaeus and Tertullian, this truth can be referred to as the "canon of truth," the "rule of truth," or the "rule of faith." This truth was passed from Christ to the apostles and then on to the leadership of the church through the line of ecclesiastical succession. It was to be preserved in the face of the gnostics and others who deviated from this truth. We have also now seen that Paul and his legacy were put in the service of early church thinkers as they articulated their theologies, their views of the church, and their critiques of patriarchy and church practice. This was a formative and vital time in the life of Christianity. For the church and its thinkers, divine truth and institutional survival were both at stake. And even as the truth of Christ needed to be worked out and developed, the church also needed to forge an identity for itself that would enable it to live in the world until Christ returned. Paul and his legacy were an important part of this story, and as nearly as I can tell, there was no Pauline silence in the early church.[20]

---

20. For a fuller treatment of scholarship on the ways Paul was reimagined in the early church, see White, *Remembering Paul*, 1–107.

130   Part 2: Foundational Texts and Traditions

Cave of Saint Paul at Ephesus:
Paul and Theocleia, mother of Thecla

9

Jesus and Other Gospels
Widening the Circle

What do the apocryphal gospels and stories about Jesus tell us about the origin of Christianity?

The New Testament gospels are only part of a much larger body of early Christian literature about Jesus. The four New Testament gospels are those texts that over time the church included in its sacred canon, but a much larger body of Jesus material was also produced. Much of that additional material has been preserved, often quite by accident, as the emerging orthodox church did its best to suppress it, believing that this material about Jesus did not conform to the church's rule of faith. Regardless of the early church's attitude toward this material, its preservation gives modern scholars important insights into the wider world of early Christianity. The early church's decisions about what was to be part of its sacred library is certainly important for understanding early Christianity, and those decisions clearly influenced the direction of the early church's ecclesiastical and theological development. But the noncanonical stories about Jesus are also important, because they give us a window into the world of those groups that lost out to orthodox Christianity. As is often said, the winners are the ones who write history,[1] and in the case of Christianity it is early Catholicism with its organizational structure and theology that ultimately prevailed. It wrote the history and created the New Testament canon, as we shall see later in

1. Pagels, *Gnostic Gospels*, 142–51.

chapter 12. But through accidental discoveries at places like Oxyrhynchus (in the late nineteenth century) and Nag Hammadi (in 1945/1946), both in Egypt, the losers are having their say as well.

These noncanonical stories do not merely provide additional material about Jesus. In many cases, they depict an entirely different way of presenting Jesus and what is important about him. Perhaps foremost among these alternate depictions are those of the gnostics who portrayed a very different image of Jesus. He is not a crucified Messiah as in the New Testament gospels but a teacher whose wise teachings lead adherents on an interior journey to attain wisdom and understanding. We know from Irenaeus's writing late in the second century that the gnostics presented a formidable challenge to emerging orthodox Christianity, and he devoted page after page to his refutation of their so-called heretical beliefs. He spares them little sympathy. Heretical or not, they are part of the early Christian record, and their theological energy illustrates that the way the early church in fact developed was not the only possibility. It could have been different. This also shatters the notion that the early church was marked by unity or uniformity. Quite the contrary: it was rent by division and it was very diverse, both in terms of belief and practice. Where we see the emerging orthodox church trying to refute, if not suppress, gnostic and other alternate expressions of Christianity, we see attempts to impose uniformity in the face of diversity and its perceived challenges. In this case, we see once again the ebb and flow between unity and diversity in the early church, the struggle for orthodox belief and practice in the face of what was thought to be unorthodox. Not that this struggle has ever completely disappeared from the church's life, but in the early period, when the church was striving to sort out who it was and what it believed, this struggle was especially acute. The struggle between orthodoxy and heresy is one lens through which to view early Christianity and to organize our understanding of it. But it is only one. This lens, though, cautions us against thinking that there was ever a golden age in early Christianity, when the church was marked by clear unity of thought and practice, where blissful harmony prevailed for all. From the very beginning there was contention. And as the church began to develop its theology and sort out its common practices, there were different options represented in different corners of the Christian community. Through different experiences and intellectual conclusions, different people argued for different ways of understanding Jesus. Not until the fourth century under the influence of Emperor Constantine would the church go through its first dramatic phase of consolidation at the council of Nicaea. This was a consolidation that sought both to ratify the power already won by emerging orthodox Christianity and to impose new levels of orthodox agreement in order that the church might help underwrite the unity of the empire. This did not bring the struggle for unity in the church to an end, but it started a process of calling church councils for the purpose of seeking agreement on potentially divisive issues.

The focus of this chapter is on Jesus and certain non–New Testament texts that tell stories about him and his teachings. Since this body of literature is extensive, I will discuss here only representative examples. This will be sufficient, however, to make the point about christological diversity in the early church. Comparing what we learned about the New Testament gospels in chapter 6 with the images and stories in these noncanonical gospels will enable us to widen our view of early Christianity. The examples will be the Gospel of Thomas, already referred to earlier in chapter 6; the Gospel of Mary; the Gospel of Truth; the passion Gospel of Peter; and the Infancy Gospels of James and Thomas. These will give us a good cross section of texts from material sometimes called the New Testament Apocrypha to see how differently Jesus and his significance were understood in different corners of Christianity.

THE GOSPEL OF THOMAS

The Gospel of Thomas is a collection of 114 sayings attributed to Jesus. The sayings are prefaced with a short prologue: "These are the hidden sayings that the living Jesus spoke and Judas Thomas the Twin (didymos) recorded." Unlike the New Testament gospels, the Gospel of Thomas makes no reference to Jesus's trial, death, or resurrection. The gospel is simply a list of sayings placed on the lips of Jesus, with little or no narrative to string the sayings together into a gospel story line. If the New Testament gospels portray Jesus's significance primarily as a crucified Messiah for the redemption of the world, the Gospel of Thomas represents Jesus as a teacher of wisdom designed to draw the hearer into an understanding of the mysteries of the cosmos. In short, there are two very different visions of who Jesus was and what his significance is.[2] The place of origin for the Gospel of Thomas is unclear, but scholars have frequently associated it with eastern Syria, perhaps the ancient city of Edessa. This was a region that honored Thomas and saw him as the twin brother of Jesus. It would certainly make sense that this area might produce a text that listed the teachings of Jesus recorded by his twin, Judas Thomas. Three fragments of the original Greek text were found

---

2. Meyer, *Nag Hammadi Scriptures*, 133.

at Oxyrhynchus, but the most complete manuscript was found at Nag Hammadi, in Coptic, an Egyptian language written largely in Greek characters.[3]

A considerable portion of Thomas sounds familiar to readers of the New Testament gospels, as the following sample of sayings illustrates.

> *Saying 9:* Jesus said, "Look, the sower went out, took a handful (of seeds), and scattered (them). Some fell on the road, and the birds came and gathered them. Others fell on rock, and they didn't take root in the soil and didn't produce heads of grain. Others fell on thorns, and they choked the seeds and worms ate them. And others fell on good soil, and it produced a good crop: it yielded sixty per measure and one hundred twenty per measure."
>
> *Saying 20:* The disciples said to Jesus, "Tell us what Heaven's kingdom is like." He said to them, "It's like a mustard seed, the smallest of all seeds, but when it falls on prepared soil, it produces a large plant and becomes a shelter for birds of the sky."
>
> *Saying 26:* Jesus said, "You see the sliver in your friend's eye, but you don't see the timber in your own eye. When you take the timber out of your own eye, then you will see well enough to remove the sliver from your friend's eye."
>
> *Saying 33:* Jesus said, "What you will hear in your ear, in the other ear proclaim from your rooftops. After all, no one lights a lamp and puts it under a basket, nor does one put it in a hidden place. Rather, one puts it on a lampstand so that all who come and go will see its light."
>
> *Saying 36:* Jesus said, "Do not fret, from morning to evening and from evening to morning, [about your food—what you're going to eat, or about your clothing—] what you are going to wear. [You're much better than the lilies, which neither card nor spin."
>
> *Saying 47:* Jesus said, "A person cannot mount two horses or bend two bows. And a slave cannot serve two masters, otherwise that slave will honor the one and offend the other. Nobody drinks aged wine and immediately wants to drink young wine. Young wine is not poured into old wineskins, or they might break, and aged wine is not poured into a new wineskin, or it might spoil. An old patch is not sewn onto a new garment, since it would create a tear."
>
> *Saying 57:* Jesus said, "The Father's kingdom is like a person who has [good] seed. His enemy came during the night and sowed

---

3. Ibid., 136.

weeds among the good seed. The person did not let the workers pull up the weeds, but said to them, 'No, otherwise you might go to pull up the weeds and pull up the wheat along with them.' For on the day of the harvest the weeds will be conspicuous, and will be pulled up and burned."

Saying 64: Jesus said, "A person was receiving guests. When he had prepared the dinner, he sent his slave to invite the guests. The slave went to the first and said to that one, 'My master invites you.' That one said, 'Some merchants owe me money; they are coming to me tonight. I have to go and give them instructions. Please excuse me from dinner.' The slave went to another and said to that one, 'My master has invited you.' That one said to the slave, 'I have bought a house, and I have been called away for a day. I shall have no time.' The slave went to another and said to that one, 'My master invites you.' That one said to the slave, 'My friend is to be married, and I am to arrange the banquet. I shall not be able to come. Please excuse me from dinner.' The slave went to another and said to that one, 'My master invites you.' That one said to the slave, 'I have bought an estate, and I am going to collect the rent. I shall not be able to come. Please excuse me.' The slave returned and said to his master, 'Those whom you invited to dinner have asked to be excused.' The master said to his slave, 'Go out on the streets and bring back whomever you find to have dinner.' Buyers and merchants [will] not enter the places of my Father."[4]

This feature of the Gospel of Thomas raises the obvious question, is the author of Thomas writing after the New Testament gospels were written and dependent on them, or does the author represent an independent Jesus tradition and hence is not directly dependent on the New Testament gospels? The examples I have cited are not the only ones that echo the words of Jesus in the New Testament,[5] but they pose quite clearly the issue of the relationship between Thomas and Jesus's teachings in the New Testament, most especially the material referred to as Q. There is no simple answer to this question. In fact, it is still one of the most divided issues in scholarship on Thomas.[6]

The date of authorship is part of this issue as well, but here too there is no unanimity. Those who see Thomas as dependent on the New Testament

---

4. Translations are by Stephen Patterson and Marvin Meyer.

5. Cameron, "Thomas, Gospel of," 536, notes that 68 of the 114 sayings have parallels in the New Testament.

6. Ibid.

often incline toward a mid-second-century dating, whereas those who see it as independent lean toward a late first- or early second-century date. Arguing for an earlier date, Marvin Meyer points to the textual tradition of Thomas that has as much claim to an early date as the New Testament gospels. He also thinks the concerns found in Thomas reflect the first century and are transmitted in forms that appear to predate the New Testament.[7] Likewise, the similarity to the Q material found in Matthew and Luke also suggests a concern for Jesus the teacher early in the first century. In that regard, Thomas is clearly not foreign to the first century. While the question I have posed above cannot be answered definitively, it nonetheless needs to be asked because it raises the possibility that parts of the noncanonical Jesus tradition might be as old as the canonical tradition itself.

Regardless of how we decide the questions of dating and of Thomas's dependence on or independence from the New Testament tradition, it is perhaps even more important to understand Thomas's Christology and religious worldview. The reference is often made to the gnostic Gospel of Thomas. But what is Thomas's relationship to Gnosticism, and is it in fact a gnostic gospel? Once again, certain Jesus sayings in Thomas do suggest a connection to some gnostic images.

> *Sayings 1 & 2*: And he said, "Whoever discovers the interpretation of these sayings will not taste death." 2 Jesus said, "Those who seek should not stop seeking until they find. When they find, they will be disturbed. When they are disturbed, they will marvel, and will reign over all. [And after they have reigned they will rest.]"
>
> *Saying 39*: Jesus said, "The Pharisees and the scholars have taken the keys of knowledge and have hidden them. They have not entered nor have they allowed those who want to enter to do so. As for you, be as sly as snakes and as simple as doves."
>
> *Saying 51*: His disciples said to him, "When will the rest for the dead take place, and when will the new world come?" He said to them, "What you are looking forward to has come, but you don't know it."
>
> *Saying 108*: Jesus said, "Whoever drinks from my mouth will become like me; I myself shall become that person, and the hidden things will be revealed to him."

The emphasis on interpretation and seeking, the claim that the keys to knowledge have been hidden, and the revealing of hidden things all seem

---

7. Meyer, *Nag Hammadi Scriptures*, 137.

to echo images known elsewhere in gnostic material. Instead of seeing Jesus as the crucified messiah, Thomas portrays Jesus as the wise teacher who leads the hearers on a journey of discovery to apprehend the mysteries of the cosmos. On this interior journey, the initiate struggles with the wise teachings of Jesus and in so doing moves to deeper levels of understanding. But is this a full-blown gnostic portrayal of Jesus? Not likely. As Marvin Meyer writes, "the *Gospel of Thomas* may most appropriately be considered a sayings gospel with an incipient Gnostic perspective."[8]

As if to challenge, if not shock, readers one last time, the text of Thomas pictures Simon Peter confronting Jesus: "Simon Peter said to them, 'Make Mary leave us, for females don't deserve life.' Jesus said, 'Look, I will guide her to make her male, so that she too may become a living spirit resembling you males. For every female who makes herself male will enter the kingdom of Heaven'" (Saying 114). It may be that this was a later addition to the text of Thomas, but even so it raises in quite offensive terms a patriarchal vision of spiritual wisdom and a narrow, gender-specific sense of who can enter the kingdom of heaven. Is this crass patriarchy, some form of incipient Gnosticism, or both? We do not know, but it contrasts sharply with our next apocryphal gospel.

THE GOSPEL OF MARY (MAGDALENE)

The Gospel of Mary is the only known Christian gospel attributed to a woman, and as this narrative unfolds it is clear she has been favored with special instruction by Jesus, a vision not given to the male disciples. The story opens with a postresurrection scene where Jesus instructs his disciples prior to commissioning them to go out and proclaim. In that sense, it might be thought to echo the scene from the Great Commission in Matthew's Gospel. That is where the similarity ends, however; for Jesus's teaching here reflects gnostic imagery about the material and spiritual natures of the world. That which has material root is subject to the passions, evil, sickness, and death.[9] The opening of the extant text illustrates this in cryptic fashion:

> Peter said to him, "You have been explaining every topic to us, tell us one other thing. What is the sin of the world? The Savior replied, "There is no such thing as sin; rather, you yourselves are what produces sin when you act in the nature of adultery, which is called 'sin.' For this reason, the Good came among you, pursuing the good that belongs to every nature. It will set it within its

8. Ibid., 133.
9. Perkins, "Mary, Gospel of," 583.

> root." Then he continued. He said, "This is why you get sick and die: because [you love] [8] what deceives [you. Anyone who] thinks should consider these matters. Matter gave birth to a passion that has no image, because it derives from what is contrary to nature. A disturbing confusion then occurred in its whole body. (7:10—8:11)[10]

But instead of going forth to proclaim boldly as instructed, the disciples fall into great distress, fearing that they too will not be spared: "If they didn't spare him, how will they spare us?" (9:21). At that point, Mary with strength and conviction stands up and comforts the hapless male disciples. The gender imagery is unmistakable. Mary is calm and resolute while the men dither in fear.

Peter speaks to Mary, acknowledging that the savior loved her more than all other women, and invites her to share with the group the private teaching Jesus gave her in a vision. Responding, she tells them she will teach them about that which is hidden from them. In very gnostic fashion, she describes for the disciples her vision of the Lord and the instruction she received. The central part of that vision describes the ascent of the soul past the cosmic powers (15:1—17:9) until finally it escapes worldly bondage and attains rest in silence. Upon finishing, Mary becomes silent, perhaps reflecting the peacefulness of her own soul.

But that is only the lull before the storm that erupts from the male disciples. Andrew is the first to object, doubting that the savior said these things because they are strange. Peter, too, pipes in with his doubts, even though he was the one who asked Mary to share her vision in the first place. The whole scene degenerates into a concern about gender, authority, and pride of place among the apostles: "Did he, then, speak with a woman in private without our knowing about it? Are we to turn around and listen to her? Did he choose her over us?" Mary is overcome and defends herself to Peter, denying as unthinkable that she has made up these things. At that point, Levi comes to her defense and challenges Peter: "Peter, you have always been a wrathful person. Now I see you contending against the woman like the adversaries" (17:10—19:5). After this unseemly episode, they go out to teach and preach.

The Gospel of Mary was composed in Greek but survives mainly in Coptic. Karen King thinks that because so many early copies of the text have survived, the gospel has a strong claim to being an early Christian work. We might suggest a late second-century date, or even a date range from 120 to

---

10. This translation comes from King, *Gospel of Mary of Magdala*.

180 CE[11] for its composition. In any case, several things are important about this text for understanding early Christianity. Once again, we see clear gnostic imagery. The distinction between the material and the spiritual natures, where the one leads to evil and destruction and the other to ascent and rest, is clear. Moreover, the gender implications of this story are self-evident—both through the central role of a woman who receives special revelation from the Lord and through the backlash among some of the male disciples, most notably Andrew and Peter. But as we see, Mary also receives support, as Levi jumps to her defense. It is hard to know how reflective this scene is of what was actually going in early Christianity, but it is not hard to think that disagreement over gender and leadership were major features of the period. Many other examples also suggest this was the case. While emerging orthodox Christianity by the late first and early second centuries seems to have taken a turn toward patriarchy (e.g., in the Pastoral Epistles), other parts of early Christianity show countermovements at work. (e.g., in the story of Paul and Thecla, in the Gospel of Mary). This part of early Christianity's story, too, is very complex and cannot be reduced too quickly to a straight line. For me, the better approach is to unearth the historical and literary diversity of early Christianity and see the gender dynamics in their wider contexts. In other words, it is important to widen the circle if the goal is to enhance our understanding of early Christianity.

THE GOSPEL OF TRUTH

Not strictly a gospel but a discourse on the gospel, the so-called Gospel of Truth sets forth a view of the Savior's appearance on earth and the meaning of the message he brought to humanity. As Einar Thomassen has pointed out, the story develops on two different levels. The first level is the earthly appearance of the Savior, who came teaching the truth only to be persecuted and crucified. Through his teaching, he awoke human beings from their slumber and forgetfulness, in order that they might return to the Father, the one from whom they have their very being. On another level, the story describes how the world came into being through ignorance.[12] Thomassen writes: "Initially, the All, the Entirety of aeons or eternal realms, existed inside the Father, who was so vast and unfathomable that they were unable to perceive him. Because of this, ignorance, anguish, and terror took hold of the aeons; Error was produced instead of truth, and on this illusive basis the

---

11. Perkins, "Mary, Gospel of," 583.
12. Meyer, *Nag Hammadi Scriptures*, 31.

world was created as a solidification of ignorance and fear, a 'fog.'"[13] Hence, the work of the Savior was to bring knowledge to mortal human beings and to undo the cosmic error of creation. The Savior, the first emanation who reveals the Father to the aeons, causes them to come into being as perfect, released from their slumber and ignorance. The material world needs to be overcome through knowledge and understanding so mortal humans might be restored to perfection in the All, the Father. (This idea is seen in other gnostic writings and images as well.) Throughout the text, these two lines of thought are woven together, and compared to the New Testament gospels present a Christian message quite alien to the one emerging in orthodox Christianity. It is probably not surprising in the early struggle to define Christian belief and practice that emerging orthodox Christianity would try to suppress such views. It is also clear how far the views expressed in the Gospel of Truth have moved away from the traditions expressed in the Hebrew Bible and more traditional forms of Judaism. While Gnosticism made inroads into Judaism as well, it developed its own rather unique ways of understanding creation and redemption. In Christian terms, Gnosticism saw the Savior, Jesus, bringing release from ignorance and bondage to the evil, material world.

Two short excerpts will illustrate the tenor and language of the Gospel of Truth about Jesus:

> The oblivion of error was not revealed. It is not a [. . .] from the Father. Oblivion did not come into existence from the Father, although it did indeed come into existence because of him. But what comes into existence in him is knowledge, which appeared in order that oblivion might vanish and the Father might be known. Since oblivion came into existence because the Father was not known, then if the Father comes to be known, oblivion will not exist from that moment on.
>
> Through this, the gospel of the one who is searched for, which <was> revealed to those who are perfect, through the mercies of the Father, the hidden mystery, Jesus, the Christ, enlightened those who were in darkness through oblivion. He enlightened them; he showed (them) a way; and the way is the truth which he taught them.
>
> For this reason, error grew angry at him, persecuted him, was distressed at him, (and) was brought to naught. He was nailed to a tree (and) he became fruit of the knowledge of the Father. It did not, however, cause destruction because it was eaten, but to those who ate it, it gave (cause) to become glad

---

13. Ibid.

> in the discovery, and he discovered them in himself, and they discovered him in themselves (18).

In this citation, we see clearly the way the text portrays Jesus bringing enlightenment to those who are in darkness, and in response error became angry and persecuted him to the point of crucifixion. Even so, Jesus became the fruit of knowledge and was not destroyed. Jesus is expressed in yet a different way in the second example.

> When he had appeared, instructing them about the Father, the incomprehensible one, when he had breathed into them what is in the thought, doing his will, when many had received the light, they turned to him. For the material ones were strangers, and did not see his likeness, and had not known him. For he came by means of fleshly form, while nothing blocked his course, because incorruptibility is irresistible, since he, again, spoke new things, still speaking about what is in the heart of the Father, having brought forth the flawless Word.
>
> When light had spoken through his mouth, as well as his voice, which gave birth to life, he gave them thought and understanding, and mercy and salvation, and the powerful spirit from the infiniteness and the sweetness of the Father. Having made punishments and tortures cease—for it was they which were leading astray from his face some who were in need of mercy, in error and in bonds—he both destroyed them with power and confounded them with knowledge. He became a way for those who were gone astray, and knowledge for those who were ignorant, a discovery for those who were searching, and a support for those who were wavering, immaculateness for those who were defiled. (30–31)[14]

Once again, the text makes clear the mission of the gnostic Jesus was to bring knowledge and light to the ignorant and defiled: "But the material ones were strangers, and did not see his likeness."

The origin of the Gospel of Truth is unclear, but it was first written in Greek and like other apocryphal texts was later translated into Coptic. Perhaps the most commonly held view is that the gospel emerged among the Valentinians, a gnostic group, and may have been written by Valentinus himself.[15] The connection to the Valentinians first appeared with Irenaeus in the late second century when he wrote:

---

14. Translations are from Attridge and MacRae, *Gospel of Truth*.
15. Brown, "Truth, Gospel of," 668.

But those who are from Valentinus, being, on the other hand, altogether reckless, while they put forth their own compositions, boast that they possess more Gospels than there really are. Indeed, they have arrived at such a pitch of audacity, as to entitle their comparatively recent writing "the Gospel of Truth," though it agrees in nothing with the Gospels of the Apostles, so that they have really no Gospel which is not full of blasphemy. For if what they have published is the Gospel of truth, and yet is totally unlike those which have been handed down to us from the apostles, any who please may learn, as is shown from the Scriptures themselves, that that which has been handed down from the apostles can no longer be reckoned the Gospel of truth. (*Against the Heresies* 3, 11, 9)[16]

Assuming Irenaeus is referring to the same text that we know as the Gospel of Truth, which appears likely, the connection to the Valentinians is clear. But even more, Irenaeus claims that the real gospels are apostolic, not these additional texts that gnostics and others claim to be the "truth" but have no apostolic foundation. For Irenaeus, the claim to apostolicity underwrites the claim to Christian authenticity and truth. As we shall see later, that claim will also become important in the formation of the New Testament canon, the process of deciding which texts are in the church's Bible. The words of Irenaeus give us a window into Christianity's struggle to sort out what Christian truth is and which texts represent it.

GOSPEL OF PETER

Unlike the other texts we have looked at in this chapter, the so-called Gospel of Peter is closer in content and even style to the Synoptic Gospels of the New Testament. Its date and place in the emerging Jesus tradition are much debated, but it reflects a central concern for the passion and death of Jesus. In fact, the text opens with a scene where Herod orders Jesus to be taken away and put to death: "But of the Jews none washed his hands, neither Herod nor any one of his judges. And when they had refused to wash them, Pilate rose up. And then Herod the king commandeth that the Lord be taken, saying to them, What things soever I commanded you to do unto him, do." With dates of origin ranging from 70 to 160 CE, it is not surprising that scholars have raised the issue of the text's relationship to the Synoptic

---

16. Irenaeus, *Against the Heresies*, translated and edited by Roberts and Rambaut *Early Christian Writings*, http://www.earlychristianwritings.com/text/irenaeus-book3.html/; see also *ANF*, vol. 1.

Gospels. Raymond Brown has argued that the Gospel of Peter is later and dependent on the New Testament gospels,[17] whereas John Dominic Crossan has claimed its independence from them. Crossan has even referred to the earliest stages of development leading to this text as the Cross Gospel. Crossan argues for an early Cross Gospel currently found in the Gospel of Peter and Q. The second stage of development is the use of this document by the four New Testament gospels. It is used by Mark and subsequently the other canonical gospels. The last stage occurs when the Cross Gospel comes under pressure to conform to the endings of the canonical gospels, with their accounts of Jesus's burial, the empty tomb, and appearances to the disciples. The gospel is then attributed to Peter.[18] If Crossan is correct, this tradition emerged and developed independently of the New Testament gospel tradition until fairly late in the process when it was compelled to conform to certain features in the canonical gospel tradition. If he is not correct, the Gospel of Peter was simply dependent on the New Testament gospels and emerged after them. Regardless of which position is finally correct, this debate illustrates the fact that unlike the gnostic gospel traditions, the passion narratives of Jesus were very important in the emerging New Testament traditions and beyond as well.

The following excerpt is sufficient to illustrate the style, tenor, and content of the Gospel of Peter:

> [25] Then the Jews and the elders and the priests, perceiving what evil they had done to themselves, began to lament and to say, Woe for our sins: the judgement hath drawn nigh, and the end of Jerusalem. [26] And I with my companions was grieved; and being wounded in mind we hid ourselves: for we were being sought for by them as malefactors, and as wishing to set fire to the temple. [27] And upon all these things we fasted and sat mourning and weeping night and day until the sabbath. [28] But the scribes and Pharisees and elders being gathered together one with another, when they heard that all the people murmured and beat their breasts, saying, If by his death these most mighty signs have come to pass, see how just he is,—[29] the elders were afraid and came to Pilate, beseeching him and saying, [30] Give us soldiers, that we may guard his sepulchre for three days, lest his disciples come and steal him away, and the people suppose that he is risen from the dead and do us evil. [31] And Pilate gave them Petronius the centurion with soldiers to guard the tomb. And with them came the elders and scribes to the sepulchre, [32]

---

17. Brown, *Death of the Messiah*, 2:1332–37.
18. Crossan, *Cross that Spoke*, xii–xiv.

And having rolled a great stone together with the centurion and the soldiers, they all together who were there set it at the door of the sepulchre; ³³ And they affixed seven seals, and they pitched a tent there and guarded it. ³⁴ And early in the morning as the sabbath was drawing on, there came a multitude from Jerusalem and the region round about, that they might see the sepulchre that was sealed.[19]

Clearly this text from the Gospel of Peter has parallels with Matthew's account of Jesus's passion, even though some of the details are unique to it. In any case, it clearly falls within the early church's christological passion tradition and develops certain features related to it. In general, it is this passion tradition that came to hold a place close to the heart of emerging orthodox Christology.

THE INFANCY GOSPELS OF JAMES AND THOMAS

It is well known to readers of the New Testament gospels that between the birth of Jesus and his baptism by John there is little information given about Jesus. Only in Luke 2:25–52 do we get any information from this period of Jesus's life. He is twelve years old and in the temple surrounded by the teachers where he amazes all with his wisdom and insight. Only after starting for home do his parents return to Jerusalem to find their Son in the temple among the religious leaders: "⁴⁸ When his parents saw him they were astonished; and his mother said to him, 'Child, why have you treated us like this? Look, your father and I have been searching for you in great anxiety.' ⁴⁹ He said to them, 'Why were you searching for me? Did you not know that I must be in my Father's house?'⁵⁰ But they did not understand what he said to them." It may come as no surprise that some in the early church would want to flesh out the story of the young Jesus and his birth. And even though Luke devotes significant attention to Mary and the birth of Jesus, there seemed a need in early Christianity to say even more.

The Infancy Gospel of James and the Infancy Gospel of Thomas seem suited to address these desires and needs. James, however, is designed primarily to defend the virgin birth from its many detractors. Hence, James's story devotes much of its attention to Mary, leading some to see the text largely as a glorification of her and her purity. While she plays a significant role in the story, the larger point seems to be an apologetic for Jesus's

---

19. Translation of the Gospel of Peter is from *ANF* 9:25–34; see also http://www.earlychristianwritings.com/text/gospelpeter.html/.

miraculous birth and his divine powers.[20] In that sense, we might call it a pre-gospel. Syria and Egypt are often suggested as its place of origin, with its date somewhere between 140 and 170 CE. The Infancy Gospel of Thomas, on the other hand, portrays miraculous deeds of Jesus before he turns twelve. Even as a youth, he is a wonder-worker, and his divine power is on display. This infancy gospel too may come from the same time frame, 140–170 CE, and from somewhere in Eastern Christianity.

Having rehearsed the story of Mary—her childhood in the temple, her marriage to the widower Joseph, the annunciation followed by her visit to Elizabeth, Joseph's doubt and her exoneration by the priests—James recounts the birth of Jesus, which takes place in a cave near Bethlehem. At this point in the story, a poignant scene underscoring the genuineness of the virgin birth unfolds:

> 19b And the midwife said: My soul has been magnified this day, because mine eyes have seen strange things—because salvation has been brought forth to Israel. And immediately the cloud disappeared out of the cave, and a great light shone in the cave, so that the eyes could not bear it. And in a little that light gradually decreased, until the infant appeared, and went and took the breast from His mother Mary. And the midwife cried out, and said: This is a great day to me, because I have seen this strange sight. And the midwife went forth out of the cave, and Salome met her. And she said to her: Salome, Salome, I have a strange sight to relate to thee: a virgin has brought forth—a thing which her nature admits not of. Then said Salome: As the Lord my God liveth, unless I thrust in my finger, and search the parts, I will not believe that a virgin has brought forth.
>
> 20 And the midwife went in, and said to Mary: Show thyself; for no small controversy has arisen about thee. And Salome put in her finger, and cried out, and said: Woe is me for mine iniquity and mine unbelief, because I have tempted the living God; and, behold, my hand is dropping off as if burned with fire. And she bent her knees before the Lord, saying: O God of my fathers, remember that I am the seed of Abraham, and Isaac, and Jacob; do not make a show of me to the sons of Israel, but restore me to the poor; for Thou knowest, O Lord, that in Thy name I have performed my services, and that I have received my reward at Thy hand. And, behold, an angel of the Lord stood by her, saying to her: Salome, Salome, the Lord hath heard thee. Put thy hand to the infant, and carry it, and thou wilt have safety and joy. And Salome went and carried it, saying: I will worship Him, because

---

20. Vorster, "Protoevangelium of James," 631.

> a great King has been born to Israel. And, behold, Salome was immediately cured, and she went forth out of the cave justified. And behold a voice saying: Salome, Salome, tell not the strange things thou hast seen, until the child has come into Jerusalem.[21]

We can hardly imagine a more vivid account of the virgin birth and its public defense.

Two examples from the Infancy Gospel of Thomas will illustrate the tenor of this text. The wonder-working young Jesus amazes those around him, and his spiritual wisdom far surpasses what might be expected from someone of such a young age:

> 6 A teacher by the name of Zacchaeus was listening to everything Jesus was saying to Joseph, and was astonished, saying to himself, "He is just a child, and saying this!" (2)And so he summoned Joseph and said to him, "You have a bright child, and he has a good mind. Hand him over to me so he can learn his letters. I'll teach him everything he needs to know so as not to be unruly." (3)Joseph replied, "No one is able to rule this child except God alone. Don't consider him to be a small cross, brother." (4)When Jesus heard Joseph saying this he laughed and said to Zacchaeus, "Believe me, teacher, what my father told you is true. (5)I am the Lord of these people and I'm present with you and have been born among you and am with you. (6)I know where you've come from and how many years you'll live. I swear to you, teacher, I existed when you were born. If you wish to be a perfect teacher, listen to me and I'll teach you a wisdom that no one else knows except for me and the one who sent me to you. (7)It's you who happens to be my student, and I know how old you are and how long you have to live. (8)When you see the cross that my father mentioned, then you'll believe that everything I've told you is true." (9)The Jews who were standing by and heard Jesus marveled and said, "How strange and paradoxical! This child is barely five years old and yet he says such things. In fact, we've never heard anyone say the kind of thing this child does." (6, 1–9)

> 9 A few days later Jesus was playing on the roof of a house when one of the children playing with him fell off the roof and died. When the other children saw what had happened, they fled, leaving Jesus standing all by himself. (2)The parents of the dead child came and accused Jesus: "You troublemaker you, you're the one who threw him down." (3)Jesus responded, "I didn't throw

---

21. This translation from the Infancy Gospel of James is from *ANF* 19B–20.

him down—he threw himself down. He just wasn't being careful and leaped down from the roof and died." (4)Then Jesus himself leaped down from the roof and stood by the body of the child and shouted in a loud voice: "Zeno!"—that was his name—"Get up and tell me: Did I push you?" (5)He got up immediately and said, "No, Lord, you didn't push me, you raised me up." (6)Those who saw this were astonished, and the child's parents praised God for the miracle that had happened and worshipped Jesus.[22]

These excerpts illustrate the spiritual wisdom of Jesus and his miraculous powers. The stories are unfamiliar to readers of the New Testament and appear to be extracanonical elaborations that display Jesus's supernatural wisdom and power. He is truly one of a kind. The writers of both infancy gospels are fleshing out the Jesus stories, most likely for the apologetic and pious needs of early Christian communities.

CONCLUSION

It is clear by now that christological thinking in the early church was diverse, contested, and complex. But the diversity also illustrates the energy the church and its early thinkers devoted to making sense out of who Jesus Christ was and what he did. If Jesus was the center of the Christian religious system, it was incumbent upon the church to figure out who he was and what he meant for the world. The Christian church writ large would spare little effort in this task, and it would seek passionately to present images of Jesus that would bring him to life for his followers. These apocryphal Jesus texts, along with the New Testament gospels, present fascinating stories about Jesus, but this entire effort to present what was important about Jesus is also set against the larger backdrop of early Christian identity formation and ecclesiastical development. To appreciate fully this wider world, we must broaden our understanding of what Christianity was and how it expressed its view of Christ beyond the portraits found in the four New Testament gospels.

---

22. Translations from the Infancy Gospel of Thomas are by Harold Attridge and Ron F. Hock from Miller, *Complete Gospels*; see also http://www.earlychristianwritings.com/text/infancythomas-hock.html/.

10

Jewish Apocalyptic Tradition and the Revelation to John

From what religious world did Revelation emerge, and what need did it satisfy in early Christianity?

One of the most enigmatic books in the Christian Bible is the Revelation to John. It is filled with highly symbolic and mysterious language, and many readers are unclear whether it contains prophecy still to be fulfilled or supplies a religious need primarily for its own time late in the first century. In any case, it is hard to overestimate the impact of Revelation on various parts of Christianity during the past two millennia. But this apocalyptic Christian text did not simply appear out of the blue. The world of the text and much of what goes on in Revelation theologically grew from Jewish apocalyptic soil that emerged in the last two centuries before the Common Era. Early Judaism and early Christianity both reflect religious impulses that today we tend to lump under the heading apocalyptic. The term derives from the Greek word *apocalypsis* which we usually translate into English as "revelation." In common speech, this term ends up being used very loosely and comes to cover a multitude of things that sound vaguely religious and mysterious having to do with expectations about the cataclysmic end of the world. Such language may be evocative, but it does little to enhance our understanding of the phenomenon. One of the most difficult things about apocalyptic material is that it is so diverse and therefore does not always lend itself easily to generalization or categorization. Just about the time we think we have it figured out, we find certain aspects that seem to deviate from the pattern. This means that a word of caution needs to be spoken at the outset of this chapter. Much of what we think and say about Revelation and apocalyptic material more generally needs to be provisional until it is tested against the relevant texts and what other interpreters have said about them. Hence, for many readers, this chapter will likely be preliminary rather than definitive, an invitation to further study rather than conclusive. If the discussion here does little more than cause us to pause and reflect further, it will have been successful.

The Revelation to John may be the final book in the Christian canon, but in the New Testament it stands in what is called the Johannine tradition: the Gospel of John, the three epistles of John, and the Revelation to John. In my view, it is highly unlikely the three bodies of Johannine material originated from the same person, although they seem in later tradition to have been lumped together. And we know that Saint John and the Johannine tradition came to be associated with western Asia Minor. This probably stems from the fact that John is said explicitly to have received his revelation on the island of Patmos off the west coast of Asia Minor. Furthermore, the John of Revelation comes to be connected with the beloved disciple in John's Gospel, presumably John himself, whom we see at the foot of the cross receiving instruction from Jesus about his mother before he dies:

> Meanwhile, standing near the cross of Jesus were his mother, and his mother's sister, Mary the wife of Clopas, and Mary Magdalene. [26] When Jesus saw his mother and the disciple whom he loved standing beside her, he said to his mother, "Woman, here is your son." [27] Then he said to the disciple, "Here is your mother." And from that hour the disciple took her into his own home. (John 19:25–27)

Hence, Mary also comes over time to be connected with Asia Minor, especially Ephesus. This illustrates the way names, traditions, and locations were often connected in Christianity, and it shows how bodies of New Testament literature linked to John were conflated. We should not presume, however, that they were necessarily connected historically or literarily. The following images show how the ancient site of Ephesus came to represent physically these connections.

Church of Saint Mary in Ephesus (fifth century)

Basilica of Saint John in Ephesus

JEWISH APOCALYPTIC

John J. Collins has tried to bring greater precision to our use of language in this field by distinguishing the respective terms and their referents: a*pocalypse* refers to a literary genre, *apocalypticism* to a social ideology, and *apocalyptic eschatology* to a set of ideas and themes that may also be found in other literary genres and social settings.[1] The value of this is that with these distinctions we have a better chance of knowing more precisely what we are talking about when we study this material and of allowing for the flexibility necessary to accommodate the nuances of such a diverse phenomenon. To illustrate, the Dead Sea community at Qumran in the Judean desert was highly apocalyptic but did not produce apocalypses. Similarly, not all apocalypses have a historically framed eschatology (end-time), focusing instead on heavenly journeys where divine mysteries are disclosed. It may be the case, too, that highly apocalyptic-sounding texts are not actually apocalypses when we begin studying them more closely. For example, is Revelation necessarily an apocalypse, even though there are all sorts of apocalyptic motifs running through it?[2] We will defer that question for the moment, but the fact that it can legitimately be asked at all illustrates the need for both terminological precision and flexibility.

Collins defines *apocalypse* this way: "a genre of revelatory literature with a narrative framework, in which a revelation is mediated by an otherworldly being to a human recipient, disclosing a transcendent reality which is both temporal, insofar as it envisages eschatological salvation, and spatial insofar as it involves another, supernatural world."[3] This definition does not attempt to describe each individual apocalypse but to get at the core of what an apocalypse is more generally in terms of form and content. There are many important features of this definition, including the emphasis on revelation, narrative frameworks, otherworldly mediators, and human recipients. But perhaps one of the most interesting features is the qualification provided by the adverb "insofar." The definition allows for the possibility that not all apocalypses disclose temporal, transcendent realities envisaged in terms of end-time salvation. Similarly, not all apocalypses exhibit a spatial sense described in terms of a new, heavenly world. In fact, Jewish apocalypses can be divided, argues Collins, into two different lines of tradition: apocalypses that display an interest in the development of history, and those that portray heavenly journeys where cosmic secrets are disclosed

---

1. Collins, *Apocalyptic Imagination*, 2.
2. For example, Roloff, *Revelation*, 7–8, would say it is not likely an apocalypse.
3. Collins, *Apocalyptic Imagination*, 4.

to a human traveler.[4] In short, not all apocalypses conform to eschatological patterns where history leads to the inauguration of a new age in a world beyond time and history. This is most closely associated with the "historical" strand of apocalypses. These various motifs may be interwoven, but they need not be.

Building on the definition above, Collins also tries to capture the worldview common to apocalypses when he writes: "Specifically, the world is mysterious and revelation must be transmitted from a supernatural source, through the mediation of angels; there is a hidden world of angels and demons that is directly relevant to human destiny; and this destiny is finally determined by a definitive eschatological judgment. In short, human life is bounded in the present by the supernatural world of angels and demons and in the future by the inevitability of a final judgment."[5] In understanding how the world really works, apocalyptists and their communities have a basis for dealing with life's struggles and turmoil. Though each apocalypse may confront a different set of problems, each provides its community with a basis for reassurance, guidance for life, and perhaps also a reason for hopefulness. It may be no surprise that the second century BCE, the period when Jewish apocalypticism first came into its own, was one of the most difficult for the people of the land of Israel. The violence and the cultural and religious stress might have seemed almost unbearable to certain traditional elements in the society, and this may have been one of the reasons they turned to new understandings and expressions of how the world works. Things may seem really bad, but all is not as it seems. There is a hidden reality that is now being disclosed to those with eyes to see and ears to hear. To be sure, this framework was never the only thing that shaped an apocalypse, but neither was it far from the evocative imagery and tenor of these texts. If apocalyptic literature is a deeply religious form of literature, it also functions on a profoundly psychological level as well.

Perhaps one of the most common interpretive mistakes we moderns make when considering apocalyptic material is to assume that its highly symbolic language is simply a code to be decoded. Each item in the text refers in code-like fashion to something behind it, and when we unlock the code, we have the meaning of the text. Apocalyptic language, however, is not computer-like language. To think of it this way would be too stiff and interpretively predictable for apocalyptic language. It is often ambiguous, indeterminate, and uncertain. If we think about it, this would seem to make perfectly good sense, for the whole content of apocalyptic literature

---

4. Ibid., 5.
5. Ibid., 7.

and its theology is marked by mystery and ambiguity. In some cases, there may have been good reasons for the apocalyptic writers to use ambiguous language in order to disguise it from outsiders who might take offense and inflict some kind of penalty on the community because of what was being said. Reading apocalyptic material too literally, in my view, misses the passion and throb of the language. This kind of literalism has often resulted in misguided predictions about the end-times. These types of readings might serve some psychological function but contribute little to the understanding of apocalyptic material as a phenomenon.

But where and how did apocalyptic tradition originate? This is a matter of considerable scholarly debate and turns on three possibilities.[6] It emerged from (1) Jewish prophecy, (2) the adaptation of Persian dualism, or (3) wisdom tradition. Each of these displays features that relate to apocalyptic language and thought. It is not for us here to enter those debates, except to say that Jewish apocalyptic need not be reduced to just one antecedent stream or influence. Apocalyptic tradition runs deep and probably has a number of tributaries feeding into it. However, I am also convinced that Jewish prophetic tradition is one of the main contributors to Jewish apocalyptic and indirectly to Christian apocalyptic material.[7] Another feature of Jewish apocalyptic that needs to be mentioned is *pseudonymity* (which means, literally, "written under a false name"). Apocalypses may bear such names as Daniel, Abraham, Enoch, Baruch, Levi, or Zephaniah, but they most certainly were not written by those important biblical figures. Apocalypses were falsely ascribed to them. The net effect of this pseudonymity is that on the one hand, the messages of these texts became deeply rooted in Israelite and Jewish religious tradition; and on the other hand, the historical author and community were disguised in the present. Once again, this last point may have served a very practical purpose.

AN EARLY CHRISTIAN FRAMEWORK

Before we look more closely at Revelation, it might be helpful to consider an early Christian apocalyptic framework that in my view shapes much New Testament eschatology and imagery. It probably emerges from the more historically oriented Jewish apocalyptic tradition and has a temporal perspective. The present reality is on the verge of passing away, to be replaced by some new, much-improved reality where the evildoers get their due and the

---

6. Ibid., 16.
7. For a fuller discussion of these influences, see ibid., 16–30.

faithful get their just reward. In other words, there will be a grand reversal of fortunes. We can diagram the image this way.

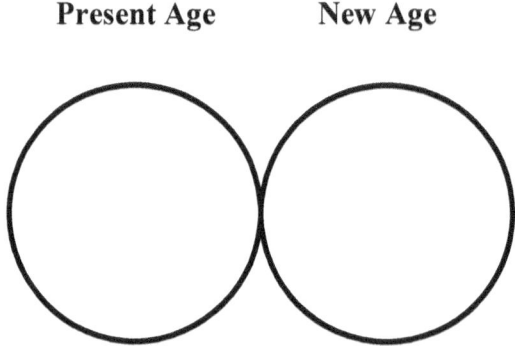

Apocalyptic Ages Old and New

The two circles in the diagram represent two realities: the earthly creation and the new creation, the present world and the world to come. The apocalypse writer stands on the edge of the present world passing away and on the threshold of the new world coming into being, and thinks the mystery of this has now been revealed. There is here a temporal dimension to these cosmic forces now unfolding. Expectation and urgency grip the community. "See" and "be prepared" become the watchwords.

This dimension of Jewish apocalyptic eschatology came to be absorbed into early Christian thinking but needed to be modified in light of the belief that Jesus was Messiah, Son of God, Son of Man, and Savior of the world. These were all titles attached to Jesus among his followers after his death and contributed to their understanding that he would return, presumably soon. But the temporal understanding of the diagram above also needed to be modified in light of the fact that in some sense the kingdom of God had already arrived in a preliminary way with Christ's coming to earth and would finally be completed at his second coming. Hence, I used the expression "now and not yet" in chapter 5 to describe the apostle Paul's eschatology. In the diagram below, the two circles overlap, indicating the time between Christ's first and second comings. The only real uncertainty is the length of time between the two.

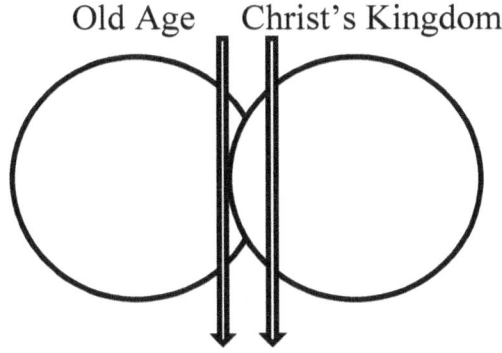

Christian Apocalyptic Ages Old and New

We know from the New Testament gospels that there was some uncertainty about precisely this issue. Some appear to have thought that Christ's return was imminent, and is reflected in texts such as Mark 9:1 (parallels in Matt 16:28 and Luke 9:27):

> And he said to them, "Truly I tell you, there are some standing here who will not taste death until they see that the kingdom of God has come with power."

Other texts—e.g., Matt 24:36, 42–44—suggest a delay of the parousia, a delay in Christ's return:

> [36] "But about that day and hour no one knows, neither the angels of heaven, nor the Son, but only the Father . . . [42] Keep awake therefore, for you do not know on what day your Lord is coming. [43] But understand this: if the owner of the house had known in what part of the night the thief was coming, he would have stayed awake and would not have let his house be broken into. [44] Therefore you also must be ready, for the Son of Man is coming at an unexpected hour.

Here the watchword is, "be prepared for you do not know the hour when Christ will return." Over time, of course, the delay of Christ's return became longer and longer. This, however, did not diminish the importance of apocalyptic for the New Testament writers and early Christianity. In fact, Ernst Käsemann, a prominent German New Testament scholar and theologian of the twentieth century, once famously pronounced that apocalyptic is the mother of all Christian theology.[8]

THE REVELATION TO JOHN

We are correct to see apocalypticism as the soil from which Revelation sprang, but it does not necessarily follow that the text itself is an apocalypse. It certainly bears many of the hallmarks of apocalyptic thinking that we have already identified: celestial journeys, visions, symbolic language, the hidden world of angels and demons, eschatological judgment, revelation of things about to take place, and conflict between the powers of this world and God. This, of course, is a Christian text, which means the figure of Christ also has a prominent place. As Craig Koester has noted, Revelation, unlike some other apocalypses, does not give a linear review of history or a linear sequence of how things will unfold in the future. Instead, it presents alternating words of warning and encouragement, intended to sustain faith in times of trouble.[9] Because of the name of the book, Revelation, many have assumed quite reflexively that it is an apocalypse. However, Jürgen Roloff is not convinced. He writes "In summary, Revelation is a prophetic writing that contains numerous apocalyptic motifs and elements of style, but whose form is chiefly characterized by the purpose of epistolary communication."[10] His description of Revelation shows how closely connected prophecy is to the apocalyptic features of the text and how the purpose of the communication resembles that found in epistolary texts. In fact, Revelation imagines seven letters written to seven churches in Asia (1:4–11; 2:1—3:22).

The narrative begins with a prologue laying out in brief the revelation from Jesus Christ made known by an angel to his servant John: "Blessed are those who read aloud these words of prophecy and hear and keep what is written." In 1:9–11, John's own voice comes to the fore and identifies that he was on the island of Patmos, where he patiently endured persecution because of God's word and the witness of Jesus Christ when he received his visions. While he was in the Spirit on the Lord's Day, a loud voice came to him and instructed him to write what he saw and to send it to the seven churches. When he turned to see whose voice it was, he saw seven lampstands, and in their midst stood "one like the Son of Man, clothed in a long robe with a golden sash across his chest." His head was "white as snow," and "his eyes were like a flame of fire" (1:11–20). So begins the Revelation

---

8. Käsemann, "Beginnings of Christian Theology," 102.
9. Koester, *Revelation*, 30.
10. Roloff, *Revelation of John*, 8.

Jewish Apocalyptic Tradition and the Revelation to John

to John, which proceeds, to use Koester's image, like spirals each looping around and advancing the series of visions in a nonlinear way.[11] Reading Revelation through from beginning to end, one gets a sense of the alternating pattern of warnings and encouragements, where each set of visions pushes the imagery and message forward. However, instead of moving forward in strictly linear fashion, the pattern seems more circular and repetitive. Koester outlines the book this way: "An outline of the book looks like a spiral, with each loop consisting of a series of visions: seven messages to the church (Rev 1–3), seven seals (Rev 4–7), seven trumpets (Rev 8–11), unnumbered visions (Rev 12–15), seven plagues (Rev 15–19), and more unnumbered visions (Rev 19–22). Visions celebrating the triumph of God occur at the end of each cycle (4:1–11; 7:1–17; 11:15–19; 15:1–4; 19:1–10; 21:1—22:5)."[12]

Among the seven letters to the churches in Asia, two are especially interesting because of the intersection of textual images with physical realities. I first quote each text and then follow it with a picture related to the site to illustrate the intersection. The visions may be presented as transcendent revelations, but that does not mean they are completely separate from physical reality. The first is the letter to the wealthy community in Laodicea (Rev 3:14–22):

> [14] And to the angel of the church in Laodicea write: The words of the Amen, the faithful and true witness, the origin of God's creation:
>
> [15] *I know your works; you are neither cold nor hot. I wish that you were either cold or hot.* [16] *So, because you are lukewarm, and neither cold nor hot, I am about to spit you out of my mouth.* [17] For you say, "I am rich, I have prospered, and I need nothing." You do not realize that you are wretched, pitiable, poor, blind, and naked. [18] Therefore I counsel you to buy from me gold refined by fire so that you may be rich; and white robes to clothe you and to keep the shame of your nakedness from being seen; and salve to anoint your eyes so that you may see. [19] I reprove and discipline those whom I love. Be earnest, therefore, and repent. [20] Listen! I am standing at the door, knocking; if you hear my voice and open the door, I will come in to you and eat with you, and you with me. [21] To the one who conquers I will give a place with me on my throne, just as I myself conquered and sat down with my Father on his throne. [22] Let anyone who has an ear listen to what the Spirit is saying to the churches."

---

11. Koester, *Revelation*, 39.
12. Ibid., 39.

If we stand today at the ancient site of Laodicea, now a ruin and archaeological site, we see an important feature of the city. It was near a thermal hot spring, and the water was piped to the city. The picture above is of the remains of corroded pipes that transported hot water to the town. These people knew firsthand about hot and cold water, and here they are chastised for being neither, only lukewarm.

The second letter is to the church at Pergamum, part of which I quote here (Rev 2:12–13): "¹²And to the angel of the church in Pergamum write: These are the words of him who has the sharp two-edged sword: ¹³ 'I know where you are living, where *Satan's throne* is. Yet you are holding fast to my name, and you did not deny your faith in me even in the days of Antipas my witness, my faithful one, who was killed among you, *where Satan lives*.'"

Jewish Apocalyptic Tradition and the Revelation to John 159

Biblical scholars often suggest that *Satan's throne* is an oblique reference to the temple of Augustus or to the so-called altar of Zeus, the sites of which are both still visible at Pergamum. The photograph above is of the altar, the remains of which were taken in the nineteenth century to Germany and reconstructed in the Pergamum museum in Berlin. The examples from the letters to the churches in Laodocia and Pergamum suggest that physical as well as religious realities from the respective cities have made their way into the text of Revelation. As revelatory as the visions (in this case, the letters) claim to be, they still reflect some earthly features of the Christian communities to which they are addressed. And as if to challenge the throne and power of Satan, the text in 4:1-11 offers a vision of God enthroned with mystery and majesty in heaven. The Christians in the seven churches have been warned about their behavior, but there is no doubt about the majesty and triumph of God.

In chapters 6-8 we read about the seals of judgment and destruction, followed in 8-11 by the blowing of the trumpets of destruction and tribulation. Throughout this section of the narrative, the imagery is vivid and deeply threatening. Creatures appear, nature convulses, pests abound, and plague threatens. But when the Lamb opens the final seal and the seventh angel blows the last trumpet, God appears triumphant. There is silence in heaven (8:1-5), and the kingdom of the world has become the kingdom of the Lord and of his Messiah (11:15). He will reign forever. Then God's heavenly temple is opened and the ark of the covenant is seen within, accompanied by thunder, lightning, earthquake, and hail (11:19). The imagery is cosmic, threatening, and at the same time strangely reassuring. God and his Messiah prevail over all this.

In chapters 12–13, a series of images rich in symbolism appears in the narrative. The first image centers on an unnamed woman pregnant with a male child and a great dragon identified as the devil, who ultimately is thrown down from heaven and defeated by Michael and his angels. While heaven rejoices because the devil has been thrown down by the blood of the Lamb, the dragon, realizing he is on earth, pursues the woman, who has given birth. But she is given wings and escapes the dragon, which only makes him angry and causes him to make war on the rest of her children, identified as those who keep the commandments and observe the witness of Jesus (Rev 12).

The second image centers on the story of the two beasts. The first beast, a grotesque creature, arises from the sea and is given the dragon's authority. Amazingly, the whole earth follows the beast. "Who is like the beast, and who can fight against it?" (13:4). For forty-two months this beast spews blasphemy and makes war on the saints, conquering them and having authority over all peoples and nations. Then a second beast rises from the earth, with two horns like a lamb, yet speaking like a dragon. It exercises the authority of the first beast and makes the earth worship him. It deceives the people of the earth, telling them to make an image of the beast, which then speaks and causes those who refuse to worship it to be killed. The image of the beast causes all to be marked either on the right hand or on the forehead with its name or with the number of its name, without which none can either buy or sell. And the number of the beast is 666.

The third set of images is much more reassuring for those who endure in the face of the devil's power (Rev 14). John looks and sees the Lamb standing on Mount Zion. There, too, are 144,000 people who have his and the Father's name written on their foreheads. A voice from heaven speaks, sounding like a beautiful new song, but only the 144,000 who have been redeemed from the earth can learn the new song. They are the firstfruits of the Lamb.

Just then an angel appears to proclaim the eternal gospel to those on earth, and a second angel announces, "Fallen, fallen is Babylon [Rome] the Great! She has made all nations drink of the wine of wrath of her fornication" (Rev 14:8). Next a third angel appears, announcing that those who receive the mark of the beast will be tormented and that those who hold fast to the commandments and the faith of Jesus will be blessed. The "One like the Son of Man" appears with a sickle in his hand, and chapter 14 ends with harvest imagery, symbolizing the judgment to come. This cycle ends in chapter 15, with the reassuring words of the son of Moses, God's servant, and the song of the Lamb:

> Great and amazing are your deeds,
> Lord God the Almighty!
> Just and true are your ways,
> King of the nations!
> ⁴ Lord, who will not fear
> and glorify your name?
> For you alone are holy.
> All nations will come
> and worship before you,
> for your judgments have been revealed.

As we pick up the narrative again in chapters 17 and 18, following the seven angels' pouring out their seven bowls of God's wrath on the earth in chapter 16, the story moves on to a thinly veiled announcement of the fall of Babylon, or Rome. In Old Testament history, Babylon was the sixth-century-BCE city and empire that destroyed Judah and Jerusalem and carried off many Israelites into exile, initiating the fifty-year period we now call the Babylonian exile. Babylon, that great city in the East, in time, too, was destroyed. In short, by referring to Babylon, Revelation harkens back to an ancient time while addressing the contemporary situation of Rome and its empire. What happened to that great city before is now about to happen to this great city. This prophetic announcement of judgment on Rome is introduced in dramatic fashion in 17:1–6:

> Then one of the seven angels who had the seven bowls came and said to me, "Come, I will show you the judgment of the great whore who is seated on many waters, ² with whom the kings of the earth have committed fornication, and with the wine of whose fornication the inhabitants of the earth have become drunk." ³ So he carried me away in the spirit into a wilderness, and I saw a woman sitting on a scarlet beast that was full of blasphemous names, and had seven heads and ten horns. ⁴ The woman was clothed in purple and scarlet, and adorned with gold and jewels and pearls, holding in her hand a golden cup full of abominations and the impurities of her fornication; ⁵ and on her forehead was written a name, a mystery: "Babylon the great, mother of whores and of earth's abominations." ⁶ And I saw that

the woman was drunk with the blood of the saints and the blood of the witnesses to Jesus.

The great beast and its client kings will make war on the Lamb, but the Lamb will conquer them, because he is Lord of Lords and King of Kings. The great city is the woman who rules over the kings of the earth and in her wickedness and fornication she shall be no more. She is the mother of whores and abominations, drunk on the blood of the saints and witnesses to Jesus Christ. She will succumb to the King of Kings. This part of the story continues throughout chapter 18 with a dirge over the fallen city, mixing language describing the pitiful state of this once great city with language that extols the triumph of God. Next the book of Revelation pauses from describing the fallen city. The text in 19:1–11 launches into praise of God and God's servants. The great multitude of heaven sings hallelujah. Next the great heavenly armies of Christ are described. The imagery is vivid, martial, and unmistakable. The army of Christ has won the decisive battle.

Revelation chapter 20 opens with the imprisonment of Satan. An angel descends from heaven, seizes the dragon, and throws him into the pit, where he will languish for a thousand years. After this, he will be let out. The text gives no reason for his eventual release. And those who were beheaded for their witness to Christ and had not worshiped the beast or its image come back to life and rule with Christ for a thousand years. This is the first resurrection. When Satan is released after a thousand years, he goes out once again to deceive the nations from the four corners of the earth. But again he and his minions are defeated; this time they are thrown into the lake of fire, where they will be tormented forever. The final judgment then takes place.

> [11] Then I saw a great white throne and the one who sat on it; the earth and the heaven fled from his presence, and no place was found for them. [12] And I saw the dead, great and small, standing before the throne, and books were opened. Also another book was opened, the book of life. And the dead were judged according to their works, as recorded in the books. [13] And the sea gave up the dead that were in it, Death and Hades gave up the dead that were in them, and all were judged according to what they had done. [14] Then Death and Hades were thrown into the lake of fire. This is the second death, the lake of fire. (20:11–14)

This text and the thousand-year period before the final judgment have generated a great deal of speculation and given rise to what is called millennialism, referring to this period before the final, decisive act of God. In light of what I said above about the ambiguity and indeterminacy of Revelation, it is hard to know exactly what to make of this, but that has hardly curtailed speculation. Rather than trying to nail down the referential meaning of this language, it might be better for readers simply to flow with the imagery and its emotional impact.

The final visions of Revelation (21:1—22:5), as if to bring the grand vision of the whole narrative to its culmination, picture a new heaven, a new earth, and a new Jerusalem coming down from heaven. It is a glorious sight—where God dwells among the people, and where death will be no more. Suffering and pain too will be no more. All things will be made new. The river of the water of life will flow from the throne of God, alongside of which grows the tree of life, producing twelve kinds of fruit and healing the nations. Nothing evil will be found there, and there will be no more night because God will be the city's light forever. The people of God will rule forever. Despite the violent and war-like tone that marks much of the narrative, the culmination of the revelation opens onto this expansive vision of peace and tranquility that even today sends a feeling of calm over readers. After having been dragged through the emotional trauma of the violence and the struggle, readers, enveloped by this new vision, feel a sense of release. Reading Revelation is an emotional and evocative experience, and the ending of the story is no different. It may be utopian, but it is powerful for those suffering persecution and feeling threatened. And even among those for whom the world seems to be spinning out of the control, Revelation may provide a comforting word.[13]

CONCLUSION

This chapter gives us a glimpse into the book of Revelation as a work of fantasy. Like all fantasy writing—whether series such as the Chronicles of Narnia, Harry Potter, or the Lord of the Rings—Revelation features stories with vivid imagery and great contending forces. But beneath the surface of the text is an important and powerful, albeit nonliteral, message. What is the message here? Great forces are contending with each other: the evil forces of the devil (the beasts) and the even greater forces of God and the messiah, Jesus Christ. These contending powers are playing themselves out in heaven and on earth, and the people of Christ are being exhorted to keep the commandments and hold firm to the faith. Remain steadfast in the face of the powers that want you to bear the sign of the beast. Not everyone resonates to this kind of language and writing but many do. Today, in fact, many flock to movie theaters to see great works of fantasy projected on the screen

---

13. The actual text of Revelation does not end at this point. There is a brief epilogue of instructions, warnings, and exhortations (22:6–21).

before them. Fantasy is a type of literature that requires imagination. In my view, the great pitfall is to literalize the language and thus miss the point and function of the message. As a reader, you simply have to go with it. It can also be problematic if people see themselves as players on the stage of an apocalyptic drama, acting out a literalistic script and perhaps even willing to go to the extreme of trying to bring about the fulfillment of the prophecy in their own time. The signs of the times are not easy to plug into the text of Revelation, and when we try, we seem to get it terribly wrong. Perhaps the word *truth* is not even appropriate to describe what fantasy writing shows us, but if it is, the truth we see is very different from the truth we refer to when we normally use the word *truth*. Some might say it is only with such extreme language, with its vivid, sometimes distorted, imagery that we can really probe certain experiential levels of meaning and truth. Be that as it may, the story of Revelation invites both fascination and caution. For people who are or who perceive themselves to be under threat, the book of Revelation may provide a word of reassurance that those who threaten them will not have the final word.

PART 3

Foundational Topics

11

Render unto God and unto Caesar
The Problem of Empire

*What are the implications for individual Christians
and for the early church that Christianity was born, survived,
and ultimately thrived in a Roman imperial context?*

For those familiar with the New Testament, it is hard to forget that compelling scene in Matt 22:15–22 where the Pharisees and Herodians try to entrap Jesus:

> [15] Then the Pharisees went and plotted to entrap him in what he said. [16] So they sent their disciples to him, along with the Herodians, saying, "Teacher, we know that you are sincere, and teach the way of God in accordance with truth, and show deference to no one; for you do not regard people with partiality. [17] Tell us, then, what you think. Is it lawful to pay taxes to the emperor, or not?" [18] But Jesus, aware of their malice, said, "Why are you putting me to the test, you hypocrites? [19] Show me the coin used for the tax." And they brought him a denarius. [20] Then he said to them, "Whose head is this, and whose title?" [21] They answered, "The emperor's." Then he said to them, "Give therefore to the emperor the things that are the emperor's, and to God the things that are God's." [22] When they heard this, they were amazed; and they left him and went away.

It can hardly be the case that Jesus is calling here for the separation of church and state rather like the contemporary political and religious situation in America. That would have been unthinkable in the world of Jesus and the early church. In the first century CE, Rome was rapidly approaching the zenith of its imperial power, and the land of Israel (Palestine) was important because it protected the empire's eastern flank. Far from being a religious wasteland, the empire was throbbing with religiosity. The Roman gods were overlaid onto the ancient Greek gods, and religious practices and ideas flooded the empire from North Africa and the East. It was a highly pluralistic and polytheistic religious environment, with temples to one god or another dotting the landscape. Perhaps most important, the religious, imperial, social, and cultural environments of Rome were inseparable. They were thoroughly interwoven, and to upset the balance in one area had implications for the entire imperial ecosystem. It is hardly the case that all parts of the empire—east and west, rural and urban, rich and poor, citizen and barbarian—looked alike or functioned in the same way in these matters. They certainly did not. But the intersections, if not convergence, of these various strands of imperial life were instrumental in negotiating Roman identity and incorporating various ethnic groups into the Roman imperial world order. It is important to keep in mind that the center of Roman power, control, and culture was always being negotiated with the periphery, and it is the case that the influence traveled in both directions. The Roman and the "other," the center and the periphery, and the upper and lower echelons of society were always being influenced and affected by each other. And Roman religion was part of that process and seems to have played a critical role in maintaining social order in the face of forces that threatened to tear it apart. Maintaining an ordered social structure and everyone's place in it was vital to Roman well-being and survival. It was into this world that the Jesus movement and somewhat later early Christianity came and sought to make their way.

In this chapter, we will look at some of the implications of this for the early church and to some extent for the empire as well. A number of features of this topic have been touched on already in previous chapters, and some of those strands will need to be brought back into the conversation. However, the focus here is on the question of empire and how that reality shaped the church, its message, its opportunities for success, and its struggles to survive in the face of opposition. In more recent scholarship, this topic has come to the front and center of academic and church discussions, probably prompted in part by contemporary concerns about empire and its implications for the contemporary world. Religiously motivated terrorism, Western global hegemony, wars that go on for years without satisfying resolution, and questions of justice have all prompted scholars and theologians to think about these issues in new ways. Alongside those concerns, interdisciplinary methodological approaches have yielded new insights and enabled us to approach the material in new ways. It is not surprising then that many scholars would bring these renewed concerns and these new methods to the study of early Christianity. It will, of course, not be possible to deal in great depth with these questions here, but we can lay a solid foundation for further study and significantly expand our sense of early Christian religion, life, and missionary activity.

IMPERIAL OPPOSITION, RESISTANCE, ACCOMMODATION, AND NEGOTIATION

In the previous chapter, our discussion of Revelation portrayed quite clearly a narrative rooted in apocalyptic dualism and opposition. Those who keep the commandments of God and hold fast to the faith of Jesus Christ stand over and against the new Babylon, which will be destroyed. The old creation is passing away, and a new creation is envisioned. The old Jerusalem is passing away, and a new one is about to descend from heaven. Revelation reflects a bipolar theological reality, if not also a bipolar social world. It is hard to miss the oppositional language of Revelation and the bipolar structure it represents. The world of Revelation may well have been prompted by persecution of Christians during the reign of Emperor Domitian (81-96). Given the threats they faced and the possibility of persecution, we can understand how Christians would come to see themselves as vulnerable. After all, their world was bipolar, marked by opposing, contending forces. Good contends against evil. For Christians, the world is not a congenial place, but rather a place of threat. They stand for truth and justice, while the decadent Roman world stands for faithlessness and the refusal to see the truth revealed in Jesus Christ. This oppositional reality is clearly, and appropriately so, part of how we today construe the relationship between early Christianity and the Roman Empire. It has often governed as well how scholars frame the issue of early Christianity and empire. This is part of the picture, but only part of it. It is this wider context that we need to examine.

In chapter 6 I referred to the work of John Dominic Crossan on the historical Jesus, and in particular to a book he coauthored with Jonathan Reed titled *Excavating Jesus: Beneath the Stones, behind the Texts*.[1] In this sophisticated work, the authors write about the clash of kingdom types, specifically the clash of the covenantal kingdom (represented traditionally

---

1. See above, pp. 89-90.

in Israel) with the commercial kingdom (represented by the Roman Empire and its minions). Four presuppositions govern the covenantal kingdom: God is just, the land of Israel belongs to God, the land was in the beginning distributed fairly among the people of Israel, and the Israelite prophets protested against the drive by fewer and fewer people to possess more and more of the land.[2] To use modern terminology, we might say that the land was intended to be in a kind of covenantal trust. During the time of Jesus, we see this represented most visibly in places like Capernaum with its houses, structures, and layout.[3] On the other hand, in the commercial kingdom, one sees a hierarchy with wealth unequally distributed, rulers with great cities and monumental buildings, and projections of power from imperial rulers to their subjects. The commercial kingdom imposes a social and economic order on society. This world is represented by Augustus, Herod the Great, and Herod Antipas, and it can be seen in the wonders of ancient Caesarea, Sepphoris, and Tiberias.[4] The realities Crossan and Reed are probing are indeed important, and their cross-disciplinary approach helps us see in new ways the conflict between what Jesus and Caesar, church and empire, represent.

Having set up the clash of kingdoms, the authors pose a penetrating question:

> This chapter raises a fundamental question that reappears at the start of the next one and returns at the end of the last one. If life in the kingdom of God as lived by Jesus and his companions was opposed to that in the tetrarchal Kingdom of Antipas around it, the royal Kingdom of Herod before it, and the imperial Kingdom of Augustus or Tiberias above it, how did all of that relate to the Christian Kingdom of Constantine?

To the extent Crossan and Reed are correct about the clash of kingdoms in the world of Jesus, their argument also illustrates a larger clash between the church and the Roman Empire. On that level too the paradigm is oppositional. Two different types of kingdoms collided and produced all the predictable kinds of conflict. But here is where we need to continue the story and see how each kingdom began over time to take on the characteristics of the other. Constantine in the fourth century legalized and privileged Christianity, and set his empire on the road ultimately to becoming a Christian kingdom. The church and the empire become married in new and not so subtle ways that eventually changed both. The point is, as that marriage

2. Crossan and Reed, *Excavating Jesus*, 108.
3. Ibid., 115–35.
4. Ibid., 54–70, 108–15.

played itself out, both church and empire became something quite different from what they had been in the beginning. It may not be too strong to posit that even as the empire became Christian, the Christian church became imperial. The influence moved in both directions. To the extent this accurately captures what was going on over those first three or four centuries of the church, it suggests that beneath the surface of the opposition between Christianity and Rome there was a process of negotiation, accommodation, and adaptation going on between the two.[5] It is probably the case that all of these things were going on at the same time in one way or another, in one corner of society or another. We know that emerging orthodox Christianity over time began to adopt Roman administrative structures (episcopal forms based on the Roman household), and architectural forms came to be patterned after Roman designs (basilicas). Christian calendars and practices were influenced by Roman festivals (Christmas and Saturnalia), and the exercise of church authority came to reflect a hierarchal model. A one-dimensional reading of the opposition between the church and Rome is insufficient to understand adequately this reality.

In a very different context, we can perhaps see something similar in Paul. The apostle spent considerable time in the city of Ephesus, located in western Asia Minor. It was one of the most significant cities in the Roman east, and it was from this city that he wrote his epistles to the Corinthians. In 1 Cor 15:24–28, Paul writes:

> [24] Then comes the end, when he hands over the kingdom to God the Father, after he has destroyed every ruler and every authority and power. [25] For he must reign until he has put all his enemies under his feet. [26] The last enemy to be destroyed is death. [27] For "God has put all things in subjection under his feet." But when it says, "All things are put in subjection," it is plain that this does not include the one who put all things in subjection under him. [28] When all things are subjected to him, then the Son himself will also be subjected to the one who put all things in subjection under him, so that God may be all in all.

God has destroyed every ruler, authority, and power and put all things, including death, under his feet. From our vantage in the twenty-first century, those words can slip by us with scarcely a thought. But imagine how they would have sounded in Corinthian or Ephesian society. In an imperial world that did not look kindly on rival powers and saw itself as the epitome of power, these words could have sounded either laughable or seditious. What

---

5 This is an important insight of postcolonial theory. See Hanges, "Response to Karl Galinsky," 28–31; and Maier, *Picturing Paul in Empire*, 1–61.

fool could think that Roman power might succumb to such nonsense? Who was Paul anyway, and what could he be thinking? As we know, of course, four hundred years later Paul's words would not have sounded so preposterous. But in their day, if taken seriously at all, they might well have sounded to many people as a challenge to Roman hegemony and social concord. I have little doubt but that Paul thought Rome was passing away, with all its power and authority. Its end was not far off. Armed as he was with this eschatological framework, it is not hard to see Paul in opposition to Rome.

Built several decades after Paul's residence in Ephesus, the so-called Fountain of Trajan provides an interesting counterpoint to his words. If today we walk down Curetes street, through the magnificent ruins of ancient Ephesus, we come upon the Fountain of Trajan. Emperor from 98 to 117, Trajan traveled extensively throughout his empire, and wherever he went buildings were built in his honor. Ephesus was no exception, as we see from this fountain or temple. Today this is what we see.

In the center, under the architrave, would have stood a larger-than-life statue of Trajan. All that remains today is a foot (presumably of the emperor) and a globe-like figure. Originally Trajan's foot might have rested on a globe. Though I have not been able to confirm it, a popular Turkish guidebook of Ephesus makes precisely this claim and further asserts that an inscription would have appeared underneath: "I conquered it all, it's all under my foot."[6] This certainly sounds plausible, and if in fact it is correct provides a vivid juxtaposition of competing claims about power and authority. Even

---

6 Seval, *Step by Step Ephesus*, 44–46.

though Trajan dates from well after Paul, and even if the reconstruction of the monument in his honor may not be entirely clear, still the presence of the monument suggests that it was built in an environment where competing powers and principalities seemed to be on a collision course.

But Paul is not simply on a collision course with the Roman Empire. In Rom 13:1–7, for example, he counsels those Christians living at the center of the empire to be subject to the governing authorities:

> Let every person be subject to the governing authorities; for there is no authority except from God, and those authorities that exist have been instituted by God. ² Therefore whoever resists authority resists what God has appointed, and those who resist will incur judgment. ³ For rulers are not a terror to good conduct, but to bad. Do you wish to have no fear of the authority? Then do what is good, and you will receive its approval; ⁴ for it is God's servant for your good. But if you do what is wrong, you should be afraid, for the authority does not bear the sword in vain! It is the servant of God to execute wrath on the wrongdoer. ⁵ Therefore one must be subject, not only because of wrath but also because of conscience. ⁶ For the same reason you also pay taxes, for the authorities are God's servants, busy with this very thing. ⁷ Pay to all what is due them—taxes to whom taxes are due, revenue to whom revenue is due, respect to whom respect is due, honor to whom honor is due.

While this passage has often been misused by later tyrants and oppressive regimes, Paul does not always position himself blindly in opposition and resistance to Rome, but here incorporates the governing authorities into his theology and understanding of God. They have been instituted by God, and those who resist what God has appointed will bring judgment on themselves. They play a divinely authorized role in society, and if you conduct yourself properly you will receive their approval. They are God's agents for your good, writes Paul to the Romans. Paul may well be addressing a particular situation in the Roman churches and not simply making a blanket statement for all times and places. But no matter how this text in Romans is interpreted, it is hard not to conclude that Paul is prepared to counsel obedience, even as a matter of conscience, to the Roman authorities, and to pay all the taxes that are due them. On the face of it, these words do not sound like the language of opposition. They sound like they come from a man who is accommodating the ruling authorities and incorporating what they represent into his sense of divine providence. He can challenge and oppose Rome, but he can also advise in some instances submission to it.

We have already met Thecla,[7] the young woman enthralled by Paul's preaching who gave up everything including her engagement to be married, in order to follow him and his gospel of chastity and resurrection. We also saw how her refusal to conform to social expectations put her on a collision course with the local authorities, who sought to put her to death. Though other women came to her defense and she was ultimately spared from death by divine intervention, this fictional story illustrates how the clash of commitments and expectations between Christianity and the Empire played itself out on another level. Was it Thecla's belief or her behavior that got her into trouble? I suggest it was less about what she believed than it was about what she did that caused her to run afoul of the men in the story and even her mother. She did not conform to social expectations regarding marriage and childbearing, and that was a serious offense. It is not hard to understand how her jilted groom might be disappointed and put out, but how would this be sufficient to cause the local authorities to agree to put her to death? She threatened good social order, and her actions threatened the society's need for children to maintain the population. This was serious business, and if one did not do their part to preserve the social order and their place in it, the powers that be were apt to react with a vengeance. Those of us who live in relatively open, tolerant societies cannot easily bring our own experience to the Roman context. Roman society was hierarchical, highly structured, and relatively inflexible. The preservation of order was important and to threaten that invited a reaction. For Thecla to opt out of the expectation to marry and instead live a chaste life was a direct challenge to that order. In that world, this was not simply a matter of personal preference. And it shows how the encounter between imperial society and Christianity manifested itself on the level of specific behaviors and not just on the level of theological ideas and beliefs.

The emperor cult is often cited in discussions of Roman religion, frequently as though it is a monolithic and centrally controlled phenomenon. More recently, interdisciplinary conversations have challenged these notions. Karl Galinsky has argued that with four exceptions, it is not centrally controlled. The four exceptions, two in the east and two in the west, were established at the behest of provincial authorities and with the permission of Augustus, but without dogma. Hence, it is inappropriate to speak about an imperial theology.[8] Galinsky does not see the imperial cult as the only or even the dominant cult with which Christians had to negotiate, and while the emperor could be praised for his blessings he was not alone in that re-

---

7. See above, pp. 125–29.
8. Galinsky, "Cult of the Roman Emperor," 3.

gard.[9] As Galinsky points out, the imperial cult was connected to other gods and cults and became especially in the East a way of constructing the reality of the Roman Empire, which Christians were also doing in their own way.[10] In that regard, imperial cults in all their diversity were part of the larger panoply of Roman religions and cults. Writing in another context, Galinsky describes Roman religion this way:

> Religion can be defined in various ways. In the Roman context, we have to be especially careful not to transpose later and Christian notions of what constitutes belief and faith to a system that was *sui generis*. But even when we use the most general definitions, it is clear that religion had to be an integral aspect of the restabilization of the Roman state and empire at the time. Fundamentally, religion is a response and alternative to chaos; it is an attempt to provide structure, order, and meaning, the very efforts that lay at the heart of the Augustan reconstitution of the *res publica*.[11]

This drive for stability too would have put Thecla and other men and women like her on a religious collision course with the authorities, who saw such behavior as opening the door to chaos.

Referring specifically to the Gospels and Paul, Galinsky raises in conclusion for us some provocative questions about seeing Christianity's response to empire as simply a matter of resistance:

> Was their resistance to empire so coded that successive generations didn't get it? Or did they mean to juxtapose rather than oppose and once the empire became increasingly Christian, empire, imperial cult, *ecclesiae*, and so forth ceased being an issue because they were appropriated in fact? Was takeover the final stage of negotiation? Was it a result of receding apocalyptic expectations?[12]

These are interesting questions and illustrate yet again the complexity of Christianity's life in the Roman Empire and how it changed over time as the church's circumstances changed. At the very least, Galinsky cautions us against reducing too quickly this complex phenomenon to just one thing.

---

9. Ibid., 5–6.
10. Ibid., 4.
11. Galinsky, *Augustan Culture*, 288.
12. Galinsky, "Cult of the Roman Emperor," 15.

PERSECUTION AND MARTYRDOM

As we have already seen, Ignatius of Antioch and Polycarp of Smyrna were both martyred during the second century.[13] Ignatius writes in his letters early in the second century about his impending death in Rome, and it is clear he does not want his fellow Christians to intercede to try and prevent his glorious destiny from being fulfilled. And we read about Polycarp's martyrdom later in that century in a text titled *The Martyrdom of Polycarp*. But we also know that well before these two bishops were martyred, James (the brother of Jesus and the leader of the church in Jerusalem), Peter, and Paul were all executed within a short period of time, probably during the reign of Emperor Nero (54–68).[14] Josephus writes in his *Jewish Antiquities* 20:200, about James's death: "Annas thought that he had a favorable opportunity because Festus was dead and Albinus was still on the way. And so he convened the judges of the Sanhedrin and brought before them a man named James, the brother of Jesus who was called the Christ, and certain others. He accused them of having transgressed the law and delivered them up to be stoned." With the death of James, the church in Jerusalem lost its leader and its familial connection to Jesus. Within a year or two after that, Peter and Paul were executed in Rome.[15] In a few short years during the middle of the first century, the church lost three of its most important figures. Written later in the first century, the so-called Letter of 1 Clement describes the situation of their deaths this way:

> But not to dwell upon ancient examples, let us come to the most recent spiritual heroes. Let us take the noble examples furnished in our own generation. Through envy and jealousy, the greatest and most righteous pillars [of the Church] have been persecuted and put to death. Let us set before our eyes the illustrious apostles. Peter, through unrighteous envy, endured not one or two, but numerous labours, and when he had finally suffered martyrdom, departed to the place of glory due to him. Owing to envy, Paul also obtained the reward of patient endurance, after being seven times thrown into captivity, compelled to flee, and stoned. After preaching both in the east and west, he gained the illustrious reputation due to his faith, having taught righteousness to the whole world, and come to the extreme limit of the west, and suffered martyrdom under the prefects. Thus was he

---

13. See above, pp. 120–22.
14. Novak, *Christianity and the Roman Empire*, 23–30.
15. Ibid., 26.

removed from the world, and went into the holy place, having proved himself a striking example of patience.[16]

And written much later still and from an even more spiritually glorious point of view, the Acts of Paul in Rome describes Paul's death in Rome with these words:

> V. . . . Then Paul stood with his face to the east and lifted up his hands to heaven and prayed a long time, and in his prayer he conversed in the Hebrew tongue with the fathers, and then stretched forth his neck without speaking. And when the executioner (speculator) struck off his head, milk spurted upon the cloak of the soldier. And the soldier and all that were there present when they saw it marveled and glorified God which had given such glory to Paul: and they went and told Caesar what was done.
>
> VI. And when he heard it, while he marveled long and was in perplexity, Paul came about the ninth hour, when many philosophers and the centurion were standing with Caesar, and stood before them all and said: Caesar, behold, I, Paul, the soldier of God, am not dead, but live in my God. But to you shall many evils befall and great punishment, you wretched man, because you have shed unjustly the blood of the righteous, not many days later. And having so said Paul departed from him. But Nero hearing it and being greatly troubled commanded the prisoners to be loosed, and Patroclus also and Barsabas and them that were with him.
>
> VII. And as Paul charged them, Longus and Cestus the centurion went early in the morning and approached with fear to the grave of Paul. And when they were come there they saw two men praying, and Paul between them, so that they beholding the wondrous marvel were amazed, but Titus and Luke being stricken with the fear of man when they saw Longus and Cestus coming toward them, turned to flee. But they pursued after them, saying: We pursue you not for death but for life, that you may give it to us, as Paul promised us, whom we saw just now standing between you and praying. And when they heard that, Titus and Luke rejoiced and gave them the seal in the Lord, glorifying the God and Father of our Lord Jesus Christ.

Here we see the way certain writers in the church not only describe the deaths of important church leaders but also embellish the accounts for

---

16. Translation is by Roberts-Donaldson.

spiritual and theological reasons. These people did not merely die, but they died meaningful and glorious deaths.

There may have been persecutions of Christians in Rome during the reign of Claudius (41–54), but the reference in Suetonius is obscure.[17] It is during the reign of Nero, however, that Christians were martyred in dramatic fashion. The great fire that devastated Rome in 64 had Nero's own fingerprints on it, and he tried to shift blame to Christians, who suffered as scapegoats for his own maniacal purposes. Mass arrests and executions of Christians took place. Yet despite Nero's edict against the Christians, it seems unlikely that persecutions extended much beyond Rome.[18] During Emperor Domitian's reign (81–96), there was further persecution of Christians. The great church historian Eusebius, writing in his *Ecclesiastical History* in the fourth century, describes the situation this way:

> When Domitian has given many proofs of his great cruelty and had put to death without any reasonable trial no small number of men distinguished at Rome by family and career, and had punished without a cause myriads of other notable men by banishment and confiscation of their property, he finally showed himself the successor of Nero's campaign of hostility to God. He was the second to promote persecution against us, though his father, Vespasian, had planned no evil (3:17–18).[19]

During most of the second and the first half of the third centuries, it was probably the case that Roman authorities were more interested in getting the Christians to recant their faith than they were in killing them,[20] but during the reign of Decius (249–251) all inhabitants of the empire were required to sacrifice to the ancient gods of Rome. Failure to do so could result in penalty and personal punishment. This was followed in 257 and 258 by the edicts of Valerian (253–260), which represented an imperial effort to stamp out the church.[21] This attempt to destroy the church did not, however, last for long, as Valerian was captured by the Persians and his son Gallienus issued his own edict of toleration.

One of the most revealing exchanges is between Pliny the Younger, governor of Bithynia and Pontus in northwestern Asia Minor, and Emperor

---

17. Suetonius, in *Life of Claudius*, 25:4 reports: "As the Jews were making constant disturbances at the instigation of Chrestus, he expelled them from Rome" (http://www.earlychristianwritings.com/suetonius.html/).
18. Potter, "Persecution of the Early Church," 232.
19. Translation is by Kirsopp Lake in *Ecclesiastical History*.
20. Potter, "Persecution of the Early Church," 233.
21. Ibid., 233.

Trajan in about 111–112. Because it provides a window into the concern of Roman authorities about how to handle the so-called Christian problem, I quote both Pliny's letter of inquiry and the Emperor's reply.

Pliny to the Emperor Trajan

> It is my practice, my lord, to refer to you all matters concerning which I am in doubt. For who can better give guidance to my hesitation or inform my ignorance? I have never participated in trials of Christians. I therefore do not know what offenses it is the practice to punish or investigate, and to what extent. And I have been not a little hesitant as to whether there should be any distinction on account of age or no difference between the very young and the more mature; whether pardon is to be granted for repentance, or, if a man has once been a Christian, it does him no good to have ceased to be one; whether the name itself, even without offenses, or only the offenses associated with the name are to be punished.
>
> Meanwhile, in the case of those who were denounced to me as Christians, I have observed the following procedure: I interrogated these as to whether they were Christians; those who confessed I interrogated a second and a third time, threatening them with punishment; those who persisted I ordered executed. For I had no doubt that, whatever the nature of their creed, stubbornness and inflexible obstinacy surely deserve to be punished. There were others possessed of the same folly; but because they were Roman citizens, I signed an order for them to be transferred to Rome.
>
> Soon accusations spread, as usually happens, because of the proceedings going on, and several incidents occurred. An anonymous document was published containing the names of many persons. Those who denied that they were or had been Christians, when they invoked the gods in words dictated by me, offered prayer with incense and wine to your image, which I had ordered to be brought for this purpose together with statues of the gods, and moreover cursed Christ—none of which those who are really Christians, it is said, can be forced to do—these I thought should be discharged. Others named by the informer declared that they were Christians, but then denied it, asserting that they had been but had ceased to be, some three years before, others many years, some as much as twenty-five years. They all worshipped your image and the statues of the gods, and cursed Christ.

They asserted, however, that the sum and substance of their fault or error had been that they were accustomed to meet on a fixed day before dawn and sing responsively a hymn to Christ as to a god, and to bind themselves by oath, not to some crime, but not to commit fraud, theft, or adultery, not falsify their trust, nor to refuse to return a trust when called upon to do so. When this was over, it was their custom to depart and to assemble again to partake of food—but ordinary and innocent food. Even this, they affirmed, they had ceased to do after my edict by which, in accordance with your instructions, I had forbidden political associations. Accordingly, I judged it all the more necessary to find out what the truth was by torturing two female slaves who were called deaconesses. But I discovered nothing else but depraved, excessive superstition.

I therefore postponed the investigation and hastened to consult you. For the matter seemed to me to warrant consulting you, especially because of the number involved. For many persons of every age, every rank, and also of both sexes are and will be endangered. For the contagion of this superstition has spread not only to the cities but also to the villages and farms. But it seems possible to check and cure it. It is certainly quite clear that the temples, which had been almost deserted, have begun to be frequented, that the established religious rites, long neglected, are being resumed, and that from everywhere sacrificial animals are coming, for which until now very few purchasers could be found. Hence it is easy to imagine what a multitude of people can be reformed if an opportunity for repentance is afforded.

Trajan to Pliny

You observed proper procedure, my dear Pliny, in sifting the cases of those who had been denounced to you as Christians. For it is not possible to lay down any general rule to serve as a kind of fixed standard. They are not to be sought out; if they are denounced and proved guilty, they are to be punished, with this reservation, that whoever denies that he is a Christian and really proves it—that is, by worshiping our gods—even though he was under suspicion in the past, shall obtain pardon through repentance. But anonymously posted accusations ought to have no place in any prosecution. For this is both a dangerous kind of precedent and out of keeping with the spirit of our age.[22]

---

22. *Letters of Pliny the Younger*, 10:96–97.

Among the many things this exchange reveals is that not all charges leveled against Christians were by any means the result of imperially motivated efforts. On the contrary, much of the threat against Christians was locally generated. As Trajan's reply indicates, Christians are not to be actively sought out. But if they are denounced and proven guilty, they are to be punished. The exception is that people who deny being Christians and can prove it should be pardoned. And no anonymous accusations should be admitted in any prosecution, as Trajan clearly understands how dangerous this would be.

In conclusion, it is interesting for us to look at the story of the Martyrdom of Perpetua and Felicitas, an account primarily of Vibia Perpetua who was executed in Carthage in 203. As we can see from the prologue and the conclusion, the account testifies to the glory of God and serves to strengthen those Christians who read it. In other words, a body of tradition and literature about the martyrs is developing expressly for the edification of those left behind and who might themselves be threatened. It is not hard to imagine the important psychological effect this might have for individual Christians, as well as for the wider church. The narrative itself is bookended with two vivid, edifying images intended for readers and for the support of the faithful.

> If ancient examples of faith kept, both testifying the grace of God and working the edification of man, have to this end been set in writing, that by their reading as though by the showing of the deeds again, God may be glorified and man strengthened; why should not new witnesses also be so set forth which likewise serve either end? Yea, for these things also shall at some time be ancient and necessary to our sons, though in their own present time (through some reverence of antiquity presumed) they are made of but slight account. But let those take heed who judge the one power of the Holy Spirit according to the succession of times; whereas those things which are later ought for their very lateness to be thought the more eminent, according to the abundance of grace appointed for the last periods of time. For *In the last days,* says the Lord, *I will pour my spirit upon all flesh, and their sons and daughters shall prophesy; and upon my servants and upon my handmaids I will pour forth of my spirit; and the young men shall see visions, and the old men shall dream dreams.* [Acts 2:17, cf. Joel 2:28] (Prologue).[23]

---

23. Translation is by Shewring, *Martyrdom*; see also http://www.earlychristianwritings.com/text/perpetua.html/.

> O most valiant and blessed martyrs! O truly called and elected unto the glory of Our Lord Jesus Christ! Which glory he that magnifies, honors and adores, ought to read these witnesses likewise, as being no less than the old, unto the Church's edification; that these new wonders also may testify that one and the same Holy Spirit works ever until now, and with Him God the Father Almighty, and His Son Jesus Christ Our Lord, to Whom is glory and power unending for ever and ever. Amen. (Conclusion).

Interestingly, Perpetua writes much of the account herself prior to her passion. She describes herself as nobly born, married with a young child, and having a mother, father, and two brothers. She is imprisoned and in great distress. The narrative turns on a series of visions, and in the first she sees her situation is to result in her passion rather than her deliverance. Although her father tries desperately to talk sense into her, she will not offer the required sacrifice in order to escape death. She will not deny her Lord. Until the day before the games, Perpetua writes her own account: "Thus far I have written this, till the day before the games; but the deed of the games themselves let him write who will" (10). Saturus continues the story. Felicitas too received the grace of God, but being eight months pregnant feared she would be held back from the games.

When the day of the games arrived, Perpetua, "glorious of presence as a true spouse of Christ and darling of God" went from her prison cell into the amphitheater. Felicitas too went to the amphitheater, having already given birth to her child so she might fight with the beasts. As the text says, she "came now from blood to blood, from the midwife to the gladiator" (18). Perpetua refuses to be dressed in the clothes of the priestesses of Ceres and goes willingly and with great resolve to her death. Throughout the most horrible distress, she persists in what can only be described as a kind of holy joy. She meets her eternal glory by her own helping hand: "But Perpetua, that she might have some taste of pain, was pierced between the bones and shrieked out; and when the swordsman's hand wandered still (for he was a novice), herself set it upon her own neck. Perchance so great a woman could not else have been slain (being feared of the unclean spirit) had she not herself so willed it" (21). So ends the story of the martyrdom of Perpetua and Felicitas.

12

People of the Book
From Text to Canon

What does it mean to say that early Christians were people of the book, and how did certain Christian texts become canon, sacred Scripture?

The short answer to the opening question above is, of course, that most of the earliest followers of Jesus were Jews, and the roots of emergent Christianity were in Judaism. Judaism by this time had already become a community of texts and traditions that defined their understanding of God and their religious practice. Given that, it would have been surprising if Christianity had not become a religion of the book. But the story of how that happened is significantly more complex and nuanced than a simple assertion of Christianity's Jewish roots. Not only did the early Christians take for themselves the Jewish sacred library, but they read and interpreted those Jewish texts in light of their conviction that Jesus was the Messiah of God foretold by the prophets of Israel. In light of that messianic conviction, the Jewish texts were read differently and seemed to point to a new understanding of salvation-history, with Christ positioned at the center of the emerging church's narrative of redemption. This new story of redemption did not appear full blown with the appearance of Jesus, but it started to develop early on and reached a surprising level of sophistication already in the first decades and centuries of the church. To put it another way, the early followers of Christ began to do a kind of biblical theology (that is, of the Jewish Bible) to work out the implications of who Jesus was and what his life, crucifixion, and resurrection meant. This is certainly not the only thing going in the early church, but it seems to have been one of the remarkable features that defined the church in the first decades.

The early centuries of the church were a time of creative ferment that produced whole new sets of texts and traditions centering on Christology, theology, and the church. But what was the value of these texts and traditions for the church, and how would they be incorporated into its life and experience of Christ? This is a process that would unfold over the first three or four centuries of the church as new texts were being written and the New Testament canon was being formed. Despite the arguments of Marcion in the second century,[1] the church would ultimately position its New Testament alongside the Jewish Scriptures, now called the Old Testament, to form the Christian Bible. With some disagreements over the Old Testament Apocryphal books (those additional books included in Roman Catholic and many Orthodox Old Testaments but not included in the Jewish Hebrew Bible or Protestant Old Testaments), all branches of the church have claimed the Bible as critical to their identity and life, but equally have continued to grapple with the nuances of its meaning and interpretation. The twenty-seven books ultimately included in the New Testament canon are, as we have already seen, not the only books produced in the church. A vast body of literature was generated by gnostics and other so-called heretical groups, as well as by other people who elaborated stories about Jesus and the apostles. But what were the processes that led to the inclusion of some books and not others? That too is part of the church's story in its early centuries, and it is this story we will examine in this chapter.

But first we must consider some of the terminology that will appear in this chapter. The English word *canon* derives from a Greek word that refers to a measuring stick in the sense of a rule or standard. In that sense, the Christian canon is the rule or standard for Christian belief and practice. More generally, we also use the word *canon* simply to refer to the body of authoritative books included in the Bible. The term *canonization*, then, designates the process of forming a canon. When referring to the Jewish Bible, we often identify it as the Old Testament. But it is important to keep in mind that this is a Christian theological designation for the Jewish Bible, and as such it stands alongside the New Testament. For Jews, strictly speaking, it is not the Old Testament because they have no New Testament, even though they have much authoritative literature that is not part of the Bible,

---

1. See above, p. 64.

such as the Mishnah and the Talmud.[2] The term *Old Testament* is perhaps appropriate to use even outside Christian circles, if we know what we mean by the term and what it implies. An even better designation might simply be *Hebrew Bible*; this term refers to the language in which it was written and distinguishes this material from the Greek New Testament. Some scholars have chosen to use the terms *First Testament* and *Second Testaments* to designate the different parts of the Christian Bible, though in general usage this is uncommon. Perhaps an even better name for the Hebrew Bible is TANAK, an acronym consisting of three consonants and two vowels. Each consonant is the first letter in the word that designates a section of the Hebrew Bible, and the three sections are the Torah, the Nevi'm (Prophets), and the Kethuvim (Writings). This acronym refers to the three traditional parts of the Hebrew Bible. Narrowly speaking, the term *Torah* designates the first five books of the Hebrew Bible, or in other words the Pentateuch: Genesis, Exodus, Leviticus, Numbers, and Deuteronomy. More broadly, the word *Torah* can also refer to the Jewish Bible as a whole and to the oral torah, represented in texts such as the Mishnah. While the term is often translated into English as "law," this word does not adequately capture the full sense of the Hebrew word, which also designates communal narratives, mythologies, and instructions. Finally, two expressions used by the author of 2 Timothy (3:15-16 NRSV) are important to keep in mind here as well because this epistolary text uses two Greek terms that are often translated as "sacred writings" and "Scripture." The passage in 2 Timothy is also the most direct biblical text referring to the "God-breathed" nature of these sacred writings. Or, should we say, the divinely inspired nature of these sacred writings? The text reads as follows: "[14] But as for you, continue in what you have learned and firmly believed, knowing from whom you learned it, [15] and how from childhood you have known the *sacred writings* that are able to instruct you for salvation through faith in Christ Jesus. [16] *All scripture is inspired by God and is useful for teaching, for reproof, for correction, and for training in righteousness.*" The writer is most likely referring to the Jewish Scriptures as the sacred writings, as there would have been as yet no New Testament texts understood as scriptural or sacred. In any case, it is clear that by the time 2 Timothy was written, certain texts were being designated as special, that is, as sacred and scriptural.

---

2. Aageson, *In the Beginning*, 19-25.

THE HEBREW BIBLE AND ITS CANONIZATION

Unlike the New Testament, which is the literature of a religious or faith community, the Hebrew Bible is closer to a national literature. It was written, revised, and edited by a people who for much of their early history were centered on a particular piece of real estate at the eastern end of the Mediterranean. And these texts, as well as the traditions upon which they were founded, developed over the better part of a millennium. These texts tell the stories of a people: their religious conceptions, to be sure, but also their history, poetry, mythology, wisdom, and prophetic challenges. It is a large body of literature that was edited and revised, and in some cases supplemented, over time. Eventually it came to be canonized and in that process separated from all the other texts and literatures produced by the people of Israel.

How that process took place is still debated, but the traditional view is that the three parts of the Hebrew Bible (Torah, Prophets, and Writings) were themselves the result of the canonization process. First, the Pentateuch and the most important part of the tradition came to be canonized, perhaps sometime during the fifth century BCE. The books of the Pentateuch were not so much in competition with other books for inclusion in the canon. Rather, the traditions and texts of this body of material were revised and supplemented over time, perhaps most especially as a result of the Babylonian exile during the sixth century BCE. In time, this material came to have a privileged place in the life and religion of the people of Israel. Somewhat later, the prophetic texts, both the Former and Latter, came to be canonized and included in the sacred library of Israel, even though they held somewhat less authority than the Torah texts. Finally, the writings, a diverse body of literature, came to define the third section of the Jewish Bible. The entire process was brought to conclusion in 90 CE at a council of rabbis at Yavneh, perhaps in response to the rise of early Christianity. While it is unclear whether this council ever officially considered the issue of closing the canon, it is the case that by the time of earliest Christianity the extent and form of the Jewish Bible was largely set. The earliest followers of Christ who produced the texts that would eventually be included in the New Testament turned to Jewish scriptural texts and cited them with regularity. For example, the writer of the Gospel of Matthew frequently quoted the Jewish Bible to show how Jesus and the events of his life fulfilled the prophecies of old, and Paul in his letters explicitly quoted from the Jewish biblical books about a hundred times. While other traditions and texts may be echoed in the words of the New Testament authors, rarely if ever are nonbiblical texts quoted directly by them.

Roger Beckwith has presented a somewhat revised version of how the Hebrew Bible was canonized. Instead of a three stage process, he argues for a two stage process where the books thought to come from Moses were considered authoritative, distinguished over time from the books not attributed to Moses, and in the end effectively canonized. Later the non-Mosaic books were grouped together, a grouping that was subsequently divided into two parts, thus constituting the sections we call respectively the Prophets and the Writings. He argues that this process was completed before the first century CE and perhaps as early as the second century BCE.[3] According to this scenario, the Hebrew Bible had effectively been canonized well before the rise of earliest Christianity, thus clearly making Judaism a religion of the book. Both of these descriptions of how the Hebrew Bible was canonized confirm this. In no way, however, should the claim that both Judaism and subsequently Christianity became religions of the book be construed to suggest other texts and traditions were not also authoritative for the respective religions. The effective closing of the respective canons hardly meant that new traditions ceased to be developed and new texts written. The contrary is the case, even as the respective biblical canons function as foundational for the two religions.

Another development associated with the Hebrew Bible also needs to be noted here because of its importance for understanding the early church's use of the Jewish Scriptures. That is the translation of the Hebrew Bible into Greek, perhaps as early as the fourth century BCE. The process of translation is described rather stylistically in the Letter of Aristeas, but the historical reality is that in the city of Alexandria, Egypt, centuries before the time of Christ the Hebrew biblical texts were systematically translated into Greek. The process was precipitated by the fact that by this time many Jews had become Hellenized and no longer spoke or read Hebrew. If the Scriptures were to be accessible to them, they needed them translated into the language they now spoke. This translation became known as the *Septuagint* (designated by the Roman numeral for 70, LXX). Greek versions of the Hebrew scriptural texts became in effect the Bible for most of the early Christians. The writings that would become the New Testament documents were in Greek, and the Old Testament for increasing numbers of early Christians was also in Greek, just as it was for many of the diaspora Jews of the Mediterranean basin.

---

3. Beckwith, *Old Testament Canon of the New Testament Church*, 164–66.

FROM ORAL TRADITIONS TO CHRISTIAN TEXTS

By the end of the first century, all or almost all of the documents that would eventually be canonized in the New Testament had been written. During Jesus's lifetime and immediately after his death, oral traditions about him and what he did began to develop and be passed down by word of mouth. This was a vibrant process of remembrance and elaboration based on the community's experience of Jesus as the living Christ. But during the last half of the first century, many of these oral traditions were woven together into gospel narratives and written down. Other teaching sayings of Jesus were also apparently written down. What prompted the tradition to be written is complex, but several factors probably played a role in this process. For one thing, the eyewitnesses to Jesus's ministry were dying or had died, and still Christ had not returned. It undoubtedly occurred to many in the early church that the time before Christ's return might be longer than they had originally expected. Thus, the tradition needed to be stabilized and preserved as only writing could do. This did not mean that oral stories came to an end. But now a written tradition developed, against which the many stories about Jesus would eventually be heard and judged. Furthermore, the church during the last half of the first century began to spread quite dramatically into the larger Greco-Roman world. With that expansion, there was likely an added need to stabilize the Jesus tradition so the message of Jesus did not expand without limits or without attention to what was actually remembered about his life. We might also speculate that as the church spread into the Greco-Roman world there were increasing numbers of Christians who could read, and for whom reading and oral performance based on written texts was possible and desirable. Another factor that may have played a role at least for those closely connected to Israel's traditional homeland, was the destruction of Jerusalem and the temple in 70. This was a catastrophe for Jews, as we have seen above,[4] but presumably it also had consequences for some in the early church as well. Some Jesus followers no doubt felt the need to develop the church institutionally, and part of this development included preserving and elaborating in writing traditions about Jesus.

Even before the gospels were written, Paul, later to become Saint Paul, wrote letters. These were written during the decade of the 50s, and today the Pauline corpus of letters makes up almost half of the New Testament books. Paul used the letter form to communicate with his churches and to address problems that had arisen. He travelled throughout the region and his churches were spread across much of Greece and Asia Minor, which

---

4. See above, pp. 44–46.

meant he could not always be present with them except through his letters. Paul was a preacher and evangelist, but he was also a letter writer, and his letters were undoubtedly read aloud to the congregations to which they were sent. However, there is evidence that they also began to circulate more broadly early on, both because of what they said, and because of Paul's own apostolic authority. In short, Paul, a man at home in the world of Greek culture and learning, was also an early contributor to the church's becoming a community of texts and eventually to the New Testament itself. Writers of other epistles also contributed to the body of early church literature and to the formation of the New Testament. Together they helped set the church on the road to becoming a community of texts.

The use of texts, however, raised a host of new issues that would affect the church's life and ability to deal with the realities associated with texts. As we know today, with the advent of the digital revolution and social media, the various platforms for communicating impose requirements on users. Our ability to communicate on a given platform depends on everything from managing our devices to coping with and constructively using an overabundance of information. In the ancient world, the use of texts also raised certain problems and imposed certain requirements on people and communities. How were texts to be reproduced? Who would copy them, and what if variations entered in the copies that were made, as they surely would? What would the texts be written on, and how would the pages be assembled? What about the cost of reproductions, and who could afford them? Given their bulk, how would texts be collected and transported? Might smaller groupings of texts circulate independently from other, related texts? How would these groupings be determined? And perhaps above all, what changes would take place as these texts were heard as documents read aloud rather than as stories told (with all the interactivity of storytelling, communicated by facial expression, voice volume, and tone)?

A lot is communicated when one is speaking face-to-face that has little to do with the words being spoken. When one is reading a text, much of that nonverbal communication disappears, and readers must interpret those dimensions of communication themselves. Or even when texts are read aloud to a group, the reader will invariably interpret the text to the audience through the subtleties of vocal inflection and emphasis. As an illustration, think about the difference between reading a comedian's joke and hearing it told with great skill. They are two different experiences. Or think about reading one of Jesus's parables as opposed to hearing it told on a hillside over a campfire. In telling a good joke or a good parable, the setup may change depending on the audience's response, but the punch line of the joke or the point of the parable must be correct and on time. But if one reads a parable from a text, an implicit repetitive uniformity sets in based on conformity to the printed words that do not change. The point of this comparison between oral texts and written texts is to illustrate that as early Christian communities increasingly began to rely on written texts and eventually on a canon, communication and information management were also affected, sometimes in profound ways. Once the church became a community of texts, it needed to develop new ways of reproducing, preserving, disseminating, and interpreting them. Its world was changing.[5]

Today one only needs to look at a critical edition of the Greek New Testament to see the result of the proliferation of copies of the same text. Since none of the original copies of any New Testament books were preserved, what we have presently in our possession are copies of copies. Not surprisingly, this process of copying led to variations entering into the copies, and when that happened, every copy made from an earlier copy reflected those variations, unless the later copies were otherwise corrected.

Families of texts emerged for separate New Testament books. Each text family bore a set of peculiarities that developed over time. Many of the variations among text families are insignificant or subtle, but not all of them. Some have important theological implications. Mark's Gospel, for instance, has shorter and longer endings depending on which manuscript tradition is followed. Did the original text end after verse 16:8, or did it continue on to verse 20?

The selection below from the critical edition of the Greek New Testament is what is generally thought to be Mark's original ending. The apparatus included shows all the variations for Mark 16:2–8. If a person knows how to interpret the symbols of the apparatus, it becomes clear how all of the various known manuscripts of Mark's Gospel read. It also becomes clear that critical editions of the New Testament are reconstructed texts based on all the known manuscripts. Furthermore, the editors of the Greek New Testament make judgments about which manuscripts and which readings are most likely original and should therefore be included in the body of the text. Various text-critical criteria have been developed to assist in this process, and virtually all serious modern-language translations of the New Testament are based in turn on these critically reconstructed texts. The texts of the New Testament as we know them today are the result of historical and intellectual processes that have developed over time.

---

5. See, Aageson, *In the Beginning*, 51–62.

16,2–8   ΚΑΤΑ ΜΑΡΚΟΝ   174

1K 16,2! 2 ⌜καὶ λίαν πρωΐ τῇ μιᾷ τῶν σαββάτων ἔρχονται⌝ ἐπὶ τὸ ²³¹
⌜μνημεῖον ᶠἀνατείλαντος τοῦ ἡλίου. 3 καὶ ἔλεγον πρὸς
15,46 ἑαυτάς· τίς ἀποκυλίσει ἡμῖν τὸν λίθον ἐκ τῆς θύρας τοῦ
μνημείου; ᵀ 4 ⌜καὶ ἀναβλέψασαι θεωροῦσιν ὅτι ⌜ἀποκε-
Mt 27,60 κύλισται ὁ λίθος· ἦν γὰρ μέγας σφόδρα⌝. ·
2Mcc 3,26.33 5 Καὶ ⌜εἰσελθοῦσαι εἰς τὸ μνημεῖον εἶδον νεανίσκον
9,3 Act 1,10! Ap 6,11! καθήμενον ἐν τοῖς δεξιοῖς περιβεβλημένον στολὴν λευ-
9,15! | κήν, καὶ ἐξεθαμβήθησαν. 6 ὁ δὲ λέγει αὐταῖς· μὴ ἐκθαμ- ²³²
1,9! βεῖσθε· Ἰησοῦν ζητεῖτε ᴰτὸν Ναζαρηνὸν⸌ τὸν ἐσταυρω-
1K 15,4 μένον· ἠγέρθη, οὐκ ἔστιν ὧδε· ⸌ἴδε ὁ τόπος⸍ ὅπου ἔθηκαν
1,36! αὐτόν. 7 ἀλλ' ὑπάγετε εἴπατε τοῖς μαθηταῖς αὐτοῦ καὶ τῷ
14,28 Πέτρῳ ὅτι ⌜προάγει ὑμᾶς εἰς τὴν Γαλιλαίαν· ἐκεῖ ᶠαὐτὸν
ὄψεσθε, καθὼς ⌜¹εἶπεν ὑμῖν.
5,14 1Hen 106,4.12 8 ⌜Καὶ ἐξελθοῦσαι⌝ ἔφυγον ἀπὸ τοῦ μνημείου, εἶχεν ²³³
5,42! γὰρ αὐτὰς ⌜τρόμος καὶ ἔκστασις· καὶ οὐδενὶ οὐδὲν εἶπαν·
4,41; 5,15.33; 10,32 ἐφοβοῦντο γάρ. ᵀ

2 ⌜και λιαν (− και λιαν W) πρωι μια των (−f¹) σαββατων ερχονται B W f¹ ¦ και
λιαν πρωι της μιας (+ των K f¹³) σαββατων ερχονται A C K Γ f¹³ 28. 579. 700. 1241.
1424. 2542ˢ 𝔐 syʰ ¦ και ερχονται πρωι μιας σαββατου D ¦ txt ℵ L Δᶜ (− των Δ*) Θ Ψ
33. 565. 892. (l 844). l 2211; Eus | ⌜μνημα ℵ* C* W Θ 565 ¦ txt ℵ² A B C³ D K L Γ Δ Ψ
083 f¹·¹³ 28. 33. 579. 700. 892. 1241. 1424. 2542ˢ. l 844. l 2211 𝔐; Eus | ᶠ ανατελλοντος
D c n q • 3 ᵀ subito autem ad horam tertiam tenebrae diei factae sunt per totum orbem
terrae et descenderunt de caelis angeli et surgent in claritate vivi Dei; simul ascenderunt
cum eo et continuo lux facta est k • 4 ⌜ην γαρ μεγας σφοδρα και ερχονται και
ευρισκουσιν αποκεκυλισμενον τον λιθον D 565 c ff² n (syˢ; Eus) ¦ και αναβλε-
ψασαι θεωρουσιν ανακεκυλισμενον τον λιθον· ην γαρ μεγας σφοδρα ℵ ¦ ⌜ανα-
κεκυλισται B L ¦ txt A C K W Γ Δ Ψ f¹·¹³ 28. 33. 579. 700. 892. 1241. 1424. 2542ˢ.
l 844. l 2211 𝔐 • 5 ⌜ελθουσαι B • 6 ᴰℵ* D ¦ ⌜ειδετε εκει τοπον (− D*) τοπον αυτου
D*·¹ (c ff²) ¦ ειδετε εκει ο τοπος αυτου εστιν W ¦ ιδε εκει ο τοπος αυτου Θ 565
• 7 ⌜ηγερθη απο νεκρων και ιδου προαγει f¹ ¦ ιδου προαγω D k ¦ ᶠμε D k. ¦
⌜¹ειρηκα D k • 8 ⌜κακουσασαι Θ ¦ και ακουσαντες 565 ¦ και ακουσασαι εξηλθον
και W (099) syˢ·(ᵖ·ʰᵐᵍ) ¦ ⌜φοβος D W it saᵐˢ

A similar situation pertains in the case of the Hebrew Bible as well. Prior to the discovery of the Dead Sea Scrolls, the earliest manuscripts we had of the Hebrew Bible were from medieval times, but with the discovery of the scrolls copies or fragments of copies of every book of the Hebrew Bible except Esther were found. This means that in one fell archaeological swoop we discovered manuscripts older by a thousand years than any we had in our possession before that time. The implications of this are still being investigated over a half century later.[6]

---

6. The copy of the Greek New Testament above is Nestle-Aland's 28th Revised Edition.

NEW TESTAMENT TEXTS AND THEIR CANONIZATION

Once a body of early Christian literature had been produced, circulated, and valued as important to the church's faith and life, it became necessary over time to define the canonical list and set its number. That process took from the late first or early second centuries to the fourth or fifth century, when the New Testament canon became fully formed and established. The two testaments of the Christian Bible were by then largely set, even though there would be debates over the place of the Old Testament Apocrypha for some time to come—for example, during the Protestant Reformation in the West during the sixteenth century. Once again, we need to be reminded that the formation of the New Testament canon did not limit the development of new traditions and theologies in the early church. We might say that early in the canonization process there was not even a very clear line between emerging Christian tradition and Scripture. In fact, the texts that came to be part of the New Testament Scriptures began as traditions that over time accrued authority as their usage and value in the church grew. Only after the New Testament canon was fixed did the line between Scripture and tradition become pronounced.

So how did the authority of certain early Christian texts grow and end up eventually being included in the New Testament canon? Let me begin by saying that in my view, this was neither an utterly random nor a tightly controlled and centralized ecclesiastical process. To be sure, it was political in the broad sense, but, even more to the point, it was a dynamic process shaped by the life, practice, piety, and experience of the early church. It was also shaped by what we might call textual "workshops" or "schools" that were devoted to preserving, collecting, and circulating certain texts. In other words, the canonical process was not a free-for-all of individual texts competing for inclusion in the New Testament canon. As Harry Gamble has said, the New Testament canon was less a collection of individual documents than it was a collection of collections: a collection of gospels, of letters of Paul, and of so-called catholic letters.[7] Beyond these were the book of Acts and the Revelation to John, which may have come to be associated with the Gospel of Luke and letters of Paul (in the case of Acts) and with the Gospel of John and the three epistles of John (in the case of Revelation).

Hence, the process of canonization began on a smaller scale as certain collections of texts about Jesus and letters by Paul came to circulate for the benefit and edification of various churches. It is also possible that this

---

7. Gamble, "Canon, New Testament," 853.

process itself started on a still smaller scale as individual letters of Paul circulated to churches other than the ones to which they were originally sent. For example, some scholars argue that Paul's letter to the Romans, because of its theological significance, circulated early on to other congregations and that this can be seen in the divided manuscript tradition of the epistle. Whether or not this is suggested by the manuscript tradition of Romans, the idea that some of Paul's letters very early on were copied and passed to other congregations seems distinctly plausible, if not likely.[8] If Paul himself was responsible for circulating them, this process would have indeed begun very early and established a pattern to be replicated over time.[9] During the early stages of this process, the church's institutional structure, though beginning to take shape, would have had insufficient centralized authority to direct this process from an ecclesiastical center. Perhaps later that may have been possible, but certainly not during the earliest phases of this canonical process. Hence, I think it likely this process began in a dynamic way on the local levels of the church and in ways that were neither centralized nor random. From there, the process spread more broadly throughout the emergent Catholic Church, until eventually the New Testament canon was more or less accepted and in that sense effectively closed.

In this process, canonization also moved in conjunction with the struggle in the early centuries of the church to define Christian orthodoxy and distinguish it from heresy. The church would develop its "rule of faith" (*regula fidei* in Latin), the norm for the church's faith, and the emerging New Testament Scriptures unsurprisingly conformed to this rule of faith. Even as the church contributed to the formation of the rule of faith, it also produced the New Testament documents. From the outside, the process certainly appears to be circular, and in many ways it was. But it was also organic, and in that sense it was a natural process that moved back and forth between the emerging New Testament texts and the desire to establish the theological heart of Christian truth. The *regula fidei* validated the New Testament texts, and the New Testament texts informed and shaped the *regula fidei*. When one appreciates the organic nature of this process, it seems, I would argue, more natural and less institutionally arbitrary. Moreover, this process took place over an extended period of time when authority accrued to certain texts because churches used and valued them, and churches turned to these same texts because they had authority and provided access to Christ, who was the one who through word, ritual practice, and experience constituted the church. In that sense, these texts were windows into ongoing life with

---

8. See the argument in Pervo, *Making of Paul*, 229–39.
9. See, Trobisch, *Paul's Letter Collection*, especially 97–98.

Christ in the context of worship and devotion. In short, the texts had redemptive significance for the community of faith and as such had authority.

The early church was built on a number of things, among them the Old Testament, the apostles, missionary work among the Gentiles, and—most important—Jesus Christ. Very quickly following his crucifixion, Jesus Christ became the foundation of the church and the wellspring for Christian faith and practice. It should be no surprise that historical and theological proximity to Jesus Christ would give certain texts special authority. The closeness to Jesus (sometimes called *apostolicity*) privileged certain texts and not others. It could be that apostolicity was determined simply on the basis of a name associated with a particular writing. So our four gospels are associated with Matthew, Mark, Luke, and John—all important names connected to Jesus's ministry. But we know that initially the gospel texts did not bear these names. They were attached to the texts only later. To claim that these texts were considered apostolic simply because they bore these apostolic names is perhaps possible, but it seems much more likely that the texts were given these names precisely because they were already considered in some sense apostolic. If that is the case, the apostolic claim must have rested on some basis other than mere authorship.[10] Whether or not the canonical writings were actually composed by one of Christ's apostles, they were thought to come from the early period of the church, and in that sense were close to the founding events of Christian life and practice. And—critically important—the canonical writings were spiritually useful, even as they were linked theologically to the foundation of the church, Jesus Christ. If usage in the church's practice was important in the process of canonization, the *catholicity*, or universal applicability, of a text was also important. But canonicity involved more than simply authorship, theological conformity, or catholicity. Inclusion in the canon rested mostly on the church's actual usage of a given document in practice. Without this, it is unlikely any document would ultimately be considered canonical by the church.[11]

While Harry Gamble categorically denies that the struggle with Marcion and Montanus motivated the church to close the New Testament canon,[12] it is still helpful to see them (and what they represented) as contributing to the church's decisions about the limits of the New Testament canon. To be sure, the canonical process began prior to Marcion and Montanus and was certainly not completed by the second or third century. However, the challenges these two men presented to the church illustrate even today

---

10. See Gamble, "Canon, New Testament," 858.
11. Ibid.
12. Ibid., 857.

the need for the church to struggle with the extent of its canon. As we saw above,[13] Marcion, a second-century convert, wished to sever Christianity from the Old Testament, believing that the God represented in it was a God of wrath and judgment whereas the God present in Jesus Christ was a God of mercy and love. Of the emerging New Testament documents, he wanted to retain only the Gospel of Luke and the epistles of Paul purged of all references to the Old Testament. If the church had adopted Marcion's position, the Christian Bible would have been a great deal smaller than it turned out to be. On the other hand, Montanus, along with the two female prophets Maxmilla and Priscilla, proclaimed that the end was near and the age of the Spirit had arrived. Believing the Spirit had spoken to them as to the apostles, they produced a body of material for which they claimed authority and perhaps even inclusion in the sacred library of the church. The Montanists persisted in the church for quite some time and attracted adherents to their cause; for example, Tertullian, a formidable Christian from North Africa. But in the end they did not carry the day in the church and ultimately receded from view. Yet both Marcion and the Montanists, and what they represented, presented the church with serious challenges. What is to be the scope of the church's canon? Obviously, in the end neither these movements nor their claims about Scripture and divine revelation satisfied the needs of the church's canonical process. But it is easy to see how such claims might prompt the church to clarify its thinking about the canonical process and about what in fact constitutes the Christian canon. Beyond this, it is not possible to be more specific about the roles Marcion and Montanus played in the canonization of the New Testament.

If the New Testament canonization process included gatherings of smaller collections of documents that were later assembled into the canon, we need to consider the features of those earlier collections. Richard Pervo argues one of the most detailed theses regarding the making of Paul and the development of the Pauline canon. He asserts that one of the first tasks of those who wished to support the communities Paul had started was to assemble his occasional correspondence into a book.[14] He contends further that by the end of the first century a collection of ten Pauline letters began to circulate, a process that involved universalizing what began in fact as occasional letters dealing with local issues.[15] If the letters were to help stabilize and nourish the Pauline and other communities, they needed to have wider

---

13. See above, pp. 64, 244-45.
14. Pervo, *Making of Paul*, 230.
15. Ibid., 230. See also my argument regarding the earliest canonical impulses in Aageson, *Paul, the Pastoral Epistles, and the Early Church*, 90-102.

applicability. Moreover, the use of common texts by different church communities helped knit churches together, which in its own way contributed to the formation of Catholic Christianity. The Paul portrayed in Acts and subsequently in the legendary Acts of Paul began to flesh out the apostle and his ministry among the Gentiles. As Pervo states, by the middle of the second century there were different Pauls competing with each other. The Pauline synthesis that finally prevailed in the church was the Paul of Acts.[16] Richard Pervo writes:

> The synthesis that became normative, however, is that of the canonical Acts, which follow a line reflected in different ways by Romans, Ephesians, and the Pastoral Epistles. Paul is a universal apostle and a heroic figure. Building upon thoughts such as those expressed in Romans, as well as Ephesians, the Paul of Acts stands in continuity with the tradition and faith of Israel, which has reached its fullest and most proper expression in the message of Jesus. Jesus and Paul are wandering teachers and social critics, but their message is milder and less antithetical to all of the roots of the social order. Paul, like Luke's Jesus, is more a reformer than a revolutionary.[17]

More than just an important figure in early Christianity, Paul became the foundational figure of early Christianity, argues Pervo.[18] And if that was the case, his letters represented and presented him and his authority in tangible form to the church.[19] The other New Testament letters, the so-called Catholic Epistles, were also assembled, and, as Gamble suggests, may have been collected to provide witness to the other apostolic figures, namely, Peter, James, and John. This collection probably did not arise until the third century and then perhaps as an attempt to counterbalance the collection of Paul's letters.[20]

Given Christianity's focus on and devotion to Jesus, it is not surprising that the church would collect traditions, both oral and written, about what he had done and said. The oral traditions about him emerged early in the postresurrection Christ communities, and written traditions about him appeared well before the end of the first century. The writing of the gospels did not mean the oral tradition ceased; but, as argued above, the writing of the

---

16. Pervo, *Making of Paul*, 233–34.

17. Ibid., 234.

18. Ibid., 237.

19. See also the arguments by Trobisch in *Paul's Letter Collection* and the essays in Porter, *Pauline Canon*.

20. Gamble, "Canon, New Testament," 855.

gospels launched the church on a new path for preserving and disseminating the stories of Jesus. As we see in the four New Testament gospels, the image of Jesus that prevailed is of a crucified messiah. All of the teachings of Jesus and the events in his life are molded into narratives that feature the redemptive significance of his death and resurrection. While the Q material and the emphasis on signs in John suggest that other approaches to Jesus's significance were also at play in the early church (for example, Jesus the teacher, Jesus the miracle worker, and Jesus the revealer of signs), even this material was incorporated by Matthew, Mark, Luke, and John into their narratives of the crucified Christ. The proliferation of apocryphal gospels in the early centuries of the church, and the presence of the *Diatessaron* of Tatian from around 170 (which wove together the four gospels into one supergospel), suggests that two impulses were at work in the gospel tradition of the early church: the desire both to elaborate and interpret the Jesus tradition and (at the same time) to condense and unify the tradition.[21] In the end, of course, the church sought a middle ground. It maintained the fourfold gospel tradition, but it did not open the door of the gospel collection wide enough to include a host of other stories about Jesus. Here too the issue was not simply the volume of tradition about Jesus but how those traditions presented him. The Jesus tradition that ultimately prevailed canonically was that of the crucified messiah. Hence, the tension in the quest for comprehensiveness and for a single, consistent gospel tradition was set alongside the desire for a gospel tradition that portrayed an appropriate christological image of Jesus as the crucified Messiah and redeemer of the world.

There are several important canonical lists, but for our purposes I will list in conclusion only the New Testament documents that appear in the Muratorian Canon and the list Eusebius gives in his *Ecclesiastical History*. The date of the Muratorian Canon is debated but may be as early as the second or early third century, or as late as the fourth century. Eusebius's *Ecclesiastical History*, and hence his canonical list, dates from early in the fourth century.

MURATORIAN CANON

Four Gospels—Presumably Matthew Mark, Luke, and John

Acts

13 letters of Paul, not including Hebrews

---

21. Ibid., 854.

Jude

1 & 2 John

Wisdom of Solomon

Revelation

Apocalypse of Peter

(Note the exclusion of the Catholic Epistles and the inclusion of the Wisdom of Solomon and the so-called Apocalypse of Peter. The Shepherd of Hermas and Pauline letters to the Laodiceans and Alexandrians were specifically rejected. We note here that twenty-four books are identified, two of which were not included in the New Testament canon, and five of which, though not listed, were eventually included: 3 John, 1 and 2 Peter, Hebrews, and James.)

EUSEBIUS'S LIST

Recognized Books

> Four Gospels—Presumably Matthew, Mark, Luke, John
>
> Acts
>
> Epistles of Paul
>
> First Epistle of John
>
> Epistle of Peter
>
> Revelation (?)

Disputed Books

> James
>
> Jude
>
> Second Epistle of Peter
>
> Second and Third Epistles of John

Not Genuine Books

> Acts of Paul

Shepherd

Apocalypse of Peter

Letter of Barnabas

The Teachings of the Apostles (Didache)

Revelation(?)

Gospel of the Hebrews (special to some)

Gospels of Peter, Thomas, and Matthias

Acts of Andrew, John, and other apostles

(We note here the considerable diversity of documents that have some status in the church and those Eusebius simply rejected out of hand.)

13

Location and Legacy, Church and Opposition, Function and Formation

What are some of the critical social currents of early Christianity that help us understand the church's complexity in its formative early years and why do these features of the church matter?

If we look at the cradle of early Christianity broadly, we see that there are regional differences and legacies, centrifugal and centripetal forces that tug at the emerging institutional church, and functional features that shape the church's life and practice. In short, the early church did not simply operate on the level of abstract theology or religious faith. It was firmly anchored in the places where it took root, and it began to absorb and reflect features of those places. The social dynamics that gave birth to the church were also important in shaping the institution that would become Catholic Christianity. Having examined a number of the New Testament and early Christian textual traditions, we now turn our attention to other factors that shaped early Christianity. So far we have looked at issues of empire, the formation of the Christian canon, and in the next chapter will investigate early Christian worship. But in this chapter we are trying to understand the contextual, regional, and social features that influenced different parts of the church.

At the risk of oversimplification, I would argue that two traditional ways of looking at the origin and development of early Christianity are equally problematic. The first is the claim that Christianity during the age of the apostles represented a unified, harmonious golden age after which the purity of the church was tarnished and corrupted. In short, we might call this view of the church, from the golden age of purity to corruption. And the second view is that the church progressed from its original primitive state to an ever more enlightened and sophisticated state as it grew and moved beyond its origin in Palestine. We might call this view the idea of Christian progress. My objection is not that there is little of value in these two portraits of Christian origins. There was a kind of simplistic purity in the apostolic age of the church where the mystical spirituality of Jesus lived on among his followers. The early church was not yet overly concerned with institutional and dogmatic debates. But that stage was probably destined to pass away naturally as the church grew, spread, and confronted a variety of challenges. And to be sure, the church certainly did develop more insightful and sophisticated ways of articulating the faith and the meaning of Jesus. In that sense, there clearly was and continued to be a progressive element in the church's thinking and practice. But that development was not always, in my view, movement from the more primitive to less primitive, from less enlightened to more enlightened. For example, the turn to patriarchy in the second or third generation of the church was not progress. It was rather conformity to a larger patriarchal culture and, if anything, was regression. Likewise, it took the church a long time to challenge the social status quo regarding hierarchy, status, and power once it had achieved these itself. On the contrary, the church seemed to exercise all these with ruthless skill for centuries.

If this is the case, how from a historical, religious, and ethical point of view might we think generally about the early church? I suggest we understand the church as a relatively pluralistic and complex phenomenon from the beginning, and as it grew, these features became even more pronounced. The people attracted to the church were diverse. The problems confronting the church were complex. The early church was marked by contention and division. And different areas of the early church exhibited distinctly regional characteristics, just as they do today. Even as there were times of consolidation when the drive for agreement marked large parts of the church, there were also times when the edges frayed and contention prevailed. In short, the early church was not normally a quiet or serene place. It was often, perhaps most often, marked by some level of contention. The irony of this is that these times of disagreement were often among the times of most creative ferment as well. To put it another way, the early church was never just one thing, and early on it struggled with its own sense of identity. It was a work in progress, and the outcome was anything but certain.

LOCATION

If we survey Christianity during the early decades and centuries of the Common Era, we see that it spread to virtually all sides of the Mediterranean basin: Palestine, greater Syria, Asia Minor, Greece, Rome, Egypt, the upper Nile, Gaul, and Spain. Most of these areas fell under the sway of the Roman Empire, but that does not mean that culturally they were all the same. For example, Irenaeus was born in western Asia Minor sometime in the middle of the second century. He also comments on having seen Polycarp, the bishop of Smyrna, as a youth. Shortly after his arrival in the city of Lyon in Gaul in either 177 or 178, he became the bishop of the church there. In his lifetime, he spanned the church in the east and the church in the west, the Greek church of the eastern empire and the Latin church of the western empire. And he engaged the gnostic problems firmly rooted in the western church, as well as the emerging episcopal polity of the church in the east.

Likewise, Tertullian was a significant theological presence in the Latin church of North Africa, and bears many theological similarities to Irenaeus.[1] We also know that Tertullian seems to have had links to Asia Minor with regard to the Thecla tradition. For instance, he wrote:

> But if the writings which wrongly (falsely) go under Paul's name, claim Thecla's example as a license for women's teaching and baptizing, let them know that, in Asia, the presbyter who composed that writing, as if he were augmenting Paul's fame from his own store, after being convicted, and confessing that he had done it from love of Paul, was removed from office. (*De baptismo* 17:5)[2]

The Thecla story, from Tertullian's point of view a fraud perpetuated by a presbyter in Asia, came to his attention as being used to authorize women to teach and baptize. He writes these words to delegitimate these practices by women and their use of the Thecla story to authorize them. He says the women who taught and baptized need to know the truth of what happened. Clearly he does not favor these practices by women, presumably by women in Asia Minor. Furthermore, later in his life Tertullian joined forces with the Montanists, who themselves were centered at a place called Pepuza, in Asia

---

1. Aageson, *Paul, the Pastoral Epistles, and the Early Church*, 158, 190–91.
2. See above, p. 128.

Minor. Irenaeus and Tertullian, both stalwarts of the Western church, had connections to the church in Asia Minor, but they (Irenaeus and certainly the pre-Montanist Tertullian) also represented notions of orthodoxy that seemed to prevail especially in the Latin west.[3]

Clement of Alexandria and Origen, both theologians from Egypt operating in the late second and third centuries, had different concerns and interests. Their work also seems to have been influenced by the intellectual traditions of Alexandria, once again reflecting the context within which they operated. Alexandria had long been Hellenized and immersed in Greek thought and culture.[4] Clement sought to bring the Christian faith and Greek philosophy together as he tried to nurture the souls of his students. Origen, on the other hand, was a scriptural exegete who tried to bring the word of God to life for those on the spiritual journey to perfection. They are both teachers and thinkers, not, as in the case of Irenaeus, a bishop charged with preserving and protecting the good order of the church. Whereas Irenaeus sought to provide a refutation to what he considered to be heresy, Clement and Origen each in their own way tried to think about the faith as teachers. Their locations and positions in the church undoubtedly left their imprint on them and may have occasionally caused them to push boundaries as Irenaeus and Tertullian might not have done. As teachers, not strictly institutional figures, Clement and Origen responded to their opponents with theological arguments and scriptural interpretations that in many ways reflected their Alexandrian environment.[5]

I have argued elsewhere that writings of Ignatius of Antioch and the New Testament letters of 1 Timothy and Titus are in the same line of development in terms of how they viewed the church. Clearly Ignatius had a more developed sense of the institutional church than the two epistles do, but generally speaking, Ignatius's writings and these Pastoral Epistles represented similar lines of thinking. If Ignatius is writing after 1 Timothy and Titus have appeared, it would stand to reason that he might have a more developed view of the church than those epistles offer. Likewise, the two epistles reflect developments in the church in Asia Minor as does Ignatius's own writing. So 1 Timothy, Titus, and the writings of Ignatius developed in one milieu and broadly share a view of the church.

If we compare the so-called letter of 1 Clement with the work of Ignatius and the Pastoral Epistles, we can detect a different development.

---

3. Aageson, *Paul, the Pastoral Epistles, and the Early Church*, 191.

4. We think of Philo of Alexandria, a first-century Jew whose writing was thoroughly influenced by Greek philosophy, perhaps most especially by Plato.

5. Aageson, *Paul, the Pastoral Epistles, and the Early Church*, 191.

Eusebius, the fourth-century church historian, identifies Clement as the third successor to Peter in Rome and marks his dates in office as 92–101. This would place him slightly earlier than Ignatius and his letters. (Ignatius dates from later during the reign of Trajan, 98–117.) Clement is in Rome when a controversy erupts in the Corinthian church. Certain people had rebelled against the local leaders, and this prompted Clement to write to the Corinthians in an effort to restore order to the church. Hence, 1 Clement, which we have in our possession today, is the letter he wrote. It is unlikely that the Corinthian church had appealed to the bishop of Rome to take action against the rebellious elements in Corinth, thereby signaling that the church in Rome had achieved superior status and could be called upon to settle disputes and bring order to the church.[6] The church in Rome with its bishop had not yet risen to that status. But Clement, the bishop of Rome, nonetheless writes to the Corinthians and addresses their problems. In the course of that discussion, Clement uses the term "bishop" or "overseer" interchangeably with the term "presbyter" or "elder."[7] On the face of it, this might suggest that the church in the Latin west did not exhibit as clearly a distinction between various church offices as did the church in Asia Minor. Even as the church grew, regional differences marked its development, and these need to be taken into account when thinking about the character of the church into the second century and beyond.

LEGACY

These developments, largely developments of the second century and later, rested on earlier views of the church. As we have already made clear,[8] perhaps the greatest controversy of the first century was Paul's notion that Gentiles could come into the church on the basis of faith and not obedience to certain torah expectations. This, of course, moved the church over time into the Gentile world of the Greco-Roman Empire, where it flourished and grew. The flipside of this is that Jewish Christianity became less and less significant over time. This was a watershed in the early church, but by the time of the second century the Pauline concern with Gentile inclusion had largely been dealt with, and the church for the most part moved on to other things. To be sure, the church would deal with Judaizing tendencies in certain corners for some time to come, but this would no longer be the major issue it had once been.

6. Quasten, *Patrology*, 1:43.
7. Aageson, *Paul, the Pastoral Epistles, and the Early Church*, 156.
8. See above, pp. 56–61.

Location & Legacy, Church & Opposition, Function & Formation 205

Another watershed in ecclesiastical development comes in the change from the Pauline notion of the church as the body of Christ to the church seen primarily in terms of leadership and offices.[9] We can see the Pauline idea most dramatically in 1 Cor 12 and Eph 4:

> 12 [14] Indeed, the body does not consist of one member but of many. [15] If the foot would say, "Because I am not a hand, I do not belong to the body," that would not make it any less a part of the body. [16] And if the ear would say, "Because I am not an eye, I do not belong to the body," that would not make it any less a part of the body. [17] If the whole body were an eye, where would the hearing be? If the whole body were hearing, where would the sense of smell be? [18] But as it is, God arranged the members in the body, each one of them, as he chose. [19] If all were a single member, where would the body be? [20] As it is, there are many members, yet one body. (12:14–20)

> 4 [4] There is one body and one Spirit, just as you were called to the one hope of your calling, [5] one Lord, one faith, one baptism, [6] one God and Father of all, who is above all and through all and in all. [7] But each of us was given grace according to the measure of Christ's gift . . . [11] The gifts he gave were that some would be apostles, some prophets, some evangelists, some pastors and teachers, [12] to equip the saints for the work of ministry, for building up the body of Christ, [13] until all of us come to the unity of the faith and of the knowledge of the Son of God, to maturity, to the measure of the full stature of Christ . . . [16] from whom the whole body, joined and knit together by every ligament with which it is equipped, as each part is working properly, promotes the body's growth in building itself up in love. (4:4–7, 11–13, 16)

The body with its many parts is here a metaphor for the unity of the church and the various gifts of church leadership.[10] The beauty and value of this image for the earliest church is perhaps self-evident, but by the late first century or early second century this image was no longer sufficient for the institutional needs of the church. It needed to cope over the longer term with the realities of life in the world. At this point we see the appearance in the church of officers and offices: bishops (overseers), deacons (servers), and presbyters (elders). Institutionally, the church began to develop beyond the image of the body to the hierarchical church, with its threefold office of

---

9. This is seen in various ways in the Pastoral Letters, Ignatius of Antioch, Polycarp, the Miletus speech of Acts 20, 1 Clement, and elsewhere.

10. See the argument by Neyrey, *Paul in Other Words*, 102–46.

ministry. This meant a profound and significant shift for the legacy of the church.

SOCIAL MAKEUP OF THE EARLY CHURCH

From the time of the early church until the twentieth century, it was commonly thought that early Christians came largely, if not exclusively, from the lower rungs of Greco-Roman society. Celsus, a second-century pagan writer, sought to disparage early Christianity by arguing that the church appealed only to the ignorant, the foolish, slaves, women, and children.[11] In more recent times, Marxist thinkers too saw the early Christians as lower-class people. They represented, even then, a proletarian movement so important to Marxist thinking and politics. Those who idealized poverty also saw early Christianity socially as part of the underbelly of Greco-Roman society. Modern scholars of early Christianity for a long time also assumed this to be the case. If we think about the life of Jesus and his disciples portrayed in the New Testament gospels, it is understandable how this view of the church's lower social standing might appear to be self-evident. Jesus and his disciples may not have been among the poorest of the poor in their world, but clearly they were rural villagers. With some exceptions, they were common laborers with limited skills and for various reasons on the margins of society. As a group, they certainly did not represent people of status and influence.[12]

But once the church moved into the larger Greco-Roman world and took root in cities such as Rome, Ephesus, and Corinth, was that still the case? This is a question that scholars concerned with the social context of early Christianity began to address starting thirty or forty years ago. People like Gerd Theissen, Wayne Meeks, E. A. Judge, and Abraham Malherbe were pioneers in this work, and with the help of social-scientific methodologies sought to examine the various status dimensions of early Christians and their communities. These efforts are based on the theoretical work of social scientists applied specifically to the history of the early church. It is painstaking work that often relies on drawing subtle inferences about the social, economic, and educational status of early Christian figures.

For example, Paul writes in 1 Cor 1:27 in a way that on the face of it gives us a clue as to the social status of the Corinthian Christians: "²⁷ But God chose what is foolish in the world to shame the wise; God chose what is weak in the world to shame the strong; ²⁸ God chose what is low and

11. Meeks, *First Urban Christians*, 51.
12. Ibid.

despised in the world, things that are not, to reduce to nothing things that are." If we were to read only these words, they would seem to confirm the perspective of Celsus. But the verse just preceding raises another possibility: "²⁶ Consider your own call, brothers and sisters: not many of you were wise by human standards, not many were powerful, not many were of noble birth." Here we notice the words "not many" repeated three times in English translation. A reasonable inference might be that at least some people in the Corinthian church were of some means, power, and social standing.[13] If correct, this would also suggest that the church in Corinth was made up to some extent of mixed-status people.

Likewise, we read in 1 Cor 11:17–34 about the problems in Corinth over the Eucharist and the common meal. Some scholars think the divisions are related to differences in socioeconomic status. Paul writes in 11:7–22 and 33–34:

> ⁷ Now in the following instructions I do not commend you, because when you come together it is not for the better but for the worse. ¹⁸ For, to begin with, when you come together as a church, I hear that there are divisions among you; and to some extent I believe it. ¹⁹ Indeed, there have to be factions among you, for only so will it become clear who among you are genuine. ²⁰ When you come together, it is not really to eat the Lord's supper. ²¹ For when the time comes to eat, each of you goes ahead with your own supper, and one goes hungry and another becomes drunk. ²² What! Do you not have homes to eat and drink in? Or do you show contempt for the church of God and humiliate those who have nothing? What should I say to you? Should I commend you? In this matter I do not commend you!
> ... ³³ So then, my brothers and sisters, when you come together to eat, wait for one another. ³⁴ If you are hungry, eat at home, so that when you come together, it will not be for your condemnation. About the other things I will give instructions when I come.

While it may not be self-evident from the text, we can imagine quite easily that in a status-conscious city like Corinth divisions might erupt in a community made up of people from different social and economic situations. People separated themselves into groups to eat based on wealth and status, which in turn threatened the unity of the community and hence required Paul's intervention. What people ate, with whom they ate, and where they ate the common meal all negatively affected the community and its Christian

---

13. Theissen, *Social Setting of Pauline Christianity*, 69–73.

sensibilities.[14] Similarly, the issue of eating meat offered to idols may also have had socioeconomic-status implications. Paul writes in 1 Cor 10:14–33:

> [14] Therefore, my dear friends, flee from the worship of idols. [15] I speak as to sensible people; judge for yourselves what I say. [16] The cup of blessing that we bless, is it not a sharing in the blood of Christ? The bread that we break, is it not a sharing in the body of Christ? [17] Because there is one bread, we who are many are one body, for we all partake of the one bread. [18] Consider the people of Israel; are not those who eat the sacrifices partners in the altar? [19] What do I imply then? That food sacrificed to idols is anything, or that an idol is anything? [20] No, I imply that what pagans sacrifice, they sacrifice to demons and not to God. I do not want you to be partners with demons. [21] You cannot drink the cup of the Lord and the cup of demons. You cannot partake of the table of the Lord and the table of demons. [22] Or are we provoking the Lord to jealousy? Are we stronger than he? [23] "All things are lawful," but not all things are beneficial. "All things are lawful," but not all things build up. [24] Do not seek your own advantage, but that of the other. [25] Eat whatever is sold in the meat market without raising any question on the ground of conscience, [26] for "the earth and its fullness are the Lord's." [27] If an unbeliever invites you to a meal and you are disposed to go, eat whatever is set before you without raising any question on the ground of conscience. [28] But if someone says to you, "This has been offered in sacrifice," then do not eat it, out of consideration for the one who informed you, and for the sake of conscience— [29] I mean the other's conscience, not your own. For why should my liberty be subject to the judgment of someone else's conscience? [30] If I partake with thankfulness, why should I be denounced because of that for which I give thanks? [31] So, whether you eat or drink, or whatever you do, do everything for the glory of God. [32] Give no offense to Jews or to Greeks or to the church of God, [33] just as I try to please everyone in everything I do, not seeking my own advantage, but that of many, so that they may be saved.

The eating of meat presumably had status implications as not everyone could afford it on a regular basis. Furthermore, it was most likely offered as a sacrifice in a pagan temple before being sold for food. Once again, we can see how the issue of eating meat would be bound up with religious sensibilities more generally and with eucharistic concerns in the Corinthian

---

14. Ibid., 145–74.

Christian community more specifically. We might assume that wealthier Corinthian Christians, who could afford meat regularly, had fewer scruples about eating it than those who did not have the means to buy it very often. With these different sensibilities at work in the church, it is not hard to see how divisions might develop over the issue on both theological and pastoral grounds. But at their root, these sensibilities would appear to have social and economic implications that affected people's practices and their willingness to eat meat without being troubled by matters of conscience.[15]

In Rom 16:23, Paul refers to Erastus, whom he identifies as the city treasurer.[16] Erastus is also a Corinthian follower of Christ (cf. 2 Tim 4:20), and this once again suggests that at least some members of the church there were of some social status. In Rom 16:1-2, Paul refers to Phoebe and suggests that she too may be a woman of some means and influence: "¹I commend to you our sister Phoebe, a deacon of the church at Cenchreae, ² so that you may welcome her in the Lord as is fitting for the saints, and help her in whatever she may require from you, for she has been a benefactor of many and of myself as well." Phoebe is identified as a deacon in the church at Cenchreae. What this means in terms of an office is unclear, but she clearly is a woman of respect and service in the church. Likewise, she is called a benefactor, which suggests she is also a woman of means. Moreover, since Paul introduces her to the Roman churches in anticipation of her trip to the imperial capital, she probably is an independent woman of means and prestige, not just in the church but even more widely in society. One can appreciate that Cenchreae during that time was a busy port city and provided ample opportunities for people to earn money and achieve some social standing. Phoebe may have been such a woman.[17] Other examples could be cited to show that some early Christians in the Pauline world had social standing and economic status and that the early church represented people of different social levels. In short, the early churches were communities of mixed status from a very early time. As Wayne Meeks says, we do not have people from the extreme top or bottom of Greco-Roman society, but the levels in between are well represented in the church.[18] This clearly challenges the previously held view about the social makeup of the early church.

---

15. Cf. 1 Cor. 8:1-13.

16. The Greek term that stands behind this translation has been much debated, but it appears that Erastus held a very important position in Corinth and one of considerable status (Meeks, *First Urban Christians*, 58-59).

17. Ibid., 60.

18. Ibid., 73.

OPPOSITION

At various points in the preceding chapters, I have made reference to the debates, arguments, conflicts, and oppositional groups that marked the early church. Jewish Christ followers, Gentile Christ followers, early Catholic Christianity, Gnosticism, Montanism, and Marcionism, to name some of the more conspicuous examples, contended with each other. Different regions of the church had different characteristics, and different personalities engaged the polemics of the church in different ways. We hear from Luke, for example, about the apparent contention between Peter and Paul in Antioch over the issue of Jewish table fellowship, and we know that Irenaeus and others fought vehemently against the gnostics. We know there was contention over issues of gender and the ministry of the church, as there was over the role and interpretation of the Old Testament. In addition to mere animosities between people, questions of authority and fine points of theology were often at issue. And overlaid onto these was an emerging institutional structure that began to exercise power and authority over a church that was growing more complex by the day. In other words, the early church was a tangle of competing ideas, social features, personalities, pieties, practices, problems, and challenges that crisscrossed life in the growing Christian communities of the Mediterranean basin.

Interwoven through all this were symbols, stories, and practices that came to constitute what we might call the Christian world. Integrating stories, beliefs, and practices as the basis of Christian understanding was an enormous undertaking filled with contentions and struggles. From a historical point of view, in the beginning no one was certain how the church would fare in the Greco-Roman world. For our purposes, an important key to its survival rested in what we might call its identity formation. The organic process of identity formation centered on a series of questions for the church: Who are we? What do we believe? How do we live? What is our past and what is our future? Who is in our group, who is not, and what are the boundaries that separate insiders and outsiders? The answers—perhaps the competing answers—to these kinds of questions would shape the early church and what it would eventually become by the fourth century. And here I would argue that the differences, contentions, and even oppositions were critical to the early church's process of identity formation.[19] It was only in the face of difference that the church could forge and fully understand what it was and what it would become. Encountering opposing ideas, the Christians could decide what the critical questions were, how they might be

---

19. Aageson, *Paul, the Pastoral Epistles, and the Early Church*, 209–10.

answered, and by whom. This process should not be romanticized because it was messy, sometimes very earthy, and often indeterminate. But looking back from our point in history, we can see it taking place, sometimes very slowly and other times more rapidly. This is not to suggest that the church at some point in time settled all of the important issues. Quite the contrary, the process of identity formation was and is always open ended. We only need to think today of the contested ethical matters of human sexuality, church and state, and gender equality to see how these identity issues continue to divide the larger church and at the same time help it forge a new way of living in the face of age-old questions.

As I have argued elsewhere, early in the Pauline tradition (that is, before the end of the first century), a series of issues emerged that would continue to occupy the church well beyond the first century, in some cases even to the present time. These are the nature of the true faith, the relationship of the church to Judaism, Christian asceticism, the problem of church unity and disunity, the formation of the Christian Bible, the relation between Scripture and tradition, the place of women in the church, and the role of church leaders in preserving the true faith and practice of the church.[20] How the church would deal with these issues over time says a lot about the identity of the church and how its identity has developed. Once again, I do not think this process can be reduced to either mere decadence and decline or progress ever upward and onward. It is a process that is much too complex to be reduced to rectilinear conceptions of history.

FUNCTION AND FORMATION

When reading and studying early Christian texts, it is important to consider the position and function of the author. I am not inclined to reduce every author and every text from the ancient church to an agent in some cynical political game, but I am fully aware that authors have agendas and the texts they produce reflect these concerns. Moreover, these texts do not simply have meanings, but they have functions as well. Hence, to ask what a given text means may not always be the most interesting or important question. It may be more important to ask how the text was intended to function, and how it may have accomplished its purposes. For example, Irenaeus developed weighty theological arguments against his gnostic opponents, but those arguments were not developed in a vacuum. Above all they existed to refute his opponents and their positions. The question then becomes, were they successful in meeting that goal? Clement of Alexandria, on the

---

20. Ibid., 16.

other hand, sought to bring Christian faith and Greek philosophy together, whereas Tertullian asked the famous question, "What indeed has Athens to do with Jerusalem? What concord is there between the Academy and the Church? What between heretics and Christians?"[21] In these three men—Ignatius, Clement of Alexandria, and Tertullian—and their arguments, we glimpse something about their intentions and how they differ from one another. Their purposes in writing are also a factor of their positions in the church: the bishop from Gaul, the legally trained theologian from North Africa, and the teacher from Alexandria in Egypt. Not surprisingly, their positions in the church shaped how they functioned and the purposes they sought to achieve. I think the same could be said about Matthew, Mark, Luke, John, Peter, and Paul as well. Their functions were conditioned by their situations in the early church, and they sought to contribute to the church in those contexts. Far from eliminating this diversity of function in the life of the church, even if it could have done so, the church preserved diversity at some important levels, which in turn contributed to the formation of the church as we have come to know it. Yes, some things deemed heretical were suppressed, but other diverse texts and traditions were not. Instead, they eventually became part of the orthodox body of Christian tradition.

The issues discussed in this chapter are not so much matters of theological argumentation as they are matters of early Christian social dynamics. My goal in this discussion has been to move our attention away from the lofty heights of early Christian theology and piety, and toward some of the more commonplace matters that affected and shaped the church. While these may have been commonplace, they certainly were not insignificant. The institutional character of the church was socially conditioned. The language and ideas that shaped the early Christian world were social constructs. And the gradual emergence of what some call the great-church tradition took place in community, with all the social dynamics at work in a religious community seeking to define itself and its mission. We have only been able to scratch the surface of this important approach to early Christianity, but our survey is sufficient to illustrate the point. Early Christianity was as much a social phenomenon as it was a religious, pastoral, and missionary phenomenon. We ought not lose sight of this fact. To do so removes Christianity from the sociohistorical context that cradled and formed it. To put it another way, we might say that this cradle is what gives the earthen vessel, the church, its texture, contour, and relief.

---

21. Tertullian, *ANF*, vol. 3, *De praescriptione haereticorum* (On the prescription of heretics), ch. 7.

Tertullian

Origen

Ignatius of Antioch

14

Worship and Religious Practice in Early Christianity

How did the early church express its piety and devotion to God through Jesus Christ in worship, ritual, and practice?

Woven through the history of early Christianity is the story of early Christian worship and practice. Following from the communal practices of the synagogue, the postresurrection Christ community found ways to express its devotion to God in light of the developing belief that Jesus of Nazareth was the Messiah and Son of God. The history of early Christianity is more than simply a story of texts, theologies, and missionary activities. It is also a story of how people expressed their devotion to Christ and how they built communities of faith that gathered for mutual edification and support. Christianity from the very beginning developed a corporate and communal way of life that has persisted throughout its history. To be sure, this corporate way of life entailed a host of social dynamics that were to make the church what it was to become. But just as important, it was a way of life that represented early Christian spirituality, both communal and individual. In the face of threat, division, and debates over correct belief, it was a way of life that developed practices that touched people's sense of meaning and views of the world. These were human aspirations that moved well beyond the purely cognitive aspects of life. In short, it was religion at its most personal and profound level. The artifacts of this spirituality and the ongoing mechanisms for shaping this spirituality are found in the liturgies and practices that came to represent early Christianity. It is hard to imagine that the early Jesus community could have survived, let alone thrived, without the spiritual passion and devotion that was part of Jesus's legacy among his followers. While we might not have direct access to people's interior spirituality, especially after almost two thousand years, we do get glimpses into this world through the artifacts, liturgies and practices they have recorded and left behind. It is these we shall explore in this chapter.

THE BEGINNINGS OF CHRISTIAN WORSHIP

The roots of early Christian worship are in the worship practices of the synagogue where the community gathered for Scripture reading and prayer. Given that the earliest Jesus community emerged from Judaism and more broadly from Jewish life, it is not surprising that the early church would reflect worship practices of this religious world. But beyond the general observation that Jewish worship practice and life influenced early Christian practice, it is difficult to be more precise about the nature of this influence, largely because prior to the writing of the Mishnah in 200 CE we know relatively little about Jewish worship practices. The Mishnah may reflect earlier practices, but it is difficult to know with certainty. However, the evidence is quite clear that there were readings from Torah in the first century CE as part of synagogue worship. We can see this, for example, in Acts 13:15 and 15:21 where Luke reports that Torah was read. As he writes in 15:21: "For in every city, for generations past, Moses has had those who proclaimed him, for he has been read aloud every Sabbath in the synagogues." And the Jewish historian Josephus, writing later in the first century CE, states in *Against Apion* 2:175: "He appointed the Law to be the most excellent and necessary form of instruction, ordaining, not that it should be heard once for all or twice or on several occasions, but that every week men [*sic*] should desert their other occupations and assemble to listen to the Law and to obtain a thorough and accurate knowledge of it." We may also presume that the reading of Torah was followed by an explanation or homily. This is suggested in Acts 13:15: "After the reading of the law and the prophets, the officials of the synagogue sent them a message, saying, 'Brothers, if you have any word of exhortation for the people, give it.'" Here we also see a reference to the reading of the prophets, which we might presume came to be a feature of synagogue worship as well. Whether the readings were conducted according to a fixed pattern or lectionary in the first century CE is unclear, but by the time of the Mishnah the evidence suggests they were.[1] The evidence for early Christian lectionaries is less clear before the fourth century.

Beyond Scripture reading, prayer was undoubtedly a feature of synagogue worship, and this carried over into early Christian practice, with the appropriate christological modifications necessitated by the conviction that Jesus was the Messiah and Son of God. Exactly how Christ was thought to mediate the prayers of the Christian faithful is not entirely clear, but by the time of 1 Timothy Christ is referred to as the mediator between God and humankind. Interestingly, this reference is in a context where the author urges that supplications, prayers, intercessions, and thanksgivings be made for everyone.

> First of all, then, I urge that supplications, prayers, intercessions, and thanksgivings be made for everyone, [2] for kings and all who are in high positions, so that we may lead a quiet and peaceable life in all godliness and dignity. [3] This is right and is acceptable in the sight of God our Savior, [4] who desires everyone to be saved and to come to the knowledge of the truth. [5] For
>
> there is one God;
> there is also one mediator between God and humankind,
> Christ Jesus, himself human,
> [6] who gave himself a ransom for all. (1 Tim 2:1–6a)

While not stated explicitly in this text, it would not be a stretch to see Christ here as also a mediating presence in the act of prayer. On the other hand, the best-known and explicitly instructed form of Christian prayer, the Lord's Prayer, clearly portrays the prayer as being addressed directly to God ("Our Father in heaven . . ."). In any case, prayer is a common feature of early Christian piety and practice, and (allowing for certain christological differences) is rooted in Jewish practice.

In Greek and Roman cults normally little emphasis was given to the temple as a congregational meeting place. However, the early church, presumably drawing on synagogue experience, was in fact an assembly or congregation. One of the common terms for identifying these assemblies was the Greek term *ekklesia*, which by extension also came to designate all the individual assemblies collectively. It is the term we normally translate into English as "church." Whether the early Christians chose the term *ekklesia* rather than the term *synagogos* to differentiate themselves from the Jewish community is hard to know.[2] Early Christians' use of *ekklesia* might

---

1. Aageson, "Lectionary," 270–71.
2. Aune, "Worship, Early Christian," 978–79.

reflect simply the fact that the Jesus community very early on moved into the Hellenistic world and began to use common Greek terminology. But even where the Jesus community continued to use Jewish thought forms, it very quickly translated them into words and categories that would be readily understandable to Greco-Roman audiences. Perhaps *ekklesia* was one of those terms.

Christians, of course, gathered for a variety of religious purposes, as did Jews, but three things especially seem to have differentiated Christian and Jewish gatherings. Christians from a very early time passed on and listened to the teachings of the apostles. Obviously, this would not have been part of Jewish practice. These stories and traditions came to have authority in Christian circles and served the religious life of people in the church. According to the book of Acts,[3] exercise of prophetic gifts also marked gatherings of the early Christians but probably did not play a significant role in synagogue communal life. Finally, Jews may have gathered for meals on occasion, but the common sacred meals of early Christians and the breaking of bread practiced in their church gatherings seem to have differentiated Christian and Jewish assemblies. Thus, while early Christian worship practice was rooted in Jewish experience, it clearly was not identical to it.[4]

While the New Testament does not describe in any detail early Christian worship practices, it does give us clues about what Christians did when they gathered. We know from 1 Cor 11:23–26, for example, that the Lord's Supper was shared and was probably preceded by a communal meal. Further on, in chapter 14, Paul writes about speaking in tongues, prophecies, revelations, and interpretations. He states in 14:22–33:

> [22] Tongues, then, are a sign not for believers but for unbelievers, while prophecy is not for unbelievers but for believers. [23] If, therefore, the whole church comes together and all speak in tongues, and outsiders or unbelievers enter, will they not say that you are out of your mind? [24] But if all prophesy, an unbeliever or outsider who enters is reproved by all and called to account by all. [25] After the secrets of the unbeliever's heart are disclosed, that person will bow down before God and worship him, declaring, "God is really among you." [26] What should be done then, my friends? When you come together, each one has a hymn, a lesson, a revelation, a tongue, or an interpretation. Let all things be done for building up. [27] If anyone speaks in a tongue, let there be only two or at most three, and each in turn; and let one interpret. [28] But if there is no one to interpret, let

3. See Acts 2:1–14; 11:27–30; 13:1–2; 15:32; and 21:8–11.

4. Aune, "Worship, Early Christian," 979.

them be silent in church and speak to themselves and to God. [29] Let two or three prophets speak, and let the others weigh what is said. [30] If a revelation is made to someone else sitting nearby, let the first person be silent. [31] For you can all prophesy one by one, so that all may learn and all be encouraged. [32] And the spirits of prophets are subject to the prophets, [33] for God is a God not of disorder but of peace.

In verses 22–25 Paul connects tongues and prophecies with church gatherings and worship, and in verse 26 he advises that when the community gathers, each person should come with a hymn, a lesson, a revelation, a tongue or an interpretation. And all this is to be done for the building up of the worshiping community. In verses 27–31, Paul becomes even more specific. Only two or at most three should speak in turn in a tongue, and one person should interpret. If there is no one to interpret, speakers in tongues should remain silent in church and speak to themselves and God. Two or three prophets are to speak while the others weigh the prophecies, and if a revelation is made to someone nearby, the first person should remain silent. Paul's rather detailed instructions are for the good order of the worshiping community and the building up of the church. If this account suggests any kind of sequence to the gathering, it appears the community began by celebrating the Lord's Supper and followed this with various hymns, lessons, revelations, tongues, interpretations, and prophecies. The Corinthian church gatherings appear relatively free and unstructured, which is why Paul sought to bring some semblance of order to these communal occasions so that the church might be built up.[5]

The Didache, also called the Teaching of the Twelve Apostles, is a text dealing with church order. The date of composition was most likely sometime between the mid-first century and the early second century. Sometime around the year 100 would be a reasonable estimate of its composition date, perhaps in either Syria or Egypt. The reason the Didache is important for our purposes is that in chapters 7–10 the text deals with the proper order for certain Christian worship practices. The text deals with the proper order for baptism (7), the days to keep fasts and the way to pray (8), the Eucharist (9), and the giving of thanks (10). For the sake of illustration, I quote Didache 7–10 in full.[6]

> *Chapter 7. Concerning Baptism.* And concerning baptism, baptize this way: Having first said all these things, baptize into the

---

5. Ibid., 975–76.
6. *ANF*, vol. 7; see also http://www.earlychristianwritings.com/text/didache-roberts.html/.

name of the Father, and of the Son, and of the Holy Spirit, in living water. But if you have no living water, baptize into other water; and if you cannot do so in cold water, do so in warm. But if you have neither, pour out water three times upon the head into the name of Father and Son and Holy Spirit. But before the baptism let the baptizer fast, and the baptized, and whoever else can; but you shall order the baptized to fast one or two days before.

Chapter 8. Fasting and Prayer (the Lord's Prayer). But let not your fasts be with the hypocrites, for they fast on the second and fifth day of the week. Rather, fast on the fourth day and the Preparation (Friday). Do not pray like the hypocrites, but rather as the Lord commanded in His Gospel, like this: Our Father who art in heaven, hallowed be Thy name. Thy kingdom come. Thy will be done on earth, as it is in heaven. Give us today our daily (needful) bread, and forgive us our debt as we also forgive our debtors. And bring us not into temptation, but deliver us from the evil one (or, evil); for Thine is the power and the glory forever. Pray this three times each day.

Chapter 9. Concerning Eucharist. Now concerning the Eucharist, give thanks this way. First, concerning the cup: We thank thee, our Father, for the holy vine of David Thy servant, which You madest known to us through Jesus Thy Servant; to Thee be the glory forever. And concerning the broken bread: We thank Thee, our Father, for the life and knowledge which You madest known to us through Jesus Thy Servant; to Thee be the glory forever. Even as this broken bread was scattered over the hills, and was gathered together and became one, so let Thy Church be gathered together from the ends of the earth into Thy kingdom; for Thine is the glory and the power through Jesus Christ forever. But let no one eat or drink of your Eucharist, unless they have been baptized into the name of the Lord; for concerning this also the Lord has said, "Give not that which is holy to the dogs."

Chapter 10. Prayer after Communion. But after you are filled, give thanks this way: We thank Thee, holy Father, for Thy holy name which You didst cause to tabernacle in our hearts, and for the knowledge and faith and immortality, which You madest known to us through Jesus Thy Servant; to Thee be the glory forever. Thou, Master almighty, didst create all things for Thy name's sake; You gavest food and drink to men [sic] for enjoyment, that they might give thanks to Thee; but to us You didst freely give spiritual food and drink and life eternal through Thy

Servant. Before all things we thank Thee that You are mighty; to Thee be the glory forever. Remember, Lord, Thy Church, to deliver it from all evil and to make it perfect in Thy love, and gather it from the four winds, sanctified for Thy kingdom which Thou have prepared for it; for Thine is the power and the glory forever. Let grace come, and let this world pass away. Hosanna to the God (Son) of David! If anyone is holy, let him [sic] come; if anyone is not so, let him [sic] repent. Maranatha. Amen. But permit the prophets to make Thanksgiving as much as they desire.[7]

We can see in the examples concerning baptism and Eucharist that the instructions are detailed and prescriptive. In the case of baptism, it is to be done in the name of the Father, Son, and Holy Spirit. If possible it is to be done with living water, presumably running water. And if cold water cannot be used, warm water will do, and if neither are available water can be poured out three times in the name of the Father, Son, and Holy Spirit. Before the baptism, the baptizer, the baptized, and whoever else can, should fast. In the case of the Eucharist, the text describes the thanks to be offered over the wine and the bread. The instruction concludes with a prohibition against the unbaptized receiving the Eucharist. In chapter 8, the community is instructed not to fast on the second and fifth days like the hypocrites but on the fourth day and the day of preparation. And they are not to pray like the hypocrites but to pray the Lord's Prayer three times each day. And in chapter 10, the community is instructed in considerable detail how to give thanks following the Eucharist. In the Didache, we see another expression of how the church, perhaps around the end of the first century, sought to bring order to its worship life. We do not yet see in the Didache a fully developed liturgical order, as no reference is made to the reading of Scripture or to homilies based on those readings, but we might presume that movement is in that direction.

I have already cited Pliny's letter to Emperor Trajan in chapter 11,[8] but I quote a portion of that letter again here because it also contains information about early Christian practice.

> They asserted, however, that the sum and substance of their fault or error had been that *they were accustomed to meet on a fixed day before dawn and sing responsively a hymn to Christ as to a god, and to bind themselves by oath, not to some crime, but not to commit fraud, theft, or adultery, not falsify their trust, nor to*

---

7. Translation by Roberts-Donaldson.
8. See above, pp. 179–80.

> *refuse to return a trust when called upon to do so.* When this was over, it was their custom to depart and *to assemble again to partake of food—but ordinary and innocent food.* Even this, they affirmed, they had ceased to do after my edict by which, in accordance with your instructions, I had forbidden political associations. Accordingly, I judged it all the more necessary to find out what the truth was by torturing two female slaves who were called deaconesses. But I discovered nothing else but depraved, excessive superstition.

The relevant parts are italicized and include a series of Christian practices known to Pliny when he wrote his letter in about 111: (1) they assemble on a fixed day before dawn; (2) they sing responsively a hymn to Christ as to a god; (3) they bind themselves to an oath not to commit fraud, theft, adultery, or betray trust; and (4) when this is over, they assemble to partake of food. These Christian practices are known to a person who stands outside the church, in this case to a Roman official.

Sometime in the middle of the second century, Justin Martyr sets forth in his *First Apology* (61–67), probably written in Rome, the most complete description of the order of Christian worship to that time. David Aune describes Justin's account of the service held on Sunday this way:

> The second section describes the type of service regularly held on Sunday (67.3), a day which Justin claims commemorates both the creation of the world and the resurrection of Jesus (67.7). At this meeting the Gospels or the Prophets are read "as long as time allows" (67.3), followed by a homily based on the reading given by the president, which concludes when all present stand and pray. Then bread and a mixture of wine and water are brought and the president offers prayers of thanksgiving, to which the congregation responds, "Amen!" (67.5). The bread and wine are then distributed and taken by the deacons to those absent. A collection is then taken up for distribution for those in need i.e., widows, orphans, the sick, prisoners, and visitors (cf. 1 Cor. 16:2).[9]

And if we extend our historical overview even further, we read the travel account of Egeria, a Galician woman who late in the fourth century (ca. 381–384) made a pilgrimage to the Holy Land. Among other things, she describes in great detail the liturgical services she observed in Jerusalem. While these accounts are too detailed to cite or describe here, it is worth mentioning them because they are an important resource for understanding

---

9. Aune, "Worship, Early Christian," 977.

early Christian liturgical development. They also illustrate how far Christian liturgical practice had come in the first three centuries.

THE PRACTICE AND MEANING OF BAPTISM

Early in the history of the church, baptism came to be one of the marks of Christianity. In fact, Matthew's Gospel concludes with Christ's charge to the disciples: "[18] And Jesus came and said to them, 'All authority in heaven and on earth has been given to me. [19] *Go therefore and make disciples of all nations, baptizing them in the name of the Father and of the Son and of the Holy Spirit,* [20] and teaching them to obey everything that I have commanded you. And remember, I am with you always, to the end of the age.'" This baptismal charge, though spoken here by the resurrected Christ to the eleven disciples in Galilee, echoed broadly through the life and experience of the early church. Not only, however, was baptism practiced as a ritual act of inclusion for converts to the new faith, it came to be invested with symbolism and meaning that separated it from the Jewish practice of ritual cleansing repeated at important times in a person's life. Through baptism and other early Christian practices, a faith community was born that moved beyond simple geographical location and ethnicity. Over time, this would mean that Christianity was universally available to people from the far corners of the world. It became a community identified and in some sense held together by its faith and practice, not by its ethnic orientation or lines of descent.

The apostle Paul, perhaps more than any other New Testament writer, presents a rich array of baptismal images. One of his most poignant images is the claim that those who are baptized are baptized into the death of Christ. In baptism, they are buried with him in order that just as Christ was raised from the dead they too might be raised (Rom 6:3-5). This is symbolic language that moves across the boundary between overt ritual action and subtle theological meaning. It is charged language that ritually connects the baptized to the central redemptive events of the Christian religious story: the death and resurrection of Christ (cf. Col 2:12). But Paul does not stop there: in 1 Cor 6:11 he implies that the followers of Christ have been washed clean of sin, and in Gal 3:27 he claims that as many as were baptized into Christ have clothed themselves with Christ. Washing and clothing, two common images, are here applied by Paul to the practice and meaning of baptism. And in the last case, Paul claims that for those who are in Christ, the distinctions between Jew and Greek, slave and free, and male and female are not defining marks. Oneness in Christ is the operative image (Gal 3:27-28). Here again, we see that Paul through his discussion of baptism redefines the nature of the community. Traditional markers of his society are set aside in favor of christological unity. It is hard to think that Paul was blind to the deep divisions in his own society between Jews and Greeks, slaves and free, males and females, but this language proposes a new religious operating system and the worldview to go with it. Participation in Christ and in the Christ community changed for Paul the nature of the community he imagined. This is imaginative language that moves beyond flat literalism, and Paul uses it to project a new way of living in community. Far from ineffectual language, this is language that helped give birth to an entirely new religious community.

The gospels portray Jesus as being baptized by John in the river Jordan (Matt 3:13–17; Mark 1:4–8; Luke 3:21–22; John 1:24–34). While there is not a direct line between the baptism of Jesus and Christian baptism, the narrative of Jesus's baptism undoubtedly undergirded the Christian practice. According to Matthew's account, Jesus insists on being baptized by John in order to fulfill all righteousness. Mark begins his narrative of Jesus with the baptism and indicates it is a baptism of repentance for the forgiveness of sins. Luke is less forthcoming about the specific meaning of Jesus's baptism, but in Luke, as in the other two Synoptic Gospels, the Spirit in the form of a dove descends upon Jesus, and the voice from heaven identifies him as the Beloved Son. The focus in these three accounts is, of course, on the role of the Spirit in Jesus's ministry and on the claim that he is the Beloved Son of God before he is cast out into the wilderness to be tempted by Satan. In John's Gospel, John the Baptist has an even more central role in the account of Jesus's baptism than he has in the Synoptics. John the Baptist is challenged by the Pharisees about why he baptizes, to which he replies that he is not worthy to untie the thong of the sandal of the one who comes after him. John is clearly not the messiah, and when he sees Jesus the next day, John announces that Jesus is the "Lamb of God who takes away the sin of the world." Jesus came after John the Baptist, but he ranks ahead of him. Here too the Spirit of God descends upon him, and unlike John he will baptize with the Holy Spirit. Rather than seeing these accounts of Jesus's baptism as part of the theology of the church's practice of baptism, we can say that these gospel stories provide a metanarrative for Christian baptism. The Gospel of John is the one gospel that ventures beyond the baptism of Jesus to make a theological claim: Jesus is portrayed as saying that no one can enter the kingdom of God without being born "of water and Spirit" (John 3:3–6). No one can see the kingdom of God without being born from above. Baptism for John the evangelist is a rebirth into a new community and a new reality.

The writer of 1 Peter in 3:20–21 sees baptism prefigured in the time of Noah when eight people were saved through water, not as a removal of dirt but as an appeal to God for a good conscience through the resurrection of Christ. The idea of baptism as cleansing is here rejected in favor of conscience. The effect of baptism has shifted: baptism no longer primarily removes dirt; baptism grants good moral standing and a clear conscience before Christ, who sits at the right hand of God. While this is the only direct reference to baptism in 1 Peter, some scholars have argued that the epistle itself reflects a baptismal liturgy.[10] Likewise, the Apostles' Creed is often thought to have been used as part of a baptismal or initiation ceremony. Whatever the merit of these arguments, it is difficult to know for sure that this is the case. Sometime after 1 Peter, Justin Martyr, writing in his *First Apology*, chapter 61, images baptism as cleansing, rebirth, and illumination. Justin echoes here two New Testament images but also interjects a third: illumination. Illumination may be implied in Eph 5:14, but is not explicit.

THE PRACTICE AND MEANING OF EUCHARIST

The three Synoptic Gospels portray Jesus's last supper with the disciples as related to the Jewish celebration of Passover (Matt 26:17–30; Mark 14:12–25; Luke 22:7–20). Moreover, this meal with the disciples serves as the foundation for Christian eucharistic practice and authorizes the church's communal sharing of bread and wine. This bread and wine, however, are not just any bread and wine. They are clearly portrayed as the body and blood of Christ. Leaving aside the later Christian theological questions of how the bread and wine could be or become the body and blood of Christ, it is clear that in partaking of the bread and wine the Christian believer was thought to become ritually and symbolically joined with Christ in his death on the cross. As things developed in the early church, the Jewish sacrificial system effectively came to an end in what was thought to be Christ's full, complete, and final sacrifice on the cross (cf. Heb 10:1–18). It would be fair to say, I think, that in receiving the bread and wine Christians saw themselves as ritually participating in the sacrificial death of Christ, the central redemptive event in their Christian religious system.

We know that the practice of Eucharist developed very early in the church, and by the time 1 Corinthians was written, sometime during the decade of the 50s, it was already well established in church practice. Paul writes in 1 Cor 11:23–32:

> [23] For I received from the Lord what I also handed on to you, that the Lord Jesus on the night when he was betrayed took a

---

10. Ibid., 987.

loaf of bread, [24] and when he had given thanks, he broke it and said, "This is my body that is for you. Do this in remembrance of me." [25] In the same way he took the cup also, after supper, saying, "This cup is the new covenant in my blood. Do this, as often as you drink it, in remembrance of me." [26] For as often as you eat this bread and drink the cup, you proclaim the Lord's death until he comes.

[27] Whoever, therefore, eats the bread or drinks the cup of the Lord in an unworthy manner will be answerable for the body and blood of the Lord. [28] Examine yourselves, and only then eat of the bread and drink of the cup. [29] For all who eat and drink without discerning the body, eat and drink judgment against themselves. [30] For this reason many of you are weak and ill, and some have died. [31] But if we judged ourselves, we would not be judged. [32] But when we are judged by the Lord, we are disciplined so that we may not be condemned along with the world.

The apostle Paul makes the claim that he handed on what he had received from the Lord. Whatever he may mean by this, he clearly believes the eucharistic words go back to Jesus and authorize the church's ongoing practice. It also seems in the words immediately following in 11:33–34 that there is controversy in Corinth over the divisive eating practices of some of the people. Presumably the Eucharist followed a communal meal and that communal meal was being practiced in a manner that was divisive to the church as the body of Christ. It may be that community members were dividing up along social and class lines to eat, and if so this was divisive to the community. Hence, Paul intercedes to give preliminary pastoral advice, which he says he will elaborate when he next visits the Corinthians.

As we saw above,[11] the Didache also addressed eucharistic practice. Beyond the prohibition against the unbaptized receiving the Eucharist, the commentary in chapters 9 and 10 focuses primarily on giving thanks to the Father for the cup as the holy vine of David and for the bread scattered upon the mountains and now gathered into one so the church may be gathered from the ends of the earth into God's kingdom. Following the Eucharist, the Didache continues by giving specific instructions to the community on how to give thanks. The one thing of special note is that in chapter 9 the cup is mentioned before the bread. In light of the Last Supper account in Luke where the cup appears first followed by the bread and a second cup, the order in the Didache suggests that early in the history of the church there were probably different traditions regarding the sequence in the blessing and giving of the bread and wine.

11. See above, pp. 221.

Justin Martyr too speaks to the issue of the Eucharist, and he is very specific about who can partake. Only the persons who believe the things that the church teaches are true, have been washed for the remission of sins unto regeneration, and live as Christ has enjoined his followers to live can receive the Eucharist. The bread and wine in the Eucharist are not common bread and wine but have been made the flesh and blood of Christ by the word of God for our salvation. In conclusion, Justin refers back to the Gospels where Jesus shares the Last Supper with his disciples. He does this presumably to show the foundation of and authorization for the Christian practice of Eucharist. They are rooted in what Christ himself did.

OTHER EARLY CHRISTIAN ACTIVITIES

As seen throughout the New Testament, prayer was a common and important feature of early Christian life. Certainly the best-known is the Lord's Prayer, but the so-called high priestly or final prayer in John 17:1–26 is another prayer attributed to Jesus. And on the night of his arrest Jesus retreated to the garden of Gethsemane where he prayed that if possible the cup of impending suffering pass from him. The earliest Christians are portrayed as people of prayer. In Acts 1:14, we are told that the disciples, together with certain women, devoted themselves to prayer. And on the day of Pentecost after Peter preaches (Acts 2:42), those who convert to the new faith are said to have devoted themselves to the teaching of the apostles and fellowship, to the breaking of bread, and prayer. When Peter and John are released from prison, their friends raise their voices to God in prayer (Acts 4:23–31). These examples are sufficient to illustrate the importance of prayer in early Christian practice and life.

Hymns were also sung in Christian worship. In 1 Cor 14:15 Paul writes: "I will pray with the spirit, but I will pray with the mind also; I will sing praise with the spirit, but I will sing praise with the mind also." This is in the context of his discussion of speaking in tongues and prophecy. Writing in Col 3:16, the author says, "Let the word of Christ dwell in you richly; teach and admonish one another in all wisdom; and with gratitude in your hearts sing psalms, hymns, and spiritual songs to God." Singing praises to God is here included among the virtues of the Christian's new life in Christ (Col 3:12–17). It is no surprise the biblical psalms were important in the early church and probably shaped its hymn tradition as well. Some scholars have also claimed that Phil 2:6–11 is in fact an early Christian hymn used here by Paul to make a point about how the Philippian Christians ought to behave toward one another.

> ⁶ who, though he was in the form of God,
> did not regard equality with God
> as something to be exploited,
> ⁷ but emptied himself,
> taking the form of a slave,
> being born in human likeness.
> And being found in human form,
> ⁸ he humbled himself
> and became obedient to the point of death—
> even death on a cross.
>
> ⁹ Therefore God also highly exalted him
> and gave him the name
> that is above every name,
> ¹⁰ so that at the name of Jesus
> every knee should bend,
> in heaven and on earth and under the earth,
> ¹¹ and every tongue should confess
> that Jesus Christ is Lord,
> to the glory of God the Father.

Whether a creedal statement or a hymn, it is clear this is an early christological statement and could easily have been sung as a kind of hymn praising Christ and describing his descent to earth and exaltation to heaven.

Closely related to the church's developing tradition of hymns were its statements of belief. We know that the great creedal statements such as the Apostles' (390) and Nicene (325, 381) Creeds were thought to describe the true and essential teaching of the church and its faith. But this impulse to state succinctly the church's belief certainly began much earlier and may have begun with the simple statement that "Jesus is Lord." From this foundational assertion, other claims about Jesus would have ultimately developed and helped shape the church's fully rounded confession of faith. What we do know for sure is that over time Christians would debate, sometimes with great zeal and bitterness, the nature of the true faith. And in some quarters of Christendom, they still do. Another feature of early Christian piety, perhaps with an implied confession embedded in it, is the giving of glory to God in the form of a doxology. Christian doxologies mention either God or Christ and ascribe glory to them, usually with the validity of the ascription being said to endure forever and ever.

Also mentioned in early Christian practice is the holy kiss, the anointing with oil, and the laying on of hands. In Rom 16:16; 1 Cor 16:20; 2 Cor 13:12; and 1 Thess 5:26, Paul invites the recipients of his letters to greet one another with the holy kiss. The holy kiss as instructed by Paul dramatizes the relationships and interconnectedness they have with one another in the church community. In Mark 6:13 and Jas 5:14, we note that the disciples and followers of Christ anointed the sick with oil. Somewhat later in the church the practice of anointing those who had just been baptized is also attested. The laying on of hands is also frequently attested in the New Testament; and in Mark 1:41; 5:23; 6:5; 7:32; and Acts 3:7 and 28:8, for example, it communicates healing through touch. But we also see the laying on of hands used as an act of commissioning in Acts 6:6 (selection of the seven deacons), 13:3 (Paul and Barnabas in Antioch), and 1 Tim 4:14 (Timothy by the council of elders). It is also seen as a means of bestowing the Holy Spirit in Acts 8:17. Anointing with oil and laying on of hands in different ways and in different contexts represent acts of healing, commissioning, and bestowing. They are deeply rooted in early Christian tradition.

CHRISTIAN LIFE AND CHRISTIAN BEHAVIOR

Christian behavior was not related only to acts of worship and piety. It is important to note in a chapter on worship that Christian behavior extended well beyond worship and other acts of devotion. Though it is not our purpose here to address the wider issue of New Testament ethics, it is noteworthy that even as many followers of Christ relativized the Jewish law in light of their faith, they certainly did not abandon a sense of proper Christian behavior and life. Quite the contrary, Paul in Gal 5:16–26 writes about life in the flesh versus life in the Spirit:

> The Works of the Flesh
>
> [16] Live by the Spirit, I say, and do not gratify the desires of the flesh. [17] For what the flesh desires is opposed to the Spirit, and what the Spirit desires is opposed to the flesh; for these are opposed to each other, to prevent you from doing what you want. [18] But if you are led by the Spirit, you are not subject to the law. [19] Now the works of the flesh are obvious: fornication, impurity, licentiousness, [20] idolatry, sorcery, enmities, strife, jealousy, anger, quarrels, dissensions, factions, [21] envy, drunkenness, carousing, and things like these. I am warning you, as I warned you before: those who do such things will not inherit the kingdom of God.

The Fruit of the Spirit

[22] By contrast, the fruit of the Spirit is love, joy, peace, patience, kindness, generosity, faithfulness, [23] gentleness, and self-control. There is no law against such things. [24] And those who belong to Christ Jesus have crucified the flesh with its passions and desires. [25] If we live by the Spirit, let us also be guided by the Spirit. [26] Let us not become conceited, competing against one another, envying one another.

Although these behaviors relate to personal matters and are rather list-like, they also establish in Paul's eyes what life in the Spirit looks like, and how it contrasts with life in the flesh. In short, Paul established the principle that life in the Spirit expressed itself in a certain manner of Christian behavior and exhorted the Galatians to follow it. In a similar manner, the author of the Didache, writing perhaps a half century after Paul, began his text with these words: "There are two paths, one of life and one of death, and the difference between the two paths is great."[12] The writer devotes the first six chapters to laying out the way of life, distinguishing it from the way of death, and exhorting the Christian community to the stand firm in the way of life. Parts of this discussion are a kind of pastiche of biblical injunctions concerning appropriate Christian behavior. Other parts are advice and exhortations for the community. In neither Galatians nor the Didache, however, does Christian liberty mean license to behave in whatever way a person wants.

Throughout this chapter, we have noted that early Christian life was rooted in worship and other communal church practices that expressed faith and common life. And closely connected to this was the conviction that Christian life and behavior had certain characteristics and qualities that marked the people of Christ and set them apart from their wider culture. Some of these worship practices were rooted in Judaism, others were not. Nevertheless, the church in its early years was in the process of developing its forms of worship and ways of being a community of faith in Christ. Part of this was also a matter of determining what it meant to live a Christian life and behave as Christ would want. In spite of having roots in both Judaism and the Hellenistic world, the church in the early years was inventing a new religious system, something that had not been seen before.

---

12 See Didache, chs. 1–6; see *ANF*, vol. 7 or http://www.earlychristianwritings.com/text/didache-roberts.html/.

15

Abraham's Children
Competition and Contention

*Does the origin of Christian anti-Semitism go back
to the period of early Christianity, and is the New Testament itself anti-Jewish or
perhaps even anti-Semitic?*

Since the catastrophe of the Holocaust, also called the Shoah, Christian communities and thinkers especially in the West have tried to figure out how this horror could have happened in the heartland of civilized, Christian Europe. What made this possible, and what was Christianity's role in this tragedy? To be sure, there were Christians in Europe who resisted the designs and machinations of Hitler and his henchmen, and in many cases they tried heroically to protect their Jewish neighbors. But it is undeniable that many more tacitly accepted or actively supported the Nazis' anti-Semitic agenda. Hitler and his thugs were certainly not sympathetic to the Christian faith, but was there something in Christianity that prepared the soil for this virulent form of anti-Semitism, and if so, what was it? The Christian church, both Catholic and Protestant, needed to confront this existential reality head-on, for the very soul of Christianity was at stake. It would not be possible or desirable to rewrite the history of the church, but it would be necessary to understand the past and face it squarely. This kind of tragedy could never happen again and certainly not with Christian complicity.

As part of this larger effort, many Christian theologians, historians, and exegetes turned to the past to unearth the roots of anti-Judaism and anti-Semitism, on the assumption that knowledge is power and that historical reflection can provide the foundation for constructive thinking about the present and the future. If Christianity emerged out of first-century Judaism, and if it eventually separated from Judaism to go its own way, how did it come to relate to its parent religion? And did the early debates between Jesus and his Jewish contemporaries come to be viewed differently once the church came into its own and began to flourish as a fully independent religious community?

For example, who can forget, let alone ignore, the implications of the explosive words of Matt 27:15–26 where Jesus stands before Pilate, and the Jerusalem crowd cries out for his crucifixion? "His blood be upon us and our children," they say. By the time Matthew wrote these words late in the first century, we know that the Jerusalem temple had been destroyed, that certain Jewish sects such as the Sadducees and Essenes had largely disappeared or morphed into other groups, and that the Christian community was meeting considerable success among the Gentiles. Regardless of what happened historically at the time of Jesus's crucifixion, it is not hard to see how these words might have come to be understood in the church as an eternal indictment against the Jews for killing God's Son. Whatever may have been the case in the time of Jesus may have come to be interpreted quite differently once the situation and fortunes of the church changed. Moreover, the religious sensibilities and the use of language by the ancients may not be ours, and hence we need to rethink how we speak about these sensitive matters and the language we use to express them. It may also be the case that over time we have learned about the dangers of certain kinds of ideas and ways of speaking about them. We can only hope that human beings have derived some sense of wisdom from history so we might not blindly repeat the mistakes of the past.

This is especially important for interpreting passages such as Matt 27:15–26 because it is liturgically situated within the narrative of Holy Week, leading up to Easter—the most holy time of year in the Christian calendar. How then can the Christian liturgical narrative function responsibly in the face of such a potentially explosive image of Jewish culpability for Jesus's death? There is no easy answer to this question, but it is precisely the kind of question contemporary thinkers must ponder if they are to deal with Christian anti-Semitism. My goal in this chapter is to explore these important and sensitive issues as they arise in early Christianity, and in this final chapter of the book to leave readers with the challenge to read the New Testament and other Christian sources with interpretive sophistication and ethical sensitivity. We should neither abandon a deep sense of the past nor be held hostage by it. But we should have some sense of the things that have shaped us and our culture, even as the culture that surrounds us is changing at breakneck speed. To state it even more sharply, it may be especially important during times of great change, when almost everything seems to be up in the air, for human beings to have a refined sense of history and culture and to have well-honed ethical sensibilities.

THE APOSTLE PAUL, THE JEWS, AND THE EARLY CHURCH

Writing almost twenty-five years ago, Jeffrey Siker asked a series of questions that are still pertinent:

> How did it happen that in a span of a hundred years the Christian conception of Judaism and of Jews' status before God changed so radically from Paul to Justin Martyr? How is it that while Paul acknowledged the Jews as children of Abraham, Justin Martyr denied them this status, reserving it for Christians alone? How is it that only the first half of Romans 11:28 was remembered by later generations of Christians: "As regards the gospel they are enemies of God"?[1]

In a real sense, these questions bring our presentation in this book full-circle to the earlier discussions in chapters 3 and 4 concerning the sibling model of Christian origins and the place of Abraham in Judaism and Christianity. But here we extend those discussions still further in order to explore how early Christians came to perceive Judaism and Jews theologically and how they sought to establish their identity by defining Judaism from their own point of view.

If Siker is correct, by the time of Justin Martyr, about a hundred years after Paul, the Pauline image of Abraham as a figure of Gentile inclusion was turned upside down and became instead a figure of Jewish exclusion. In Christian hands, the figure of Abraham came to represent something radically different by the mid-second century. Siker takes great pains to show how Paul in Romans and Galatians argues for Gentile inclusion in the promises of God through faith apart from works of law, even though the two letters deal with the issue of non-Christian Jews differently. In short, the Letter to the Romans deals with the topic directly, whereas Galatians does not.[2] In Paul, Abraham is not turned against the Jews so as to show how their lack of faith in Christ excludes them from the promises of God.

---

1. Siker, *Disinheriting the Jews*, 14.
2. Ibid., 74–76, 187–94.

Rather, the focus for Paul is on the inclusion of Gentiles. By the second generation of Christianity (60–90), Matthew, Hebrews, and Luke-Acts still focus on Gentile inclusion, but by this time the notion of Jewish exclusion begins to appear. Matthew, for example, holds fast to the idea of Gentile inclusion—he has not completely broken his ties to synagogue—but points increasingly toward the idea of Jewish exclusion from the promises of God. Hebrews uses Abraham to criticize the Levitical priesthood and to show how the covenant with the Jews is inferior to the new covenant in Christ.[3] Even though Gentile inclusion has not disappeared during this period, the issue of Jewish exclusion is becoming more prominent.

During the third generation of the church (90–120), Siker looks at the Gospel of John, the Epistle of Barnabas, and Ignatius, material that in different contexts we have already discussed. He poses the same questions to them and concludes that the issue of Gentile inclusion has become more and more an unspoken assumption in the thinking of these writers. John does not speak directly to the issue of Gentile inclusion, whereas Barnabas and Ignatius assume it to be the normative form of Christianity. In the third generation, the exclusion of non-Christian Jews from the promises of God has become even more pronounced. John, for example, denies that Abraham is the father of the Jews. Their father is the devil. Both Barnabas and Ignatius too use Abraham, at least implicitly in the case of Ignatius, to highlight the exclusion of the Jews. According to Siker's schema, the third generation represents further development on the continuum toward the exclusion of Jews from the economy of divine salvation.[4] We might also assume that this development had more than theological implications for Christians. It probably also had very practical implications in terms of how Christians interacted with Jews and their synagogues in the Mediterranean communities in which they lived. It is difficult to know this for sure, but it would certainly seem plausible.

With the fourth generation of the church (120–160), the situation has turned fully 180 degrees from the first generation. Here, Siker examines material from people like Aristides, Heracleon, Philip (the Gospel of), and Justin Martyr. Christianity by this time is largely a Gentile phenomenon. According to Siker, it is during this period that Jewish exclusion becomes virtually a matter of Christian doctrine and normative for early Christian thinking. As he points out, Justin Martyr uses the words "Christian" and "Gentile" interchangeably, which indicates for him that Gentile Christianity has moved beyond Judaism and is now the typical form of Christian faith.

---

3. Ibid., 190–91.
4. Ibid., 191.

Further, Justin uses Abraham to argue that the promises of God have been taken from the Jews and bestowed now on the Christians. Jews are not the true children of Abraham; Christians are.[5]

We may disagree with Siker's overly schematic view of how the church regarded these questions over the first hundred years, but his argument illustrates in an overarching fashion the trajectory of the church's thinking. To me, his general argument seems correct, which also means that by the second century the replacement understanding of Christianity had come to predominate and to provide the rationale for the church's emerging view of Judaism. The church has superseded the synagogue, and Christianity has superseded Judaism as the true faith. It is clearly not a big step from this claim to what we might call Christian anti-Judaism. Not only is it anti-Jewish, but it also has the theological rationale to support it.

However, while this theological view may obviously lead to anti-Semitism, it is not precisely the same thing. Being against the religion of the Jews is one thing; being sworn enemies of the Jews because of who they are as people and as an ethnic group is something even more insidious. No doubt the one can shade into the other very easily, and the two may be difficult to separate, but conceptually it is important to distinguish *anti-Judaism* and *anti-Semitism*. Clearly, what we experienced in the mid-part of the twentieth century in Europe was anti-Semitism. Jews could convert to Christianity to spare themselves from the wrath of the Nazis, but it made no difference. In the warped view of those who held to this reprehensible ideology, Jews as Jews were less than human. No matter what they believed religiously, and no matter where they worshiped, they were still beneath contempt and needed to be eradicated. We need to be exceedingly careful and conceptually nuanced in how we use the term *anti-Semitism* in the context of the early church. It may or may not be appropriate to the situations we find in the first hundred years of Christianity. Neither, however, should we exclude the possibility that it is there. If it is, it needs to be faced squarely. This question will very likely turn on the nuanced way we define the terms *anti-Judaism* and *anti-Semitism*. Later in this chapter we will take up this issue in a more careful and precise manner.

We have already looked at parts of Paul's rather lengthy conversation about the "unbelief" of the Jews in Rom 9–11;[6] and while we do not need to repeat that discussion here, it is important to make certain comments about this section of Romans in relation to the issues raised in this chapter. The discussion in Rom 9–11 is the most direct and sustained discussion

---

5. Ibid., 192.
6. See above, pp. 69.

anywhere about Israel, the Jews, and the fact that even by Paul's day the vast majority of Jews had not come to faith in Christ. And it is significant that this discussion appears in the Letter to the Romans, the most theologically mature of Paul's letters. It is also the case that Rom 9–11 displays Paul struggling to make sense out of what for him must have been one of his most perplexing theological dilemmas: what can it mean that his own kinfolk have not in any significant numbers come to believe that Jesus is the Jewish messiah? Paul simply cannot avoid these issues for three reasons: (1) he does not believe that the coming of Christ means God has abandoned the people of Israel and the covenant with them; (2) he does not believe that he himself has abandoned Israel or its people, the Jews; and (3) his theology only makes sense if it is fundamentally rooted in Israel's covenant with God. To put it another way, Paul's own theological convictions are running headlong into the reality that he is experiencing in his own ministry, and he needs to try to make sense out of what this means. From a theological and conceptual point of view, it would have been a lot easier for Paul if he had simply adopted the Marcionite position and abandoned the Jewish God, who was after all a wrathful and judgmental God according to Marcion, unlike the God represented in Jesus Christ. By the second century of the church, that was a conceptual option for some Christians, but not for Paul in the mid-part of the first century. He would not, or rather could not, go there.

If one reads Rom 9–11 from beginning to end, it is virtually impossible not to feel Paul's angst for his own people and to sense his theological struggle as he wends his way through this tortuous discussion. From the claim that not all Israel is really Israel because not all Abraham's offspring are his descendants to the assertion that God's election was bestowed on Jacob and not Esau, Paul attempts to show that God's word has not failed. In fact, a remnant of God's elect people has been preserved (9:6–29). From there, Paul presses on to argue that the Gentiles who did not strive for righteousness have nevertheless attained it, whereas those who sought righteousness by the law did not attain it and stumbled. In the Old Testament, the people of Israel heard God's call, but they were a disobedient and contrary people. Even now the Jews have heard the preaching about Christ, but they have not listened. Instead, God has been found by those who did not seek God (9:30—10:21). What does all this add up to? Has God abandoned the people of Israel? Heaven forbid! This could never be the case. God has saved a remnant. In an interesting twist, Paul argues that the "unbelief" of the Jews is so that the Gentiles might come to the way of salvation. And in turn, the Jews will become jealous because they will see what abundance the Gentiles have received. Not yet finished, Paul presses on once again. The wild olive branches (the Gentiles) have been grafted into the tame olive tree

(Israel). If you are a Gentile, says Paul, do not become haughty, because it is not you who support the root, but it is the root that supports you. Yes, some of the branches were broken off because of their "unbelief," but you, the wild branches, stand only because of faith (11:1–20).

Having led readers on this circuitous and sometimes troubling journey, Paul then writes these words in 11:20b–32:

> [20b] So do not become proud, but stand in awe. [21] For if God did not spare the natural branches, perhaps he will not spare you. [22] Note then the kindness and the severity of God: severity toward those who have fallen, but God's kindness toward you, provided you continue in his kindness; otherwise you also will be cut off. [23] And even those of Israel, if they do not persist in unbelief, will be grafted in, for God has the power to graft them in again. [24] For if you have been cut from what is by nature a wild olive tree and grafted, contrary to nature, into a cultivated olive tree, how much more will these natural branches be grafted back into their own olive tree. [25] So that you may not claim to be wiser than you are, brothers and sisters, I want you to understand this mystery: a hardening has come upon part of Israel, until the full number of the Gentiles has come in. [26] And so all Israel will be saved; as it is written,
>
> "Out of Zion will come the Deliverer;
>   he will banish ungodliness from Jacob."
> [27] "And this is my covenant with them,
>   when I take away their sins."
>
> [28] *As regards the gospel they are enemies of God for your sake; but as regards election they are beloved, for the sake of their ancestors;* [29] *for the gifts and the calling of God are irrevocable.* [30] *Just as you were once disobedient to God but have now received mercy because of their disobedience,* [31] *so they have now been disobedient in order that, by the mercy shown to you, they too may now receive mercy.* [32] *For God has imprisoned all in disobedience so that he may be merciful to all.*

It may not be entirely clear what Paul means when he says that when the full number of Gentiles has come in, then all Israel will be saved, but it is clear that Israel is beloved by God and the covenant with Israel is not null or void. While these claims probably fall more easily under the canopy of religious mystery than rigorous logic, it is easy enough to see how Paul is seeking to provide a satisfying explanation for God's enduring commitment to Israel, despite the fact that most Jews do not believe in Christ. Whether his explanation is satisfying or not, Paul has given it his best shot. In the end, he writes, "how unsearchable are the divine judgments and how inscrutable his ways!

> 'For who has known the mind of the Lord?
> Or who has been his counselor?'" (11:33–34)

In a moment of theological candor, Paul all but admits he does not fully understand how all of this will work out. What he is sure of is that Israel is not finally cut off from God's promises and God's care.[7]

THE GOSPELS, THE JEWS, AND THE EARLY CHURCH

As we turn to the New Testament gospels, I will deal with the gospel texts as documents that appeared in the last third of the first century. In other words, in this section of the chapter, I will not be asking primarily about the historical Jesus's attitude concerning the issue of the Jews and Judaism, but rather the perspectives actually represented by the gospel texts themselves. These perspectives may or may not be the same as those held by Jesus. To try and untangle the various layers of the Jesus tradition is a complex matter and for our purposes here would take us too far afield. This also means that the gospels are in fact early Christian documents and not simply pre-Christian accounts recording the events surrounding the life and death of Jesus in the first third of the first century. A lot had changed between the time of Jesus and the writing of the gospels, and by the late first century the church's attitude toward Judaism had certainly shifted and developed.

Recognizing that the anti-Jewish polemics in the gospels vary, Douglas Hare proposed a threefold system of classification to distinguish the different kinds of polemics: "prophetic anti-Judaism," "Jewish Christian anti-Judaism," and "Gentilizing anti-Judaism." The first category identifies the kind of criticism that comes from within Judaism itself and has a long tradition in Israel as the prophets challenged the Jewish people for their failure to live as God expected. Hare would place the historical Jesus in this category. The second type of anti-Judaism describes the non-Christian Jews who because of their failure to accept Jesus as the Messiah are condemned. This type of anti-Judaism would be representative of Jewish Christian missionaries who

---

7. For further reading, see Gaston, "Israel's Misstep in the Eyes of Paul," 135–50; Hall, *Christian Anti-Semitism and Paul's Theology*; and Aageson, *Written Also for Our Sake*, 89–104.

tried to convert Jews to the new faith. The final type of anti-Judaism, according to Hare, is the view that Israel's refusal to believe in Christ means that God has rejected the Jewish community. The old Israel has been replaced by a new Israel: the church. These categories bring greater precision to the issue of anti-Judaism in the New Testament, and we note that the term *anti-Semitism* does not appear in this context.[8]

George Smiga, in his book *Pain and Polemic: Anti-Judaism in the Gospels*, builds on Hare's work but makes certain adjustments, especially in the terminology he uses to describe the categories.[9] Smiga objects, in these matters, to the use of the Jew-Gentile distinction to differentiate forms of anti-Judaism, largely because early Christianity cannot easily be reduced to a single Jewish or Gentile point of view. In short, to speak of Jewish or Gentile Christianity is problematic for Smiga.[10] Instead of using the terms associated with the Jew-Gentile distinction, he prefers to use terms that reflect the character of the polemic itself. Hence, he prefers the terms "prophetic polemic," "subordinating polemic," and "abrogating anti-Judaism" to describe the three categories.[11]

In turn, Smiga surveys each of the New Testament gospels and tries to position them in one of these three categories. Beginning with Mark, we can see already the difficulty he has assigning each gospel to one of the categories because Mark is subject to being read differently. Depending how the narrative is read, it could possibly fit any of the three. Nevertheless, he thinks Mark's Gospel fits best under the heading "subordinating polemic." To be sure, Mark proposes a redefinition of Judaism in view of Christ, but he does not suggest that Israel's place before God has been taken away. While there are things in the text that might imply that Israel has been replaced, Mark never actually says this. The better part of interpretive wisdom is not to assume something the gospel writer never actually says. Thus, Smiga refrains from putting the Gospel of Mark in the category "abrogating anti-Judaism."[12]

Adding further refinement to his categories, Smiga describes Matthew as representing an abrogating polemic (with violence). Matthew represents a rather ambivalent position with respect to Judaism. On the one hand, he seems at home in Judaism and the Jewish law; and on the other, he says things that seemingly depreciate it. Certain Jews and Jewish practices come in for

---

8. Hare, "Rejection of the Jews in the Synoptic Gospels and Acts.
9. Smiga, *Pain and Polemic*, 13–18.
10. Ibid., 17.
11. Ibid., 18–21.
12. Ibid., 49–51.

harsh, or at least tacit, criticism by Matthew. We think again about the text cited above that takes place before Pilate and the Jewish crowds during Jesus's passion. The Jewish crowds certainly do not come off very well in this episode. Similarly, during the infancy narrative of Jesus, Matthew portrays the magi believing that Jesus is the newborn king, but the Jewish leaders in Jerusalem do not. And in the resurrection account, the Jewish authorities devise a scheme to deny and cover up the resurrection of Jesus. But Matthew does seem to be at home with the Jewish law and is not prepared to do away with it. Adopting the point of view held by Matthew himself, not his adversaries or a third-party observer, Smiga seeks to situate the anti-Judaism of the gospel. For Smiga, the idea of abrogating anti-Judaism would be inaccurate. Matthew does not direct his polemic against Jews or Judaism, but he does hold the view that any theological claims other than his own are invalid. In that sense, he holds to an absolutist position. Hence, for Smiga, the category "abrogating polemic" describes the absolute nature of Matthew's position without claiming that he attacked Jews or Judaism per se. We might say that Matthew did not oppose Judaism—just everyone's take on Judaism other than his own. Of course, it is a small step for later interpreters of Matthew to move from this abrogating polemic form of anti-Judaism to a form of abrogating Judaism, especially among those who saw themselves as distinct from Jews and Judaism in their own day. To be sure, Smiga himself is drawing a fine line between Matthew's representing an abrogating polemic and Matthew's representing an abrogating-Judaism type of polemic.[13]

After a nuanced analysis of Luke-Acts, Smiga concludes that these texts represent a disjunctive view of Judaism and Christianity. The church claims for itself Jewish roots, while at the same time Jews have been rejected. Those Jews who do not enter the community of Christ and become followers of Christ are forever rejected by God. Though there are in Luke-Acts positive portrayals of Jews, these are not finally central to understanding Luke's presentation of Jews and Judaism. As Smiga says, "those images are not primary and serve another purpose, namely to demonstrate continuity with roots, which have been left in the past."[14] Luke is a sophisticated writer, and according to Smiga he weaves together a subordinating polemic with other more positive images of Judaism. But in the end, Luke sees the rejection of Israel, and this causes Smiga to argue for an abrogating form of anti-Judaism (with sophistication) as the most appropriate description of the anti-Judaism in Luke-Acts.[15] Once again, Smiga refrains from associat-

---

13. Ibid., 52–96.
14. Ibid., 133.
15. Ibid., 97, 133.

ing the anti-Judaism in Luke-Acts with particular groups, opting instead to describe it in terms of the form of anti-Judaism itself. We can see how Luke-Acts, probably written sometime during the decade of the 80s of the first century, already represents a relatively sophisticated portrayal of the relationship between Judaism and Christianity. Luke is clearly moving in the direction of a replacement model of Christian origins.

John's Gospel is probably the latest of the New Testament gospels and brings some entirely new images to the gospel tradition. No matter how we read John, however, the anti-Jewish polemic simply cannot be removed from the gospel. Christ alone is the way to salvation, and in that sense the gospel clearly represents an abrogating form of anti-Judaism, according to Smiga.[16] Other views of Jesus are not to be tolerated. While the Synoptic Gospels have a linear kind of historical progression, the Gospel of John also has a vertical dimension that marks the presentation of Jesus: the heavenly and the earthly. Through the signs of Jesus, the heavenly is seen to be manifested on earth. The heavenly light has come into the earthly darkness. These christological realities predominate in John's presentation, not issues of Judaism and Jewish law. This contrasts with Matthew's Gospel, which often takes up issues related to Judaism and Jewish law and practice.[17] One of the conspicuous features of John's Gospel is his repeated references to the "Jews." No matter whether we read these references symbolically or as simply referring to Jesus's Jerusalem opponents, it seems clear that John sees the "Jews" as prime manifestations of unbelief. In that, they run up against John's absolute claims for the role of Christ in salvation. For John, Jesus is the way of salvation: "Jesus said to him [Thomas], 'I am the way, the truth, and the life. No one comes to Father except through me'" (John 14:6). Despite the fact that these words are spoken only to Jesus's disciples, it sounds unmistakably like all those, including Jews, who do not believe in the Christ of John's Gospel are excluded from salvation. Non–Christ believing Jews are rejected, and in that sense traditional Judaism itself is abrogated.[18]

With the help of George Smiga, our survey of anti-Judaism in the Gospels helps us see with much greater clarity the nature of the church's thinking about Judaism in the latter part of the first century. It is also the case that the church was defining itself over and against its chief adversary, the Jews. Over time as Christianity succeeded and grew, Jews would need to respond to Christians, and respond they did. They would question the very identity of Christ—the illegitimate child of a Roman soldier—and claim that

---

16. Ibid., 173.
17. Ibid.
18. Ibid.

he did not really rise from the dead.[19] They would be compelled to defend their Scriptures against the seemingly unusual interpretations of these same texts by the Christians, and would retreat into their own worlds when the church eventually rose to the pinnacle of political and religious power in the fourth century and beyond. It is my view that in the New Testament period of Christianity we do not find anything that can reasonably be called anti-Semitism, if by that term we mean racially and ethnically inspired hatred of Jews by Christians. To be sure, there was probably more than enough hatred to go around in the ancient Mediterranean world, but were the Jews singled out by the Christians or others as a racial group for special condemnation? That, of course, would come. But if it is already at work in the earliest period of the church, that case still needs to be made. It is not self-evident to me from the work already done on this topic.

THE ROOTS OF ANTI-SEMITISM

Having said this, I have no doubt that many of the roots of anti-Semitism are to be found in Christian anti-Judaism, especially as it developed over time and took on more and more virulent forms. As the church gained power, it was in a position to enforce its decrees against Jews, and from this it is not hard to see how Jews would eventually be vilified because of who they were rather than what they believed. When was the tipping point between anti-Judaism and anti-Semitism reached? That may be hard to determine precisely, and that question is certainly beyond the scope of this discussion. But it is important to be mindful of anti-Judaism's antecedent connection to anti-Semitism, even if it is not the only antecedent. It may be difficult to separate religion from other social and cultural features that contributed to anti-Semitism, but the Christian religion cannot be exonerated for its role in this insidious reality.

There were, however, other features of post–New Testament Christianity that also contributed to anti-Judaism and through it to anti-Semitism. The first of these is what is often called Judaizing. The verb "to Judaize" appears only once in the New Testament (Gal 2:14) but refers to a phenomenon more common in the post–New Testament period. It usually refers to the taking over of Jewish customs and practices without conversion to

---

19. In fact, the claim in Matthew's Gospel that guards were posted by Jewish authorities at the tomb of Jesus so that his body could not be taken by his followers, who would then fabricate a story about his resurrection, was probably the gospel writer's attempt refute Jewish claims about the falsity of the resurrection. The story shows dramatic divine intervention that sends the guards running away in fear. Therefore, the resurrection must be true despite what the Jews were saying.

Judaism.[20] For example, there were Jews who converted to Christianity but still continued to observe some of the Mosaic commandments and other Jewish practices. Other Christians may also have participated in certain Jewish practices and were thus considered by church authorities to have Judaized. Judaizing was more prevalent in the fourth century than in the first and brought blistering criticism from people like John Chrysostom, who thought this was nothing short of an abomination.

In 386 while a presbyter in Antioch, Chrysostom preached a series of eight sermons addressed to the members of his congregation. While this preaching did not address specifically the Judaizers themselves, he urged his own members to seek out those who Judaized and dissuade them from their pernicious ways. If his audience members were people from his own congregation, the intended targets were those who continued to celebrate Jewish festivals and practice their fasts. As he says, they submit to circumcision and observe the Sabbath. In short, they have high regard for the Jews and think what they do is holy. Such apparent abominations sent Chrysostom over the edge to unrestrained and violent language. His vehemence was shocking, and in him we can see how close anti-Judaism could get to incitement of violence against Jews. Chrysostom obviously felt that in the practice of Judaizing the boundary between Jews and Christians was being blurred, and that was clearly a problem for him. Christians should have nothing to do with Jews and their customs.[21]

We have already mentioned Marcion several times above,[22] but he is relevant to this discussion as well. As we recall, Marcion wanted the church to abandon the Jewish Bible as part of its own body of scriptural material. He argued for this because he saw in the Old Testament a God who was concerned with justice and punishment rather than kindness and mercy, both of which in contrast he saw in the God of Jesus Christ. It is not hard to see how this would be seen minimally as anti-Jewish. It was a not so veiled condemnation of everything upon which Judaism rested: its God, its Scriptures, and its Torah-based way of life. But what is not so often remembered is the way important church thinkers actually rejected Marcion's position. That was to add a whole new layer of anti-Judaism. Tertullian, the North African theologian, was not particularly incensed by Marcion's view of the Mosaic law. That had already been set aside by Jesus and the new covenant. What he really objected to was the idea of two different Gods. To be sure, the picture of God in the Jewish Bible may indeed be of a harsh figure, but what was

---

20. Aageson, "Judaizing," 1089.
21 Gager, *Origins of Anti-Semitism*, 118–20.
22. See, e.g., above, pp. 64, 194–95.

the reason for this? It was not due to the inherent harshness of God but to the faithless and disobedient nature of the people of Israel themselves. God was not the problem; the Jews were. In Tertullian's refutation, we can see clearly how responsibility is shifted from God to the Jews. By shifting this responsibility to the Jews, Tertullian was able to rescue the Jewish God for Christianity. It was at a price, however. And that price focused not just on Judaism but on the Jews. This argument was an important and insidious step on the way to anti-Semitism.[23]

In his *Dialogue with Trypho*, Justin Martyr takes a related line of argument as he seeks to refute the legitimacy of Judaism through a dialogue with his Jewish interlocutor, Trypho. The law of Moses is no longer binding, and Israel's prophets themselves spoke directly about Israel's faithlessness. The law was given only as a means to keep Jewish disobedience in check. While the Jews read their Scriptures, they do not understand them, reading them in only the most superficial manner. They are the murderers of Christ, and because of that at present suffer punishment and judgment. It is a tough indictment but one delivered with Justin's typically polite tone.[24] As with Tertullian, so with Justin, we see definite movement in the direction of blaming the Jews themselves for their unbelief and their present predicament. The problem is not simply the religion or its God but the people.

The evidence for early Christian anti-Judaism, if not anti-Semitism, could be multiplied, but I have presented enough here to make the point. Anti-Judaism is rooted deeply in early Christianity and ultimately contributes to anti-Semitism. I repeat what I said earlier. There is no point in trying to whitewash the tradition and thereby sanitize it. That approach only sweeps the tragedy under the rug and makes it more difficult to deal with responsibly. It is far better to learn from the theological and ecclesiological mistakes of the past and vow never willingly to repeat them. This tragic past also provides an opportunity for Christians and Jews to build new relationships and shared traditions. The past need not be the future. Indeed, it must not be. In the present day, the circle of conversation must also expand to include Muslims. Given the anti-Muslim rhetoric often heard in the West, it may be that dialogue between Jews, Christians, and Muslims is among the greatest religious and human challenges of our time. To withdraw from this challenge in fear will only compound our problems and prevent us from dealing constructively with the shared histories of these three great religions.

---

23 Gager, *Origins of Anti-Semitism*, 160–64.
24 Ibid., 165.

Abraham's Children 245

Synagoga (Synagogue) and Ecclesia (Church),
column figures, South Transept Portal, Strasbourg Cathedral

The Jewish Ghetto in Venice, described as the first Jewish Ghetto in Europe

Epilogue

The fifteen windows in this book have provided readers with important lines of sight through the religious history of early Christianity. Rather than survey all the relevant information, the discussions in each chapter orient us to the topics and questions at hand. Yet these sight lines are rarely separated from one another. They intersect, creating a web of interconnections, reminding us that the whole of early Christianity is more than the sum of its individual parts. The underlying theoretical basis for this book is less about a concept of history or a notion of conflict or a struggle between orthodoxy and heresy than it is about the intersections among diverse features of early Christianity. In the end, these sight lines and intersections produce perspectives and patterns that help us make sense of what early Christianity was and how we might understand it in our own contexts.

While it is my goal in these fifteen chapters to bring a sense of order to our understanding of early Christianity, I have no desire to eliminate the messiness or diversity of the phenomenon. It is often appealing to tie up some aspect of early Christianity in a neat and clean theoretical package, but the effort can hone the rough edges and create coherence where little may exist. This is not to disparage these kinds of studies. I have learned much from them over many years. It is, however, an argument for what I have called a multiplex approach to the study of Christian origins. We need, this book has argued, to come to the study of early Christianity from different directions, with different lines of sight if we are to grasp fully the rough-edged complexity of this material. The argument for a multiplex approach to the study of Christianity's origins acknowledges that there are gaps in our information and that a great conceptual, cultural, and social divide separates us and our world from the period of the early church. But even when we use a multiplex approach, we must recognize that what we see and what we produce in terms of our understanding of early Christianity are constructs of the modern mind. The questions we ask are ours. They are not necessarily the questions the early Christians would have asked. And the conclusions we draw are ours and may bear only a limited relationship, if any, to the way the ancients thought about their own beliefs, practices, and hopes. In short, the study of early Christianity, whether multiplex or otherwise, is always a contemporary enterprise; but likewise it can never be separated from serious study of the evidence, both textual and material. Contemporary theoretical perspectives and insights will always help us understand the ancient material in new and helpful ways. And the way the traditions played themselves out over time will also give us a perspective on their character and meaning in hindsight. Hence, there is invariably a dynamic interplay between the ancient sources and contemporary perspectives in the study of early Christianity.

In the first chapter, I laid out in brief my approach to the study of early Christianity, and in many ways that has governed the way I have thought about the origins of Christianity in this book. Having now read the chapters in this volume, readers should be clear that I have not so much argued a thesis about the emergence and development of early Christianity as I have provided a framework for the study of this phenomenon. Many will disagree with a number of the ideas stated in the first chapter and would prefer a different way of approaching the material. In some cases, disagreements turn on my distinction between religion and theology or on my stated sequence of these for the study of early Christianity. Other readers will prefer to ask different questions than mine, and in some cases will prefer more overtly theological or spiritual questions. In response to that, I continue to argue passionately that good theology rests on critical study of the Bible and history of the church. When spirituality and religious experience cut themselves off from serious scholarship, Christianity and the Christian church suffer and open themselves to questionable ideas and dangerous conduct. Throughout the process of doing scholarship and theology there also needs to be an acute moral and ethical sensitivity. Without this, both scholarship and theology run the risk of losing their way.

Hence, as the readers and I part company at the end of this book, I leave you with a question: What do the ideas and arguments in this book mean for the way people might rethink their own religious assumptions—whether they are openly hostile to religion, devoutly committed to religion, or oblivious to religion? Rather than focusing in the end on conceptual disagreements, I challenge readers to think about how my approach might alter their own thinking about what religion and theology are or are not. My ideas are certainly not beyond criticism, but the more interesting ideas are often those that cause us to think differently, regardless of whether we like or agree with them. Hence, I urge you to continue to refine your questions in these matters and to pursue your answers to them with passion and openness. If the ideas and arguments in this book have contributed to that process, it will have been a success.

Bibliography

Aageson, James W. "'Control' in Pauline Language and Culture: A Study of Rom 6." *NTS* 42 (1996) 75–89.

———. "Genesis in the Deutero-Pauline Epistles." In *Genesis in the New Testament*. edited by Maarten J. J. Menken and Steve Moyise, 117–29. LNTS 466. London: Bloomsbury T. & T. Clark, 2012.

———. *In the Beginning: Critical Concepts for the Study of the Bible*. Boulder, CO: Westview, 2000.

———. "Judaizing." In *ABD* 3:1089.

———. "Lectionary, Early Jewish Lectionaries." In *ABD* 4:270–71.

———. *Paul, the Pastoral Epistles and the Early Church*. Library of Pauline Studies. Peabody, MA: Hendrickson, 2008.

———. "Scripture and Structure in the Development of the Argument in Romans 9–11." *CBQ* 48 (1986) 265–89.

———. "Typology, Correspondence, and the Application of Scripture in Romans 9–11." *JSNT* 31 (1987) 51–72.

———. *Written Also for Our Sake: Paul and the Art of Biblical Interpretation*. Louisville: Westminster John Knox, 1993.

Aslan, Reza. *No God but God: The Origins, Evolution, and Future of Islam*. New York: Random House, 2005.

Attridge, Harold W., and George W. MacRae, trans. *The Gospel of Truth*. The Nag Hammadi Library. Website: *The Gnostic Library*, http://gnosis.org/naghamm/gostruth.html/.

Aune, David E. "Worship, Early Christian." In *ABD* 6:973–89.

Barth, Karl. *The Epistle to the Romans*. Translated from 6th ed. by Edwyn C. Hoskyns. Oxford: Oxford University Press, 1972.

Bassler, Jouette M. et al., eds. *Pauline Theology*. 4 vols. Minneapolis: Fortress, 1991–1997.

Beckwith, Roger. *The Old Testament Canon of the New Testament Church and its Background in Early Judaism*. Grand Rapids: Eerdmans, 1985.

Berger, Peter L. *The Sacred Canopy: Elements of a Sociological Theory of Religion*. Garden City, NY: Anchor, 1967.

Blasi, Anthony J. *Making Charisma: The Social Construction of Paul's Public Image*. New Brunswick, NJ: Transactions, 1991.

Borg, Marcus J. *Jesus in Contemporary Scholarship*. Valley Forge, PA: Trinity, 1994.

Brodd, Jeffrey, and Jonathan L. Reed, eds. *Rome and Religion: A Cross-Disciplinary Dialogue on the Imperial Cult*. WGRWSup 5. Atlanta: Society of Biblical Literature, 2011.

Brown, Raymond E. *The Death of the Messiah: From Gethsemane to the Grave; A Commentary on the Passion Narratives in the Four Gospels*. 2 vols. ABRL. New York: Doubleday, 1994.

Brown, S. Kent. "Truth, Gospel of." In *ABD* 6:668–69.

Bultmann, Rudolf. *Theology of the New Testament*. Translated by Kendrick Grobel. 2 vols. New York: Scribner, 1951–1955.

Cadbury, Henry J. *The Making of Luke-Acts*. London: SPCK, 1968.

Cameron, Ron. "Thomas, Gospel of." In *ABD* 6:535–40.

Collins, John J. *The Apocalyptic Imagination: An Introduction to the Jewish Matrix of Christianity*. New York: Crossroad, 1984.

Collins, Raymond F. *1 & 2 Timothy and Titus: A Commentary*. NTL. Louisville: Westminster John Knox, 2002.

Crossan, John Dominic. *The Cross that Spoke: The Origins of the Passion Narrative*. 1988. Reprinted, Eugene, OR: Wipf & Stock, 2008.

Crossan, John Dominic, and Jonathan L. Reed. *Excavating Jesus: Beneath the Stones, behind the Texts*. San Francisco: HarperSanFrancisco, 2001.

Dibelius, Martin. *The Book of Acts: Form, Style, and Theology*. Translated by Mary Ling and Paul Schubert. Edited by K. C. Hanson. Fortress Classics in Biblical Studies. Minneapolis: Fortress, 2004.

———. *Studies in the Acts of the Apostles*. Edited by Heinrich Greeven. Translated by Mary Ling. London: SCM, 1956.

Dunn, James D. G., ed. *Jews and Christians: The Parting of the Ways, A.D. 70–135*. Grand Rapids: Eerdmans, 1999.

———. *The Theology of Paul the Apostle*. Grand Rapids: Eerdmans, 1998.

Eliade, Mircea. *Myth and Reality*. Translated by Willard R. Trask. World Perspectives. New York: Harper & Row, 1963.

Fiorenza, Elisabeth Schüssler. *In Memory of Her: A Feminist Theological Reconstruction of Christian Origins*. New York: Crossroad, 1984.

Flannery, Edward H. *The Anguish of the Jews: Twenty-Three Centuries of Antisemitism*. Rev. ed. Studies in Judaism and Christianity. New York: Paulist, 1985.

Gager, John G. *The Origins of Anti-Semitism: Attitudes toward Judaism in Pagan and Christian Antiquity*. New York: Oxford University Press, 1985.

Galinsky, Karl. *Augustan Culture: An Interpretive Introduction*. Princeton: Princeton University Press, 1996.

———. "The Cult of the Roman Emperor: Uniter or Divider?" In *Rome and Religion: A Cross-Disciplinary Dialogue on the Imperial Cult*, edited by Jeffrey Brodd and Jonathan L. Reed, 1–22. WGRWSup 5. Atlanta: Society of Biblical Literature, 2011.

Gamble, Harry Y. "Canon, New Testament." In *ABD* 1:852–61.

Gaston, Lloyd. "Israel's Misstep in the Eyes of Paul." In *Paul and Torah*, 135–50. Vancouver: University of British Columbia Press, 1987.

Goldberg, Michael. *Jews and Christians, Getting Our Stories Straight: The Exodus and the Passion-Resurrection*. Nashville: Abingdon, 1985.

Haenchen, Ernst. *The Acts of the Apostles: A Commentary*. Translated by R. McL. Wilson. Philadelphia: Westminster, 1971.

Hall, Sidney G., III. *Christian Anti-Semitism and Paul's Theology*. Minneapolis: Fortress, 1993.

Bibliography

Hanges, James Constantine. "To Complicate Encounters: A Response to Karl Galinsky's 'The Cult of the Roman Emperor: Uniter or Divider?'" In *Rome and Religion: A Cross-Disciplinary Dialogue on the Imperial Cult*, edited by Jeffrey Brodd and Jonathan L. Reed, 27–34. WGRWSup 5. Atlanta: Society of Biblical Literature, 2011.

Hare, Douglas R. "The Rejection of the Jews in the Synoptic Gospels and Acts." In *Antisemitism and the Foundations of Christianity*, edited by Alan Davies, 27–47. New York: Paulist, 1979.

Hays, Richard B. *Echoes of Scripture in the Letters of Paul*. New Haven: Yale University Press, 1989.

Hengel, Martin. *Acts and the History of Earliest Christianity*. Translated by John Bowden. Philadelphia: Fortress, 1979.

Hennecke, E., ed. *New Testament Apocrypha*. Vol. 1. Edited by W. Schnemelcher. Translated by R. McL. Wilson. London: Redwood, 1973.

Hoffman, Daniel. "The Authority of Scripture and Apostolic Doctrine in Ignatius of Antioch." *JETS* 28 (1985) 71–79.

Hussain, Amir. *Oil and Water: Two Faiths; One God*. Kelowna, BC: CopperHouse, 2006.

Johnson, Luke Timothy. *The First and Second Letters to Timothy*. AB. 35A. New York: Doubleday, 2001.

Käsemann, Ernst. "The Beginnings of Christian Theology." In *New Testament Questions of Today*, 82–107. Translated by W. J. Montague. Philadelphia: Fortress, 1969.

King, Karen L. *The Gospel of Mary of Magdala: Jesus and the First Woman Apostle*. Santa Rosa, CA: Polebridge, 2003.

Kingsbury, Jack Dean. *Matthew as Story*. 2nd ed. Philadelphia: Fortress, 1988.

Koester, Craig R. *Revelation and the End of All Things*. Grand Rapids: Eerdmans, 2001.

Lake, Kirsopp, trans. *The Ecclesiastical History*. Vol. 1, *Books 1–5*, by Eusebius. LCL 153. Cambridge: Harvard University Press, 1926.

Levenson, Jon D. *Inheriting Abraham: The Legacy of the Patriarch in Judaism, Christianity, and Islam*. Princeton: Princeton University Press, 2012.

MacMullen, Ramsay. *Roman Social Relations: 50 BC to AD 284*. New Haven: Yale University Press, 1974.

Maier, Harry O. *Picturing Paul in Empire: Imperial Image, Text and Persuasion in Colossians, Ephesians and the Pastoral Epistles*. Biblical Studies. London: Bloomsbury, 2013.

Meeks, Wayne A. *The First Urban Christians: The Social World of the Apostle Paul*. New Haven: Yale University Press, 1983.

Meyer, Marvin, ed. *The Nag Hammadi Scriptures: The Revised and Updated Translation of Sacred Gnostic Texts*. New York: HarperCollins, 2007.

Miller, Robert J., ed. *The Complete Gospels: Annotated Scholars Version*. Rev. ed. San Francisco: HarperSanFrancisco, 1992.

Neusner, Jacob. *From Testament to Torah: An Introduction to Judaism in Its Formative Age*. Englewood Cliffs, NJ: Prentice-Hall, 1988.

———. *Judaism when Christianity Began: A Survey of Belief and Practice*. Louisville: Westminster John Knox, 2002.

———. *Rabbinic Judaism: Structure and System*. Minneapolis: Fortress, 1995.

Neyrey, Jerome H. *Paul in Other Words: A Cultural Reading of His Letters*. Louisville: Westminster John Knox, 1990.

Noormann, Rolf. *Irenäus als Paulusinterpret: Zur Rezeption und Wirkung der paulinischen und deuteropaulinischen Briefe im Werk des Irenäus von Lyon.* WUNT 2/66. Tübingen: Mohr/Siebeck, 1994.

Novak, Ralph Martin, Jr. *Christianity and the Roman Empire: Background Texts.* Harrisburg, PA: Trinity, 2001.

Pagels, Elaine. *The Gnostic Gospels.* New York: Vintage, 1989.

Pelikan, Jaroslav. *Jesus through the Centuries: His Place in the History of Culture.* New Haven: Yale University Press, 1985.

Perkins, Pheme. "Mary, Gospel of." In *ABD* 4:583–84.

Pervo, Richard I. *Acts: A Commentary.* Hermeneia. Minneapolis: Fortress, 2008.

———. *The Acts of Paul: A New Translation and Commentary.* Eugene, OR: Cascade Books, 2014.

———. *The Making of Paul: Constructions of the Apostle in Early Christianity.* Minneapolis: Fortress, 2010.

Porter, Stanley E., ed. *The Pauline Canon.* Pauline Studies 1. Leiden: Brill, 2004.

Potter, D. S. "Persecution of the Early Church." In *ABD* 5:231–35.

Powell, Mark Allan. *Jesus as a Figure in History: How Modern Historians View the Man from Galilee.* Louisville: Westminster John Knox, 1998.

Quasten, Johannes. *Patrology.* 4 vols. Utrecht-Antwerp: Spectrum, 1964–1966 (vols. 1–3); Westminster, MD: Newman, 1986 (vol. 4).

Quinn, Jerome D., and William C. Wacker. *The First and Second Letters to Timothy.* ECC. Grand Rapids: Eerdmans, 2000.

Rankin, David. *Tertullian and the Church.* Cambridge: Cambridge University Press, 1995.

Rhoads, David et al. *Mark as Story: An Introduction to the Narrative of a Gospel.* 2nd ed. Minneapolis: Fortress, 1999.

Roloff, Jürgen. *The Revelation of John.* Translated by John E. Alsup. CC. Minneapolis: Fortress, 1993.

Sanders, E. P. *Paul, the Law and the Jewish People.* Philadelphia: Fortress, 1983.

Schoedel, William R. *Ignatius of Antioch: A Commentary on the Letters of Ignatius of Antioch.* Hermeneia. Philadelphia: Fortress, 1985.

Schwartz, Daniel R. "The End of the Line: Paul in the Canonical Book of Acts." In *Paul and the Legacies of Paul,* edited by William S. Babcock, 3–24. Dallas: Southern Methodist University Press, 1990.

Segal, Alan F. *Paul the Convert: The Apostate and Apostasy of Saul the Pharisee.* New Haven: Yale University Press, 1990.

———. *Rebecca's Children: Judaism and Christianity in the Roman World.* Cambridge: Harvard University Press, 1986.

Seval, Mehlika. *Step by Step Ephesus.* Istanbul: Minyatur Publications, n.d.

Shedinger, Robert F. *Was Jesus a Muslim? Questioning Categories in the Study of Religion.* Minneapolis: Fortress, 2009.

Shewring, W. H. *The Passion of Perpetua and Felicity.* London: Sheed & Ward, 1931.

Siker, Jeffrey S. *Disinheriting the Jews: Abraham in Early Christian Controversy.* Louisville: Westminster John Knox, 1991.

Smiga, George M. *Pain and Polemic: Anti-Judaism in the Gospels.* A Stimulus Book. New York: Paulist, 1992.

Stark, Rodney. *The Rise of Christianity.* San Francisco: HarperSanFrancisco, 1997.

Bibliography

Stendahl, Krister. "Paul among Jews and Gentiles." In *Paul among Jews and Gentiles, and Other Essays*, 1–77. Philadelphia: Fortress, 1976.

Taqi-ud-Din Al-Hilali, Muhammad, and Muhammad Muhsin Khan, trans. *Interpretation of the Meanings of the Noble Qur'an*. Riyadh: Dar-us-Salam, n.d. http://noblequran.com/translation/.

Thackeray, St. J., trans. *The Life, Against Apion*, by Josephus. LCL 186. Cambridge: Harvard University Press, 1926.

Theissen, Gerd. *The Social Setting of Pauline Christianity: Essays on Corinth*. Edited and translated by John H. Schutz. 1982. Reprinted, Eugene, OR: Wipf & Stock, 2004.

Trobisch, David. *Paul's Letter Collection: Tracing the Origins*. Bolivar, MO: Quiet Waters, 2001.

Vermes, Geza. *Christian Beginnings: From Nazareth to Nicaea*. New Haven: Yale University Press, 2013.

Vorster, Willem S. "James, Protoevangelium of." In *ABD* 3:629–32.

Walton, Steve. "The State They Were In: Luke's View of the Roman Empire." In *Rome in the Bible and the Early Church*, edited by Peter Oakes, 1–41. Grand Rapids: Baker Academic, 2002.

White, Benjamin L. *Remembering Paul: Ancient and Modern Contests over the Image of the Apostle*. Oxford: Oxford University Press, 2014.

Index of Modern Authors

Aageson, J. W., 64n, 65n, 66n, 69n, 109n, 113, 117n, 121, 128n, 190n, 195n, 210–11, 238n
Aslan, R., 20n
Attridge, H. W., 141n, 147n
Aune, D. E., 222

Barth, K., 64
Bassler, J. M., 64n
Beckwith, R., 187
Berger, P. L., 7n
Blasi, A. J., 108, 109n
Borg, M. J., 87n, 89n
Brown, R. E., 143
Brown, S. K., 141n
Bultmann, R., 87

Cadbury, H. J., 96n
Cameron, R., 135n
Collins, J. J., 151–52
Collins, R. F., 113
Crossan, J. D., 88–90, 92, 143, 169–70

Dibelius, M., 96n
Dunn, J. D. G, 51n, 63

Eliade, M., 26

Fiorenza, E. S., 117n
Flannery, E. H., 40n, 43n

Gager, J. G., 243n, 244n
Galinsky, K., 171n, 174, 175
Gamble, H. Y., 192, 194, 196
Gaston, L., 238n

Goldberg, M., 13, 18n

Haenchen, E., 96n
Hall, S.G., III, 238n
Hanges, J. C., 171n
Hare, D. R., 238–39
Hays, R. B., 64
Hengel, M., 96n
Hennecke, E., 82n
Hoffman, D., 116n
Hussain, A., 20n, 23

Johnson, L. T., 113n

Käsemann, E., 155, 156n
King, K. L., 138
Kingsbury, J. D., 75n
Koester, C. R., 156, 157

Lake, K., 178n
Levenson, J. D., 26, 29–30

MacMullen, R., 61
Maier, H. O., 171n
MacRae, G. W., 141n
Meeks, W. A., 206, 209
Meyer, M., 135n, 136–37, 139n
Miller, R. J., 147n

Neusner, J., 47n
Neyrey, J. H., 205n
Noormann, R., 123

Pagels, E., 131n
Pelikan, J., 6n, 79n

Perkins, P., 137n, 139n
Pervo, R. I., 96n, 128n, 193n, 195–96
Porter, S. E., 196n
Potter, D. S., 178n
Powell, M. A., 87n

Quasten, J., 124n, 204n
Quinn, J. D., 113n

Rankin, D., 125
Reed, J. L., 169–70
Rhoads, D., 75n
Roloff, J., 151n, 156

Sanders, E. P., 61n
Schoedel, W. R., 120
Schwartz, D. R., 108n
Segal, A. F., 46n, 57, 107n

Seval, M., 172n
Shedinger, R. F., 8n, 13n
Shewring, W. H., 181n
Siker, J. S., 233–35
Smiga, G. M., 239–41
Stark, R., 99
Stendahl, K., 57n

Theissen, G., 206, 207n
Trobisch, D., 193n, 196n

Vermes, G., 17n, 90–92
Vorster, W. S., 145n

Walton, S., 109
Wacker, W. C., 113n
White, B. L., 129n

Index of Topics

Absolutism, 10
Anti-Judaism, 41–44, 58, 231, 235, 238–44
Anti-Semitism, 41, 43–44, 231–32, 235, 239, 242–42
Apocalypsis (apocalypse), 48, 151
Apocalyptic eschatology, 151, 154
Apocalypticism, 151–52, 156
Apocryphal gospels, 82, 131, 197
Apostles' Creed, 22
Apostolicity, 142, 194
Aqedah, 29–30, 32

Baptism, 14–15, 22, 50, 78, 83–84, 101–2, 104, 123, 205, 219–21, 223–25

Canon, 184
Canonization, 74, 184, 186, 192–95
Catholicity, 194
Chrysostom, 41, 243
Commercial kingdom, 89, 170
Comparative study of religion, 8
Constantine, 13, 82, 90, 92, 114, 132, 170
Cornelius's conversion, 101–4
Covenantal kingdom, 89, 92, 169–70
Cross gospel, 143

Dead Sea Scrolls, 46, 191
Diaconoi (deacons, ministers), 115–16, 205
Diatessaron, 81, 197

Ekklesia, 217–18

Episcopoi (bishop, overseer), 82, 112, 114–16, 176, 205
Emperor cult, 174–75
Essenes, 19, 46, 58, 232
Eucharist, 15, 22, 49–50, 81, 207–8, 219–21, 225–27
Eusebius's canonical list, 198–99

Gnosticism, 82, 136–37, 140, 210
God fearers, 60, 104
Great Commission, 79–80, 137

Heterodoxy, 23, 82, 114

Islam, 20–24

Jerusalem council, 106

Life in the Spirit, 229–30
Life in the flesh, 229–30

Marcion, Marcionism, 64, 122, 184, 194–95, 210 236, 243
Mishnah, 47–48, 185, 216–17
Monotheism, 19, 21, 22, 37
Montanus, 194–95
Muratorian canon, 197–98
Muslim, 6, 20–24, 37, 244

Nag Hammadi, 132–34, 136, 139
Nicaea, 82, 91–92, 114, 132
Nicene Creed, 22, 82, 88
Noahide Commandments, 107

Off-Shoot Model, 44–46

Orthodoxy, 23, 82, 114, 122, 126, 132, 193, 203, 247
Orthopraxy, 23
Oxyrhynchus, 132, 134

Paidagogos, 67
Paul's conversion/call, 57–59
Passover, 19, 32, 48, 225
Patmos, 149, 156
Pentecost, 81, 96–97. 227
Pharisees, 19, 45–47, 50, 57–58, 136, 143, 167, 224
Phenomenological study of religion, 5
Pillars of Islam, 21
Presbuteroi (elders), 115–16, 205
Pseudonymity, 153

Quelle (Q), 76, 81–82
Qur'an, 20–24, 37
Qumran, 151

Rabbinic Judaism, 39, 44–48, 50–51, 57
Relativism, 9–10
Religion, study of, 5–8
Replacement Model, 40–44
Righteousness by faith, 59–61

Rule of faith, 124, 129, 131, 193
Rule of truth, 123, 129

Satan's throne, 158–59
Sadducees, 19, 46–47, 54, 58, 86, 97, 232
Septuagint (LXX), 187
Shema, 64
Sibling Model, 46–50
Synagogos, 217
Synoptic gospels, 76, 80–81, 142, 224–25, 239, 241
St. Augustine, 64, 66, 124

Talmud, 47, 186
TANAK, 185
Theology, study of, 7
To Judaize, 242–43
Torah, 17–23, 26, 29–30, 33–37, 45, 47–48, 50, 61 67, 185–86, 216, 243
Trinity, 22
Two-source hypothesis, 76, 78

Ummah, 21

Zealots, 19, 47, 58

Index of Ancient Sources

SCRIPTURE

Genesis

9:4–6	107		
12–50	27, 31		
12:1–3	27		
15:1–6	27, 33		
15:6	32, 59		
16:1–15	28		
17	33		
17:1–22	28		
18:9–19	28		
21:1–7	28		
21:12–14	28		
22:1–19	28		
23–50	28		
25:12–18	28		
32:22–32	28		
49:1–33	28		

Leviticus

17–18	107

Isaiah

52:13—53:6	16
53:7–8	101

Joel

2:28	182

Matthew

1:1	14, 36
1:1–2	14, 36
1:5	14
1:17	14, 36
1:21	14
1:22–23	15
1:23	14
2:5–6	15
2:17–18	15
3:13–17	224
5:17–20	17, 45
5:21–48	17, 45
5:38–42	45
13:54–58	78
16:28	155
21:36–44	42
22:15–22	167
24:1–2	43, 48
24:36	155
24:42–44	155
26:17–30	225
26:59–61	43
26:61	48
27:15–26	232
27:20–26	41
28:16–20	79–80
28:19–20	223

Mark

1:4–8	224
1:11	84

Mark (continued)

1:15	84
1:16–20	84
1:41	229
2:13–17	84
3:13–19A	84
3:31–35	84
4	84
4:11–12	85
5	85
5:23	229
6:1–6	78
6:5	79, 229
6:13	229
7:32	229
8:22	84
8:22—10:33	85
8:27–38	85–86
9:1	155
9:7	84
9:30–37	86
10:32–40	86
11	86
11:12–24	77
13	86
14–15	84
14:12–25	225
15:39	84
16:1–8	79
16:2–8	190–91
16:8	87, 190
16:9–20	79
16:20	190

Luke

2:25–52	144
3:21–22	224
9:27	155
22:7–20	225

John

1:24–34	224
2:11	81
2:13–22	48
3:3–6	224
3:16	32
8:37–59	36
13:31—17:26	81
14:6	241
17:1–26	227
19:25–27	149
20:30–31	81

Acts

1:8	95
1:14	227
2:1–14	218
2:17	182
2:23–31	227
2:42	227
3:7	229
4:32–37	97–98
5:1–11	98
6:1–6	98
6:6	229
6:8—8:1a	99
8–10	101
8:17	229
8:26–40	100
8:27–40	100
9:1–9	56
10:1–35	102–3
10	101
11:1–3	59
11:1–18	104
11:26	104
11:27–30	218
13:1–2	218
13:3	229
13:15	216
14:15	227
15:1–29	59
15:7	106
15:14–29	108
15:19–22	106
15:21	216
15:32	218
20	107
21:8–11	218
27–28	108
28:8	229

Romans

3:23	66

3:30	64	**2 Corinthians**	
4	32	3:7–18	34–35
4:1–3	59–60	5:17–18	65
4:9–12	33, 60	13:12	229
5:12–21	65–66		
6:3–5	223	**Galatians**	
7:5–13	67–68	1:12–17	58
9–11	69, 235–36	2:7–10	107
9:1–3	69	2:14	242
9:6–29	236	3	117
9:27–29	69	3:6–9	32, 59–60
9:30—10:21	236	3:19	67
10:1–21	69	3:20	64
11:1	69	3:23–29	33
11:1–6	69	3:23–26	67
11:1–20	235	3:27–28	223
11:17–24	69	3:27	223
11:20b–23	237	4:21–31	34
11:25–26	69	5:13–14	68
11:28	233	5:14	67
11:33–36	69	5:16–26	68, 229–30
11:33–34	238	5:19–20	68
13:1–7	173	5:22–23	68
15:14–29	108	6:15	65
16:1–2	209		
16:16	229	**Ephesians**	
16:20	229	4:4–7	205
16:23	209	4:11–13	205
		4:16	205
1 Corinthians		5:14	225
1:27	206–7		
5:7	32	**Philippians**	
6:11	223	2:6–11	227–28
7:21–24	63	3:5	57
8:1–13	209	3:20	125
8:4	64		
10:14–33	208	**Colossians**	
11:7–22	207	2:12	223
11:17–34	207	3:12–17	227
11:23	49–50	3:16	227
11:23–32	225–26		
11:23–26	218	**1 Thessalonians**	
11:33–34	207, 226	5:26	229
12:12–31	114		
12:14–20	205		
14:22–33	218–19		
15:24–28	171		
16:1–2	222		

1 Timothy

1:5-9	115
2:1-6a	217
2:8-15	116-17
3:1-13	115
4:1-5	118
4:14	229
5:3-16	118

2 Timothy

1:8	120
1:12-14	114
1:12	120
2:3	120
2:9	120
3:11	120
3:15-17	116, 185
4:5	120
4:20	209

Titus

1:10-11	119
1:13-14	119
3:4-5	119

Hebrews

2:17	49
7:27	49
10:8-10	49
11	35
11:8-12	36
11:17-22	36

James

2:23-24	35

1 Peter

3:20-21	224
5:14	229

Revelation

1-3	157
1:4-11	156
1:9-11	156
1:11-20	156
2:1—3:22	156
2:12-13	158
3:14-22	157
4:1-11	157, 159
4-7	157
6-8	159
7:1-17	157
8-11	157, 159
8:1-5	159
11:15-19	157
11:15	159
11:19	160
12-15	157
12-13	160
12	160
13:4	160
14	160
14:8	160
15	161
15:1-4	157
16	161
17-18	161
17:1-6	161-62
19:1-11	162
19:1-10	157
19-22	157
20:11-14	162
21:1—22:5	157, 163
22:6-21	163

APOCRYPHAL TEXTS

Acts of Paul and Thecla

5	126
12	126
37	128
38	128

Acts of Paul in Rome

V-VII	176

Gospel of Mary

7:10—8:11	138
9:21	138

15:1—17:9	138
17:10—19:5	138

Gospel of Peter

9:25-34	143-44

Gospel of Thomas

1-2	136
9	134
20	134
26	134
33	134
36	134
39	136
47	134
51	136
57	134-35
64	135
108	136
114	137

Gospel of Truth

18	140-41

Infancy Gospel of James

19b-20	145-46

Infancy Gospel of Thomas

6:1-9	146
9:1-6	146-47

EARLY JEWISH AND CHRISTIAN AUTHORS

Clement

1 Clement

5	176

Didache

1-6	230
7-10	219

Ignatius

Ign. *Rom* 4:3	120-21
Ign. *Eph* 12:2	120

Irenaeus

Adversus haereses

1:9:4	123-24
1:22:1	123
3:11:9	142

Josephus

Jewish Antiquities

20:200	176

Against Apion

2:175	216

Justin Martyr

First Apology

61-67	222

Martyrdom of Perpetua and Felicitas

Prologue	181
Conclusion	182
9-21	182

Polycarp

Phil 3:2	122
Phil 3:3	121-22
Phil 11:2	122

Tertullian

De praescriptione hereticorum

20-21	124-25
7	212

De baptismo

17:5	128, 202

ROMAN AUTHORS

Pliny's Letter to Trajan	179, 221–22
Trajan's Letter to Pliny	180

QUR'AN

3:65–68	37

www.ingramcontent.com/pod-product-compliance
Lightning Source LLC
Chambersburg PA
CBHW022003220426
43663CB00007B/935